God, Jesus, and Other Foolishness

D1572380

God, Jesus, and Other Foolishness

Why Biblical Christianity Makes Sense

Jeffrey A. Kramer

WIPF & STOCK · Eugene, Oregon

GOD, JESUS, AND OTHER FOOLISHNESS
Why Biblical Christianity Makes Sense

Wipf & Stock
An Imprint of Wipf and Stock Publishers
199 W. 8th Ave., Suite 3
Eugene, OR 97401

www.wipfandstock.com

PAPERBACK ISBN: 978-1-6667-4108-7
HARDCOVER ISBN: 978-1-6667-4109-4
EBOOK ISBN: 978-1-6667-4110-0

09/09/22

This book is dedicated to the memory of my eleventh-grade English teacher, Mr. Robert F. Hollenbach, who first impressed upon me a love of reading.

Contents

List of Illustrations and Tables

Preface

As AN AVID READER and a scientist with a PhD in chemistry, it seems as if not a day goes by that I do not read or hear something that implies or states outright that religious belief is the purview of the foolish and the ignorant, or that the question of religious belief has been definitively settled in favor of non-belief. Methodological materialism (and the atheistic assumptions that underlie it) was part and parcel of my education. I have read numerous books that openly challenge (and criticize) belief in a divine Creator and in the Bible, and I have read many more books that take the occasional verbal swipe at "irrational" religious beliefs. Yet I persist in my Christian belief. Perhaps you think that, like many Christians in your estimation, I inherited my faith from religious parents, and I have simply never challenged or tested my beliefs. I can state categorically that you would be wrong on that assumption. I have challenged and tested virtually every aspect of my religious beliefs, and this book is my humble, honest attempt to make the case that a biblical Christian faith is neither irrational nor illogical. Many of the presuppositions that underlie any worldview cannot be proven with scientific or empirical vigor, and acceptance of many of the truth claims of atheism and postmodernism requires just as much faith as acceptance of the fundamentals of Christianity. In this book I will try to demonstrate that Christianity is true, in the sense that it is a logical interpretation of reality and our lived experience, and that the implications of the biblical worldview and the Christian faith make more rational sense than the alternatives.

Given this aim, it is worth noting at the outset the tension between the work and the lives of some of the individuals cited in this book. In particular, I have cited Ravi Zacharias several times throughout the book. It has been revealed recently that Mr. Zacharias was guilty of serious sexual misconduct. As our culture works, quite rightly, to weed out injustices toward women, it is important that crimes and allegations do not go unmentioned. Much of the content in this book was written before the charges against Mr. Zacharias were made public. As I reviewed this book, I struggled with whether or not to remove references to his work. In the end, I have left these citations in the book, and I hope that this does not dissuade you from reading and possibly benefitting from the content in this book. As George MacDonald said, "Truth is truth, whether from the lips of Jesus or Balaam."[1] Even within the Bible, great truths are sometimes uttered by those who neither knew nor acknowledged Christ (see for example Mark 5:7 and Acts 16:17). If I were to remove all citations to those guilty of great sin, I would necessarily limit myself to only the red letters in my New Testament.

1. MacDonald, "New Name," 65.

Acknowledgements

As N. T. Wright once wrote, "in this book I am standing in the noble tradition of continuing my theological education in public." I thank you the reader for considering this, my first foray into Christian apologetics. I hope that you find this book (or at least the references contained in it) thought-provoking, winsome, and helpful.

I would like to thank all those who have contributed in any way to the publication of this book. Any merit that you may have found in it is a tribute to their contributions. Any errors, issues, or shortcomings are mine alone. This includes my editor, Matt Wimer; copyeditor, Nathan Rhoads; cover designer Savanah Landerholm; and all the people at Wipf and Stock; Karen Graham for assistance with some of the figures; and those who reviewed the book while in manuscript form: Rev. David Parish, Mr. Cliff McNeely, Dr. Matt Lambro, and Dr. Dionisio Fleitas.

I would also like to thank several early and current influences in my life and my thinking. This includes, but is not limited to, my eleventh- and twelfth-grade English teacher, Mr. Robert F. Hollenbach, who first instilled in me a love of reading; my college roommate, Curt Salada, who first taught me to challenge my presuppositions; and friends Greg Finfrock, Boyd Crawford, Mark Garcia, David Parish, and Tanner Selinger, who have sharpened me over the years as iron sharpens iron.

I would like to thank my wonderful and loving parents, who raised me in the church (even though it didn't quite catch until later in life, as is often the case). As Proverbs 22:6 says, "Train up a child in the way he should go, and when he is old he will not depart from it"—even if he may put it down for a while. My mom and dad have been a constant source of love and support all my life, and they also provided early proofreading and editing of this work.

I would like to thank my wife, *ezer*, and true love, Jenny, and our beautiful little boy, Samuel, for their patience, love, and support through the writing and countless revisions of this book. More than anyone else in my life my Jenny sharpens me, supports me, and gives her love and her life to me and to our little boy. I could not imagine a better life partner if I tried.

Finally, I would like to thank my Father God, my Savior and Lord, Jesus Christ, and the *Ezer* (the Holy Spirit of the living God) for creating and sustaining me, redeeming me, and beginning the work of restoring me to oneness with God.

List of Abbreviations

A   adenosine (used in chapter 2 in reference to the nitrogenous base found in DNA)

AA   amino acid

ABC   American Broadcasting Corporation

AP   Advanced Placement

C   cytosine (used in chapter 2 in reference to the nitrogenous base found in DNA)

CBS   Columbia Broadcasting System

CF   cystic fibrosis

CFTR   cystic fibrosis transmembrane conductance regulator

DNA   deoxyribonucleic acid

EMBO   European Molecular Biology Organization

Fig.   figure

G   guanine (used in chapter 2 in reference to the nitrogenous base found in DNA)

ISV   International Standard Version

JAMA   *Journal of the American Medical Association*

K_c equilibrium constant (based upon molar concentration)

M   molarity (molar concentration in moles per liter)

MAFFT   multiple alignment using fast Fourier transform

List of Abbreviations

mM	millimolar
μM	micromolar
MRSA	methicillin-resistant *Staphylococcus aureus*
myc	an oncogene with homology to the avian myelocytomatosis virus
NASA	National Aeronautics and Space Administration
NBC	National Broadcasting Corporation
NIV	New International Version
NPR	National Public Radio
PBS	Public Broadcasting Service
PNAS	Proceedings of the National Academy of Science
RNA	ribonucleic Acid
T	thymidine (used in chapter 2 in reference to the nitrogenous base found in DNA)

Introduction

For the foolishness of God is wiser than men, and
the weakness of God is stronger than men.

—1 CORINTHIANS 1:25 [1]

OXFORD PHILOSOPHER OF SCIENCE Richard Dawkins, famous for his outspoken atheist views, has said, "Faith is the great cop-out, the great excuse to evade the need to think and evaluate evidence. Faith is the belief in spite of, even perhaps because of, the lack of evidence." [2] This opinion is shared by many in the sciences, educated and intelligent individuals who identify themselves as atheists or agnostics, and whose experiences with organized religion may be limited to occasional church attendance as children and coverage of religious fringe groups by an unsympathetic media. Dawkins's opinion is also shared by many non-scientists as well. There is a widespread sense in contemporary Western cultures that religious belief is the hallmark of ignorance, and that intelligence, rationality, and a healthy dose of skepticism dispel any such nonsensical beliefs. It is widely assumed that any open-minded and educated individual in the twenty-first century could not possibly accept most of the teachings of the major religions; and that people gullible enough to believe such archaic and superstitious nonsense are

1. Note that, unless otherwise specified, all biblical quotations are from the Revised Standard Version.

2. Dawkins, quoted from a speech at the Edinburgh International Science Festival, (April 4, 1992), cited in "Scientist's Case against God."

either not very smart, not very educated, or simply intellectually lazy. Dawkins has said, "religion . . . teaches us that it is a virtue to be satisfied with not understanding."[3] Dawkins is wrong. He has satisfied himself with not understanding (or willfully ignoring) countless historical truths concerning the history of religion, most notably the history of Christendom. He misunderstands or misrepresents organized religion and a significant proportion of the people he is criticizing, believing things about religion in spite of, or even perhaps because of, the lack of a fair consideration of the supporting evidence.

Christianity has a deep legacy of thought and logic.[4] Indeed a convincing case can be (and has been) made that the entire modern scientific enterprise could only have sprung from a Judeo-Christian worldview. Many critics of religion claim that adherents of a particular religious faith believe what they do only because they were born into a family and a culture that shared those beliefs. If they had been born in a majority Hindu or majority Muslim society, the argument goes, they would have been Hindu or Muslim rather than Christian. It is true that with respect to religion (as with political affiliation), many people are what they are because they were "born into it." But for many, their religious beliefs (whether those they grew up in, or those they came to later) became "real" to them only after "something happened" in their life to change their beliefs, something traumatic or particularly painful that caused them to draw closer to God. Few people are "reasoned into" religious faith on purely rational grounds. But it is also true that the vast majority of people do not leave religion as a result of careful intellectual consideration alone. Many, distracted by other passions and other cares, simply drift away. Others leave because "something happened," something particularly traumatic or painful for which a fragmentary and inherited religious worldview is unable to cope. Too often people neglect religious faith until some crisis arises, at which time they find their faith, like muscles atrophied from disuse, insufficient to face their crisis.

Religious beliefs, like most philosophical beliefs and unlike much of what may be called the "hard" sciences, are not easily proved true in a "scientific" or empirical sense; however, things can be true without hard empirical proof. Short of God appearing and submitting Himself[5] to

3. Dawkins, *God Delusion*, 152.

4. See for example Schaeffer, *Escape from Reason*; Mangalwadi, *Book That Made Your World*; and Metaxas, *Is Atheism Dead?*

5. "Himself" here refers to God and is thus capitalized. It is a common practice

questioning and experimentation, there can be no empirical proof of the existence of a spirit God or of much else that is claimed by religion to be true. However, it does not follow that God does not exist, that religion is untrue, that religious belief is for the credulous and the gullible, or that religious persons do not think about and challenge their beliefs. Many of the presuppositions underlying any worldview, be it religious, atheist, or postmodern, cannot be proven empirically. But they may be tested. In order to be successful a worldview must deal with four questions relating to origins, meaning, morality, and destiny; and it must do so in a manner that is logically consistent (that is, it corresponds with reality, and it is internally consistent), empirically adequate, and existentially relevant. Too many people are *apetheists*[6] (they simply don't care enough to really investigate and challenge their belief system) rather than genuinely thoughtful atheists or agnostics. Too few people really consider or challenge the presuppositions that undergird their worldview.

I believe an honest evaluation of what one believes and why will show that Christianity makes sense. The great twentieth-century author and apologist C. S. Lewis wrote, "I believe in Christianity as I believe that the sun has risen: not only because I see it, but because by it I see everything else."[7] It is not the purpose of this book to prove empirically the existence of a divine entity, or that Jesus Christ is part of the triune Godhead and the only means by which we may be saved. Such beliefs always require an element of faith (as do very many non-religious beliefs). Rather, it is an attempt to tease apart truth and reasonable belief from cheap, shallow criticism of religion in general and of the Christian faith in particular. It is an attempt at thinking through and comparing the issues with both a religious worldview as well as an atheist, agnostic, or postmodern worldview. It is an attempt to demonstrate that many of the fundamental religious beliefs that some have loudly dismissed as illogical and irrational are actually based on something other than blind faith. I

---

in the Judeo-Christian tradition to capitalize "He," "Him," "His," etc. when referring to God, Jesus, or the Holy Spirit. Ancient Hebrew did not have capital letters, so this is of course not in the original of any biblical passage. Please forgive me for sticking with this tradition. With R. C. Sproul (*Holiness of God*, 21), "I cannot bring myself to refer to Him as 'him.'" Even if you do not admit the existence of God or the divinity of Christ, this use of capitalization clears up potential uncertainties with pronouns, such as may occur in a passage like "And he kissed Him" (Mark 14:25).

6. I first came across the word "apatheist," defined as "someone who just hasn't put much thought into religious questions," in Downing, *Looking for the King*, 210.

7. Lewis, "Is Theology Poetry?," 64.

am not arguing that belief in the Christian God is true simply because it makes sense, but rather that it makes sense because it is true. A thinking individual can indeed believe in the fundamental tenets of the Christian faith because they make sense. In fact, Christianity and the Christian worldview fit with our experience of reality on a variety of levels, particularly when compared to the most common alternative beliefs put forward by the most outspoken opponents. A blind acceptance of many of the truth claims of atheism and postmodernism requires just as much "faith" as does religious belief.

Greater and smarter men and women than I have struggled with these topics, and many have found their faith strengthened and encouraged. Occasional doubts in one's faith do not prove that the object of that faith is untrue. Nor does slavish acceptance without any doubts prove that a point of view is true. Even atheists have doubts—or at least they ought to. It is my purpose in writing this book to demonstrate that acceptance of the tenets of atheism and postmodernism requires just as much faith as acceptance of the fundamentals of Christianity. Christianity is true, in the sense that it is a logical interpretation of the facts of reality, and the implications of religious faith make more rational sense than the implications of a rejection of that faith. Scientific empiricism is not the only way to truth, and something may be true without being able to be demonstrated with the same empirical rigor that we routinely require of mathematics and the mathematical sciences. It is therefore my hope that you will read this book with an open mind and an open heart, accepting the possibility that science, though a useful and beautiful tool for understanding how our world works, is not the only way to truth, and that religious faith is not intellectual laziness or evading the need to think and evaluate evidence.

1

Believing in God Is Irrational

Religion . . . allows . . . millions to believe what only
lunatics or idiots could believe on their own.

—SAM HARRIS[1]

IN THE 1600s AND 1700s educated Europeans increasingly began to see
reason as the key to human progress. Called the Enlightenment, or Age of
Reason, this movement rose from the Scientific Revolution, itself a product of the Renaissance and the Protestant Reformation. As with these
earlier movements, Enlightenment thinkers challenged many of the accepted beliefs of their times. They challenged authority as well, including
one of the primary authorities in Western civilization at the time—the
church. Newtonian physics and calculus gave rise to a mechanistic view
of the universe—an idea that the physical laws being discovered and described by science were sufficient in and of themselves to explain nature
(though Newton himself did not share this idea). As confidence in science and the human intellect increased throughout the Enlightenment
and the Industrial Revolution, educated elites increasingly came to view
religious belief as unnecessary, irrational, and backwards. They began
instead to place their faith and hope for the future in science and human

1. Harris, in "Sam Harris Extended Interview."

reason. Although a deity was still required to explain the origins of the universe, God was considered to be an "absentee landlord," a distant and external agency that had created the universe and its immutable laws, then left it to fend for itself. Called deism, this belief system held that praying to such a God was moot. The focus instead ought to be on studying the created order and seeking the perfectibility of man with an eye toward improving the lot of humanity through rational and scientific means, without reference to or reliance upon God.

Although the optimism ended with the horrors of the wars and bloody revolutions of the early twentieth century, faith in the sufficiency and infallibility of science persists. There remains implicit in the world today an idea that religion and science are at odds and that science is the sole source of verifiable truth. Science is thought to have disproved, or at least made unnecessary, such foolish religious beliefs as the existence of a divine being that can be called God, and it is assumed that one cannot rationally pursue science while also holding to religious belief. In short, it is widely assumed that good scientists, and any other reasonable person, cannot (or should not) be religious. Yet countless scientists, including some very famous ones through the ages up to and including the present day, have been devoutly religious. Religious belief is undeniably waning amongst scientists in the present day, as it is amongst non-scientists, but this reflects a pervasive cultural shift rather than any actual scientific evidence that refutes religious belief. This cultural shift is due at least in part to an overtly secular humanist educational system, which has expunged even the mention of religious faith from the curriculum in the name of pluralism and political correctness. Every day in schools throughout the world students are taught science and other subjects in environments where the very mention of religion is absent. The curricula include descriptions of how the universe came into being and how life evolved, the deeds of noteworthy historical figures, the themes of literary works, and political and social movements, often without any mention of religious belief. If religion is mentioned at all, it is usually only to list a series of errors and misdeeds attributed to the religious authorities of an unenlightened past, and the noble efforts of scientists and Enlightenment reformers to rise above injustice, religious intolerance, and persecution. This is in spite of the fact that religious conviction has been a contributing factor to virtually every major development in Western culture, and not only in an adverse sense, as is often portrayed. Implicit in these curricula (through the absence of any serious mention of the vast beneficial impacts of organized religion through the ages) is the idea, sometimes stated outright, that the existence of a divine creator God is at the very least unnecessary, that modern man no longer needs to cling to discredited and outdated religious beliefs, and that science has replaced religion as the primary source of truth in our world.

Fact vs. Truth

The notion that science has done away with religious belief misunderstands the nature of the questions asked and the answers sought by science and by religion (and more generally by philosophy) and belies an underlying bias regarding our understanding of truth and knowledge. Science is an empirical pursuit—that is, it deals with observable, repeatable, and measurable phenomena. Empiricism is a theory of knowledge that presumes that all knowledge is derived only from firsthand sense-experience, from observations made with the five senses. As an empirical pursuit, science deals with the study of the physical world, the realm that can be sensed and measured physically. Whereas science deals with observable and physically verifiable fact, religion and philosophy deal with truth—with matters of morality, purpose, and meaning. Scientific theories and religious doctrines can both be said to be true (or denied as false), but in very different ways. Science seeks to address questions of how something came to be the way it is; that is, it seeks to measure reality and explain how things work. Science is the practice of observing phenomenon, forming hypotheses and theories based on those observations, and then testing those theories by evaluating their ability to predict future observations. Religion (and philosophy) deals with a search for the basis of knowledge, beauty, truth, and morality, and for transcendent meaning or purpose. It does not necessarily seek to explain the "nuts and bolts" of how things happen, but rather why they happen and what they ultimately mean. Although one's philosophy or religion can be impacted by science, the two fields need not be at odds. The perception that they are opposed represents not just the proliferation of misinformation regarding what science has and has not proven and what religion has and has not preached, but also a lack of understanding of the primary role and purpose of both pursuits. As Thomas Aquinas wrote, "It is the abuse of [both] science and philosophy which provokes statements against faith."[2]

2. Aquinas, *De Trinitate*, exposition 2.3. Referenced in Clouser, *Myth of Religious*

Biola University professor Paul Spears delineates five broad categories that comprise the study of philosophy.[3] These are metaphysics (the branch of philosophy that explores fundamental questions of existence, reality and purpose), logic (the science of constructing and arguing ideas), aesthetics (which seeks to answer the question "what is beauty?"), ethics (the basis of right and wrong behavior), and epistemology (the study of the origin, composition, and limits of knowledge). Much of what is studied in these five broad areas does not submit to empirical investigation, but empiricism is not the only way of knowing. In the philosophy of knowledge (epistemology) there are a number of theories of how we come to truth and knowledge. Theories of knowledge other than empiricism include historicism, which suggests that knowledge is dependent upon (and often relative to) the specific historical or cultural context; idealism, the assertion that reality as we can know it is fundamentally mentally constructed; skepticism, the idea that absolutely certain knowledge is not possible; and rationalism, which regards reason as the chief source for and test of knowledge. The belief that empiricism is the only way to truth is not itself an empirically provable position. Furthermore, although science is often characterized as a purely empirical pursuit, it very often "employs a mixture of inference and observations."[4] Much scientific knowledge is based upon rationalist (and sometimes skeptical) epistemology. *The Stanford Encyclopedia of Philosophy* states of the competing claims to epistemological truth:

> The dispute between rationalism and empiricism concerns the extent to which we are dependent upon sense experience in our effort to gain knowledge. Rationalists claim that there are significant ways in which our concepts and knowledge are gained independently of sense experience. Empiricists claim that sense experience is the ultimate source of all our concepts and knowledge. Rationalists generally develop their view in two ways. First, they argue that there are cases where the content of our concepts or knowledge outstrips the information that sense experience can provide. Second, they construct accounts of how reason in some form or other provides that additional information about the world.[5]

Neutrality, 102.

3. Spears, "Introduction to Philosophy," 5–15.

4. Stewart, *In Pursuit*, 62.

5. Markie and Folescu, "Rationalism vs. Empiricism."

While it is true that philosophy does not lend itself to empirical methods, it does not follow that the fruit of philosophy cannot be said to be true. Humans know intuitively that molesting a child is morally reprehensible, but the truth of this cannot be proved empirically. Many today wrongly ask, how can something be said to be absolutely true if it does not yield to empirical proofs? Is not such moral and religious truth, they ask, relative to one's culture, one's situation, and one's point of view? Theologian Francis Schaeffer and others have commented on the split in our modern culture described variously as public/private, facts/values, or rationality/faith.[6] Implicit in this idea is the notion that only empirically verifiable scientific facts are absolute, and that values are relative to the times and circumstances and cannot be said to be absolutely true. Author Nancy Pearcey has called this division "the single most potent weapon for delegitimizing the Biblical perspective," noting that upon accepting this idea, "Secularists can then assure us that of course they 'respect' religion, while at the same time denying that it has any relevance to the public realm."[7] Such slavish submission to empiricism is unfounded, and entirely unsuited to non-empirical pursuits. The application of the principals of empiricism to matters of morality and philosophy is a recent development, beginning with Auguste Comte in the nineteenth century. Such approaches are ill-conceived. One can scarcely hope to prove empirically that rape is evil. Even allowing that a testable hypothesis could be imagined, testing that hypothesis would be so obviously immoral that the very idea is repugnant. This does not mean that matters of morality, philosophy, and religion can never be said to be absolutely true.

Oxford philosopher Richard Swinburne has argued that belief in God can be tested and justified (though not necessarily proven empirically) in that the hypothesis that there is a God leads us to expect many of the things that we observe; for example, that there is a universe with scientific laws operating within it, and that it contains human beings with consciousness and an apparent inborn moral sense.[8] Looking at the same "data," Richard Dawkins draws a very different conclusion, specifically that "The universe that we observe has precisely the properties we should expect if there is, at bottom, no design, no purpose, no evil,

6. Schaeffer, *Escape from Reason*, 261.

7. Pearcey, *Total Truth*, 20–21.

8. Swinburne, *Is There a God?*, 2.

no good, nothing but pitiless indifference."[9] Can we say that one or the other of their interpretations is true? Is not the fact that two highly educated individuals draw such different conclusions from the same facts evidence that philosophical truth is subjective? The answers to these two questions, respectively, are yes and no. We must not assume that only those things that can be demonstrated empirically can be said to be true. A great many scientific theories gain credibility and wide acceptance in spite of being unprovable via empirical methods (consider much of the field of cosmology). In such cases, scientists routinely use *abduction*, what Oxford mathematics professor John Lennox has called "the method of inference to the best explanation."[10] Just as a scientific theory can be tested rationally (and non-empirically) using thought experiments to see if the implications of accepting the theory fit with other observed data, so the implications of a moral or philosophical belief can be evaluated to determine if they make sense in light of other observations, or if a particular belief leads to inescapable logical flaws. For example, if one believes, as do some pantheists, that "god" is an impersonal force that is comprised of the combined spirit of all creation—a sort of universal entity with which we all become one when we die—then how could this life force have existed before the creation of everything which underlies its existence? If this entity is comprised of everything in creation, without that created order it would not exist; so who or what was responsible for the initial act of creating? Clearly such a belief does not explain the source of the created order, and thus additional beliefs (or entirely different ones) must be entertained to explain the existence of the universe. Using our reason and inference to the best explanation, we can seek to understand if a belief makes sense, if it follows logically from the data at hand, and if it rationally explains our observations of reality. Note that pantheism is not challenged in the previous example because the existence of the life force is empirically proved or disproved. It is called into question because of a logical flaw—because it does not explain how the universe could have been created by something that is a product of that very creation.

9. Dawkins, *River Out of Eden*, 131–32.

10. Lennox, *God's Undertaker*, 32.

How We Know What We Know

The twentieth-century philosopher and professor of law Herman Dooyeweerd proposed fifteen aspects of how we perceive reality, which have been summarized by Roy Clouser.[11] We experience these aspects routinely in daily life. These fifteen aspects can be related to the topics typically taught in secondary and post-secondary liberal arts curricula (Table 1).[12] They include math (e.g., algebra and geometry) and science (e.g., physics, chemistry, and biology) as well as the humanities and the arts. The aspects and subjects are not organized in order of importance, but rather in order of abstraction. That is, the aspects near the bottom of Table 1—algebra, geometry, physics, and chemistry—deal with the direct observation of the physical world. These subjects are particularly well suited to the scientific method, that is, to empirical methods. Measurements can be made, calculations performed and confirmed, experiments performed, and the results carefully observed and recorded. This is true also of biology, insofar as it involves the study of biochemical mechanisms, metabolic pathways, responses to stimuli, and adaptations to a changing environment. In other words, when science limits the scope of its investigations to the physical world, the empirical method is perfectly appropriate. But where the study of living matter intersects with perception and cognition, the empirical method becomes less authoritative. If we have ten dollars and spend five, it is simple quantitation that tells us that we have five dollars left. The concept of money, though, or how we use it, may touch on several other of the fifteen aspects, such as economic, social, moral, and logical.

---

11. Clouser, *Myth of Religious Neutrality*, 66–67.
12. Greene, *Reclaiming*, 180.

Table 1. Aspects by Which We Experience Reality.

Herman Dooyeweerd proposed that our ordinary experience of reality includes a unified combination of a number of different aspects, or ways of experiencing reality. These aspects turn out to represent the areas that make up the subjects of academic study. Those aspects below the line deal with the study of the physical world and are particularly suited to the scientific method and empiricism.

Aspect	Subject
fiduciary (pistical)	theology
ethical	ethics, morality
justicial	civics
aesthetic	fine arts
economic	economics
social	sociology
linguistic	language
historical	history, culture
logical	reasoning, logic
sensory	psychology
biotic	biology
physical	chemistry
kinematic	physics
spatial	geometry
quantitative	algebra

The aspects highest up on the table—ethics, morality, and theology—deal ultimately with meaning and purpose (teleology). Teleology is the explanation of phenomena in terms of the purpose they serve rather than of the cause by which they arise. One of the primary reasons for the success of the Scientific Revolution and it's scientific method was the removal of purpose or teleology from the questions being asked. In addition, and contrary to Dawkins's charge that Christians satisfy themselves with not understanding, the pioneers of the Scientific Revolution also focused on the immediate cause rather than the ultimate or first cause. To use Aristotelian terminology, they focused their studies on the material and the formal cause, to the exclusion of efficient and final cause (see Text Box 1). This was not, as many moderns assume, because they saw purpose as unimportant, or because they discounted the God of the Bible as the first and ultimate cause. Quite the contrary, for the leaders of the Scientific Revolution, the matter of purpose and ultimate cause was settled. The leaders of the Scientific Revolution were almost uniformly deeply religious. They believed that the world was created by the God of the Bible—a God of reason, logic, and order. Newton and Galileo, two of the greatest scientific innovators of their time, "believed that the universe was mathematically designed by God and that mathematics and science should strive to uncover that glorious design."[13] They saw their science as a form of worship. Johannes Kepler wrote of the laws of nature that "God wanted us to recognize them by creating us after his own image so that we could share in his own thoughts."[14]

> **Text Box 1.** Aristotle proposed four "causes" for any particular item, specifically, material, efficient, formal, and final cause. By way of example, consider a simple chair.[15]
>
> The *material* cause is the actual physical properties or makeup of a thing that is. Our hypothetical chair is made of wood, and therefore the wood is the material cause.
>
> The *efficient* cause is the thing or agent that actually brings something about, the actual force that brings something into being. The carpenter who made it is the efficient cause of our chair.
>
> The *formal* cause is the structure or design of the thing in question. We may call this the blueprint, or the plan. The formal cause is what makes it one thing rather than another. The carpenter could have chosen to make the very same wood into a box or a table, but he didn't. Instead, his plan, or design, called for putting the wood together as a chair. According to Aristotle, our carpenter's design is the formal cause.
>
> The *final* cause is the ultimate purpose for being; it is why the carpenter made the chair in the first place.

13. Kline, *Mathematics*, 337.

14. From a letter (April 1599) to the Bavarian chancellor, cited in Baumgardt and Callan, *Johannes Kepler*, 50.

15. Falcon, "Aristotle on Causality."

For all the good that it has brought, one of the more dubious and damaging bequeathals of the Enlightenment is the notion that empirical methods, which were proved so useful for the hard sciences in the Scientific Revolution, could be applied to the social, political, and philosophical realms. As philosopher of education Jack Layman points out, "Karl Marx related economic laws to cultural matters, Herbert Spencer applied Darwin's biological evolution to philosophy and ethics, and Sigmund Freud revolutionized scientific psychology and founded psychoanalysis. And in the last decade of the nineteenth century, in the hands of the scientific humanist John Dewey, education arrived as a social 'science.'"[16] These men have sought to remove the discussion of purpose from consideration in these studies. Theologian and missionary Lesslie Newbigin has pointed out, "it is difficult to describe human behaviors without using the category of purpose."[17] Newbigin goes on to write, "While the methodological elimination of final causes from the study of nature has been immensely fruitful, the attempt to explain all that exists solely in terms of efficient cause leads to conceptual absurdity and to social tyranny."[18] Although empirical methods (e.g., statistical analysis) can provide useful statistical information regarding the behaviors of populations, and may even provide correct predictions regarding the behavior of population groups, reducing individuals to numbers on a spreadsheet can never capture the cares and motivations of individual persons. This de-humanizing treatment of individuals as cogs in a larger mechanism has resulted in the postmodern revolt against purely rational and empirical truths.

When science limits itself to the mechanistic study of the natural (physical) world, empiricism is the proper epistemology; but when scientists make statements regarding meaning or purpose (e.g., teleology), they are dealing with metaphysics, not science. Many of the most outspoken atheists appeal to a lack of empirical evidence for God, never admitting that a spiritual being *cannot* be disproved by strictly empirical means— nothing can. The fact that (as they claim) there is no empirical evidence for the existence of God can only prove that they have not observed (or recognized) God, not that God does not exist. They are using rationalism to defend what is claimed to be an empirical conclusion. Their error also points to an important underlying bias—that the material world is all

16. Layman, "Early History," 32.

17. Newbigin, *Foolishness*, 34.

18. Newbigin, *Foolishness*, 93.

there is. If the material world is all that exists (this belief is called materialism), if there is no transcendence, empiricism is the obvious and only epistemology that makes sense. Upon this materialist assumption many believe (consciously or unconsciously) that empiricism is the only way to truth, but, like empiricism itself, materialism cannot be proven to be true by any empirical method.

Can We Know Religious Truth Is True?

If, as asserted above, empiricism is unsuited for investigations into aspects above the line (Table 1), how can one determine that a religious belief is universally true? We must begin with the recognition that empiricism is not the only valid epistemology, and that empiricism is itself not empirically verifiable. The eighteenth-century English theologian John Wesley described four ways to religious truth, often referred to as the Wesleyan quadrilateral. These are: tradition, reason, experience, and Scripture.[19] Although most religious beliefs rely on all four sources to some extent, different religious traditions may rely on one source of truth more than the others. Within Christianity, evangelical denominations, those that hold to a theology of biblical inerrancy, favor Scripture (often called "special revelation"[20]) as the primary source of truth. Wesley himself held this view. The Catholic Church may be seen to favor tradition (in the form of papal encyclicals and the writings of great theologians such as Augustine and Aquinas) as the primary source of theological truth. The so-called mainline denominations, as well as the Unitarians, can be thought of as favoring human reason as the primary source of theological truth. Experience as a source of truth represents the sum total of all of our personal experiences (in this case, religious experiences, such as answered and unanswered prayers or worship experiences). Pentecostal and charismatic denominations place a premium on religious experience (sometimes called "personal revelation") as a primary source of religious

19. Outler, "Wesleyan Quadrilateral," 9.

20. Special revelation as a source of truth within Wesley's quadrilateral depends upon direct input from deity and refers to divine revelation that God spoke through a specific medium, captured in time, and translated forward for future individuals to know and understand (in other words, Scripture). The Bible, comprised of sixty-six books written by ~forty authors over more than one thousand years, is considered by Christians to be a special revelation from God. This is dealt with in more detail in chapter 5.

truth.[21] In some ways, Wesley's quadrilateral might also be applied to knowledge in a more general sense. Tradition as a source of truth (linked to historicism) relies on the teachings and interpretations of the assembled body of thought leaders through the ages, and the consensus that has developed through years of thought and practice. Reason and experience as sources of truth relate to rationalism and empiricism, respectively. As it relates to a quest for truth and knowledge in general, revelation may be thought to relate to personal insights, and "aha" moments that come to knowledge seekers;[22] or to defining experiences such as Sartre's "act of will," or Jaspers' "final experience."[23]

Although some tend to rely more heavily on one or two of the four sources truth, or to discount one or two of them, in many ways moral and philosophical beliefs are arrived at by a combination of these sources of truth. The way we get to truth in our daily lives is not necessarily—in fact not predominantly—based upon empirical evidence. We rarely use the scientific process of analyzing all of (and only) the empirically verifiable data, then postulating, testing, and evaluating our hypotheses (that is, our beliefs) in light of the evidence. Most of the time people simply ignore or discount any evidence that does not fit with their presuppositions. Even what we know scientifically is not arrived at by strictly or uniformly empirical means. Data that do not seem to fit with the prevailing theories are often ignored, discounted, or explained away as results that science does not yet fully understand. In other words, to a greater or lesser degree, we all rely on multiple forms of epistemology in all of our knowledge.

Strict Empiricism and Empirical Proof

Science, as an empirical pursuit, claims to seek observable, verifiable evidence to support truth claims. The classic concept of the scientific

21. Christians believe that individuals can be inspired by personal revelations from God, but these revelations are not typically considered to be inerrant, or authoritative by most Christians. Charismatics tend to put a greater influence on such personal revelations.

22. One example of a famous "aha" moment of personal revelation is when the nineteenth-century chemist Auguste Kekulé reportedly came to the (correct) structure of the aromatic hydrocarbon benzene as the result of a daydream, in which he saw a snake eating its own tail (Kekulé, *Benzolfest*, 1302).

23. Note however that I am not here defending of any part of Jasper's philosophy. As noted by Francis Schaeffer (*How Should We Then Live?*, 167–81), these sorts of existential self-actualization are highly individualistic and entirely divorced from reason.

method begins with a question to be answered. Experiments are performed and empirical data are gathered and reviewed, after which the scientist proposes a hypothesis or theory that explains the data. Additional experiments are conducted, data gathered, and observations made to determine how well the theory explains the data at hand and how well it predicted the outcome of the additional experiments. Strictly speaking, a staunch empiricist would hold that a theory can never truly be "proven"; a theory can only be strengthened by repeatedly observing a particular outcome and never observing a reliable contradictory result. It may work a million times, successfully predicting the outcome of future experiments, but one cannot say definitively that it will always be correct without first testing every eventuality. For example, it is a widely held tenet of criminal law that fingerprints are unique to each individual. To a strict empiricist the theory cannot be proven unless the fingerprints of every human being are collected, compared, and shown to be unique. No scientific theory rises to this level of proof.

> **Text Box 2.** Johann Mayer in 1788 was the first to suggest that although specific friction ridge arrangements (fingerprints) may be similar between two individuals, they are never duplicated.[24] Fingerprints were first introduced as reliable legal evidence in 1911.[25] The admissibility of fingerprint evidence has since been debated and challenged in the courts beginning in 1999.[26] The infallibility and uniqueness of fingerprint evidence was challenged as "non-science" because the theory behind them had never been scientifically validated. Specifically, there had been no verification of the uniqueness of every individual's fingerprints based on conventional sciences, no statistical analyses, and no empirical validation process, all of which are essential for being a valid science according to the law. Yet fingerprints remain admissible as evidence in courts throughout the world. Although the fingerprints of every single individual have not been compared to confirm that they are all unique, a reasonable person can conclude that if your

24. Mayer, *Anatomische*.

25. *People v. Jennings.* Supreme Court of Illinois, 252 Ill. 534, 96 N.E. 1077, 1911.

26. *United States of America v. Byron Mitchell*, US District Court for the Eastern District of Pennsylvania, 1999.

fingerprints are at a crime scene, this is evidence that you were there, and not some hypothetical individual with fingerprints identical to yours.

If a theory may be accepted by experts in the absence of absolute, empirical proof, what is required in order to state definitively that a particular theory is actually scientific fact? In fact, much of what is widely accepted to be scientific fact is actually difficult or impractical to prove empirically. The mathematical equation $2 + 2 = 4$ can be conveniently proven empirically. If I have two coins and you have two coins, and I give you my coins, one can prove by a simple act of counting that you now have four coins. This relates back to Dooyeweerd's "quantitative" aspect (Table 1). Provided that we both recognize the same definitions for the characters 2, 4, +, and =, we can prove the mathematical equation quickly, conveniently, and repeatedly. However, there is no experiment that can empirically prove (or disprove) that our moon formed as the result of a collision of a proto-earth and a second celestial body. Mathematical models can demonstrate the plausibility of such an event, and even delimit the mass, momentum, and trajectory of the two colliding bodies. The theory may explain other observations, but all of this does not rise to the level of strict empirical proof. Short of inventing time travel and traveling back to that event to observe it firsthand, we are left with theories that make more or less sense of the data at hand.

By definition, there is no experiment that can empirically prove or disprove the existence of a supernatural (literally, outside of the natural world) divinity. It is possible to theorize mechanisms by which the universe came into being or life evolved that do not require the involvement of a divine being, but this does not mean that no divine being exists. When French physicist Pierre-Simon Laplace was asked by Napoleon why God was conspicuously absent from his hypothesis regarding the formation of matter over millions of years, he reportedly replied, "Sire, I had no need for that hypothesis."[27] Not only did Laplace not empirically prove his theories concerning the formation of the solar system, neither did he prove or disprove anything about God. Even if his mechanisms were definitively and empirically proved to be true, this would only mean the existence of God is not necessary to explain how the universe

27. Attributed to Simon Laplace (referenced in Lennox, *God's Undertaker*, 46).

formed—it would not prove or disprove anything about the existence of a divine spirit being. Statements supposing that a particular scientific theory has disproved the existence of God are metaphysical, not scientific, statements—no matter the scientific credentials of the one making such claims.

Just as no empirical data can definitively prove or disprove the existence of the supernatural, many of the scientific theories that we take for granted cannot be "proved" by strict empirical criteria. For example, the big bang theory of how the universe came into being cannot be proved or disproved empirically, simply because we are limited to the present—we cannot travel back in time to witness firsthand if the event happened. We can only study the nature of things as they are presently and hypothesize about earlier states. For this reason, scientists will often continue to refer to something as a "theory" long after it has been nearly universally accepted and considered by most to be a fact. However, a lack of strict empirical "proof" does not mean that a theory cannot be useful, or that the theory cannot be used to make correct predictions. Even partly true or incomplete theories can be immensely useful. Einstein's theory of general relativity made possible many remarkable predictions, some of which are still being verified, yet relativity has been used for decades in advanced research programs in multiple disciplines. Furthermore, Einstein's theory largely superseded Newtonian physics, yet Newtonian physics is still exceptionally useful in our everyday life. A theory can be useful while being wrong or incomplete (as with Newtonian physics), or in the absence of a strict empirical demonstration of all of its predictions (as with general relativity). A lack of absolute empirical proof of every aspect of a theory most certainly does not preclude the theory from being widely accepted and being useful for explaining observations and predicting future outcomes. The same allowances can be made for religious belief. Even in the absence of absolute empirical proof for the existence of God, the existence of God is uniquely useful for explaining many observations in life—in many cases more useful than conflicting beliefs favored by atheists.

Surprisingly little of what we "know" individually (much less what we believe) rises to the level of empirically proven fact. Adhering to extreme empirical requirements is impractical. Simply watching the daily news would be useless, as one could not believe any news item without traveling to the site to witness the events as they take place. Believing weather reports would not be possible without a thorough, firsthand understanding of the predictive models used to generate the predictions. Living with such a person, if such a person even exists, would be tedious in the extreme. Furthermore, evidence of past errors of theory or interpretation are not a reason to disregard a theory entirely. In the past scientists claimed that the earth was flat, and more recently that all life could be divided into two broad categories (bacteria and eukaryotes, with what are now referred to as "archaea" being included in the classification of bacteria). As additional data is gathered, some scientific theories must be revised, while others are discarded entirely in favor of newer theories. Science is not discarded simply because it has been wrong in the past. Should not the same consideration be afforded religion? Just because religious persons and organizations in the past have believed things that have since been proven incorrect or have supported actions that have been shown to fall short of the standards of that religion, the entire enterprise of religious belief need not be discarded.

Faith and Knowing

An honest assessment of knowledge would show that how we know what we know and what we believe is inexact at best, and most certainly not based on strict empiricism. Many of us "know" things simply because we trust the source from which we learned them, and because that knowledge fits with our overall worldview and our other preconceived notions. The very first things we learn beyond our own experiences come from parents and teachers. Children do not routinely possess the capability of questioning the source of the knowledge they gain. Many adults (and not just the religious) seem just as unable or unwilling to honestly question their sources of information, or, perhaps worse, only question information that disagrees with their own preconceptions. Often the effort that would be needed to verify information empirically and discredit misconceptions may not be trivial. Few will exert the effort either to evaluate the data that they consume or the validity of their underlying preconceptions.

But what if much of what we "know" about science and the supposed evidence obviating the existence of God is simply incorrect or incomplete? In reality, the way that we come to most scientific knowledge is not very different from how one comes to religious truth. Although science is ultimately an empirical pursuit, a search for knowledge and understanding through the study of testable and verifiable facts, scientific knowledge is not always arrived at through empirical means. Much of what is known in the sciences is not based on firsthand empirical data, but rather through our preconceptions and on what we have learned from what we consider reliable experts. Broad parallels can be made to Wesley's ways to religious truth: tradition, reason, and experience.[28] Tradition is when we learn from teachers and textbooks. Experience and reason are used when we make experimental observations ourselves and when we consider and interpret our own data and data collected and reported by others. Much of what we "know" comes from the tradition part of the Wesleyan quadrilateral. We take what we "know" (often simply what we learned from authorities that, for various reasons, we trusted), along with our own past experiences, and interpret the new data accordingly. We use rationality to interpret data and experiences. I am *not* saying that empirical scientific fact can only be accepted by faith. It is true, however, that our presuppositions inform how we process evidence. Neither am I advocating for *rationalism*,[29] though we most certainly use our (albeit flawed) reason to evaluate empirical and non-empirical evidence. When teaching students to write a conclusion for a laboratory experiment, I refer to the "C-E-R method" (for Claim, Evidence, and Reasoning). Their conclusion should start with a restatement of the purpose of the experiment, and then make a claim. The claim must be supported by evidence (their empirical data), and they must then demonstrate how or why this data supports their claim. This last part is the reasoning, and relies not on the actual data (empiricism) but on their underlying theories and suppositions. Twentieth-century theologian and Christian apologist G. K. Chesterton said, "If I am asked, as a purely intellectual question, why I believe in Christianity, I can only answer, 'For the same reason that an intelligent agnostic disbelieves in Christianity.' I believe in it quite rationally upon the evidence."[30] The different conclusions

---

28. Note that there is no parallel to Scripture in this analogy, only to Wesley's other three pillars. However, although science does not routinely ascribe inerrant authority to the writings of other scientists, there are some theories that are considered orthodoxy despite an absence of empirical evidence. Macroevolution has become one such anti-theory. Few scientists will risk questioning any part of evolution, since any such questions will result in damage to career and denouncement (with a religious fervor) from the scientific establishment.

29. As described by Francis Schaeffer (*God Who Is There*, 9), rationalism, the theory that human reason is the foundation of certainty in knowledge, is really just humanism, and is itself not a rational position since it is based on speculation and circular reasoning.

30. Chesterton, *Orthodoxy*, 150.

drawn are not due to issues with the empirically verifiable data, but differences in abduction—that is, differences in the interpretation of what constitutes the best explanation which they infer. These differences in interpretation of the evidence are related to underlying presuppositions. It is not often that an individual challenges, or is even aware of, his or her presuppositions.

For primitive man, steeped in superstition, any unexplained occurrence was attributed to the gods. The perceived character and nature of the universe and the gods was then informed by those occurrences. Prior to the Scientific Revolution, missing explanations for natural events were simply attributed to God. This approach has rightly been criticized as a "god of the gaps" mentality. But people today have a totally different set of presuppositions—presuppositions that often include the "certainty" that there is no god and that there is nothing beyond the natural world. The modern scientific enterprise demands anti-supernaturalism as a necessary first principle. This is referred to as "methodological materialism"—the belief that the material universe is all that exists. It intentionally removes teleology and the supernatural from consideration, in order to focus on the material and formal cause and only upon the proximal efficient cause. However, materialism is neither a scientific nor even an empirical belief. Materialism, like empiricism itself, cannot be demonstrated empirically. Furthermore, this presupposition is certainly not necessary to doing good science.

Math and science are typically taught at a time when students have neither the ability nor the inclination to effectively evaluate the source material or weigh the ramifications. It is often easier to accept (and to teach) incomplete and unscientific conclusions. But when, upon further examination, questions are raised for which there are no scientific answers, seekers are assured that we will one day understand, as our scientific theories are refined and new theories are put forward. They are fed a diet of bad metaphysics disguised as science and espoused by degreed experts. We need not entertain ideas of supernatural agencies, we are assured; we should instead put our faith in science and in the inexorable power of the human intellect. Nobel laureate Erwin Schrödinger wrote, "The obvious inability of present-day physics and chemistry to account for such events [the events which take place within the spatial boundary of a living organism] is no reason at all for doubting that they can be accounted for by these sciences."[31] This is "science of the gaps." It makes a religion of science and of human reason. For modern man, who believes that science has demonstrated that no god exists, any unexplained occurrence has him running to the theoreticians for a science-based explanation—a new theory that can explain the observations. No data, no facts, no findings are even momentarily considered to point to a supernatural answer, and no such belief is allowed regardless of the accumulated evidence. If science has no explanation at present, we're told that we can rest assured that one day our theories will address this new data. We need not resort to belief in religion or God; what is glibly dismissed as a "god of the gaps" belief. Instead, we replace faith in God with faith in man's ability to (some day) understand.

Science education is routinely done in a manner that puts off the possibility of divergent opinion, the "conclusions" blindly and uncritically accepted by scientists, educators, and every-day people alike. Students are taught bad metaphysics disguised as science without a frank discussion of the underlying biases. High school and college textbooks routinely include scant details or discussion of underlying assumptions and presuppositions. Textbooks include only brief mention (if any) of a theory of an "external agency," but this is quickly dismissed because it does not permit the construction of "testable hypotheses," and therefore does not provide a "scientific explanation." As Clouser reminds us, "Everyone in philosophy and the sciences knows that theories have un-provable assumptions."[32] These unprovable assumptions (and philosophical presuppositions) that underlie virtually all scientific theories should cause us to proceed "with caution and humility, retaining a judicious agnosticism about the limitations of the scientific understanding of man."[33] Yet no attention is given to alternate theories that are opposed to the materialist presuppositions of the text—theories that have been held by educated men and women of science through the ages up to and including the present day. The very suggestion of such alternatives are dismissed as unscientific (with the implication being that these alternatives are thereby illogical and untrue). We're taught that we should not expect a "scientific" (read empirical) answer to a "non-scientific" (that is metaphysical)

31. Schrödinger, *What Is Life?* 4.
32. Clouser, *Myth of Religious Neutrality*, 3.
33. Zacharias, *Shattered Visage*, 33.

question, and we should dismiss as "unscientific" conclusions that dis-agree with our unproven and unprovable materialist presuppositions.

Are Science and Religion Opposed?

Although some of the evidence supporting the existence of God is pro-vided in the next chapter, and in many of the references cited therein, the purpose of this chapter has been to show that science and religion are not opposed, provided that we do not insist on unscientific materialist presup-positions. Rather, they are simply answering difference questions—ques-tions that cannot be answered by the same methods of inquiry. Empirical methods cannot adequately answer some of the most important questions we can ask. If you believe there is no God, science cannot take His place in providing moral truth, purpose, or a sense of meaning.

The question remains, however, whether religion, as some have claimed, precludes good science. Richard Dawkins has said, "one of the truly bad effects of religion is that it teaches us that it is a virtue to be satisfied with not understanding" the world,[34] and "Faith is the great cop-out, the great excuse to evade the need to think and evaluate evidence. Faith is the belief in spite of, even perhaps because of, the lack of evidence."[35] Such statements are unsupported by the facts, but they are echoed endlessly in popular culture in spite of all of the evidence to the contrary. Believing in God need not stop someone from seeking to understand the universe in which we live and seeking ways to apply that knowledge to improve our lot in life. The founders of the Scientific Revolution were almost uniformly deeply religious. Mathematician Morris Kline rightly reminds us that Newton and Galileo "believed that the universe was mathematically designed by God,"[36] and that "The mathematicians and scientists of the Renaissance were brought up in a religious world which stressed the universe as the handiwork of God . . . Copernicus, Brahe, Kepler, Pascal, Galileo, Descartes, Newton, and Leibniz accepted this doctrine. These men were in fact orthodox Christians."[37] They saw science as a form of worship. This is not simply

34. Dawkins, *God Delusion*, 152.

35. Dawkins, quoted from a speech given at the Edinburgh International Science Festival, April 4, 1992 (cited in "Scientist's Case against God").

36. Kline, *Mathematics*, 337.

37. Kline, *Mathematics*, 206.

true of early scientific thought leaders in olden days, who might have been influenced by a nearly universal cultural bias. More recently, the religious faith of Norman Borlaug, the Nobel laureate referred to as "the man who saved a billion lives," did not stop him from performing research in plant breeding and genetics that led to the green revolution and provided a more stable food supply for billions in the developing world.[38] Nor did religious faith keep Francis Collins from a career in genomics research highlighted by discovering the genetic mutations responsible for both cystic fibrosis and Huntington's disease, then leading the publicly funded effort to sequence the human genome.[39] In fact, between 1901 and 2000 over 60 percent of Nobel laureates were Christians, and several more were Jewish.[40]

Perhaps the only argument in support of the assertion about religion being "belief in spite of evidence" can be found in a challenge put forward by noted atheist and philosopher Anthony Flew. In debates with Christians, Flew would ask, "What would have to occur to constitute the disproof of the existence of God?" To a strict empiricist this question is nonsense—like materialism itself, the transcendent can neither be proved nor disproved. But I am not an empiricist, and in truth I have no easy answer to this question. I do not know what evidence would be sufficient for me to give up my belief in God. Although this in and of itself does not prove or disprove anything, it does give me pause. After decrying the unwillingness of atheists to recognize and challenge their own preconceptions, I too must evaluate my own preconceptions. But in fairness, the atheist must also ask himself what would have to occur to constitute proof of the existence of God, and more importantly, does he require that same level of proof for the other things that he accepts as truth? It is interesting to note that Anthony Flew did honestly ask himself these questions and challenge his own preconceptions, and "converted" to theism. His account of his logic and rationale for this change is detailed in *There Is a God*.[41] It is just as important for each of us to reevaluate our preconceptions, and the evidence for and against them. This is as true of atheists ("there is no God and there is no evidence for God") and agnostics ("there is no way to know for sure") as it is for religious people.

38. Hesser, *Man Who Fed the World*.

39. Collins, *Language of God*.

40. Shalev, *100 Years of Nobel Prizes*, 57.

41. Flew, *There Is a God*.

Science and religion need not be opposed, provided that the purview and limitations of both enterprises are kept in mind. If science will insist on methodological materialism and strict empiricism, it should limit itself to only those questions and conclusions below the line that lend themselves to strictly empirical methods. In our time, many in the sciences demand anti-supernaturalism as a necessary first principle, but this is not scientific. As Madalyn Murray O'Hair noted in her description of an atheist, materialism is a "philosophy which cannot be discredited."[42] Neither can it be empirically proven, which makes hers a statement of metaphysics and religion, rather than one of empirical science. It is true that a theory of an "external agency" does not permit empirical proof or empirical experimentation. But it does not follow that, based on an overwhelming combination of evidence, concluding that an external agency exists is illogical or irrational. Those who insist on strict empiricism themselves routinely point to data not in evidence, while espousing whimsical "hypotheses" devoid of any supporting evidence. They are unwilling to even entertain the possibility of an answer, no matter how well it fits the data, that relies on a supernatural deity. The charge that our inability to explain all things through science is not, as some have claimed, a belief in a "god of the gaps." Rather, it is a recognition of the shortcomings of strict empiricism and materialism in answering questions of transcendent importance. As astronomer Allan Sandage has said, "It was my science that drove me to the conclusion that the world is much more complicated than can be explained by science. It was only through the supernatural that I can understand the mystery of existence."[43] Science alone cannot answer all questions. An open-minded reading of the data will demonstrate that there is a great deal of evidence, both philosophical and scientific, that supports the existence of the supernatural, provided that it is interpreted without the hubris and unscientific presuppositions insisted upon by atheistic materialism. Francis Bacon, credited with developing the scientific method, wrote that "A little science estranges man from God. A lot of science brings him back."[44]

We must dispel the idea that science is opposed to religion and that an empirical pursuit such as science could ever disprove the existence of a transcendent God. Empirical methods can only measure empirical

42. Murray O'Hair, *What on Earth*, 16.

43. Quoted in Strobel, *Case for a Creator*, 20.

44. This quote is most often attributed to Sir Francis Bacon (and occasionally to Louis Pasteur), though I have been unable to find an actual reference.

(physical) phenomena. The scientific method, which intentionally limits itself to empirical methods and the study of the physical world, cannot address things outside of the material realm. By definition a spiritual being will not be observable using physical (empirical) means. Although science cannot empirically prove the existence of a non-physical God, neither can it disprove God. One need not put aside science in order to believe. Scientific study of the physical world is most certainly not opposed to a belief in a transcendent deity, and very many scientific facts can be reasonably interpreted to support the existence of a creator God.

Additional Reading

For additional reading on the topics of epistemology and the use of reason to arrive at a convincing rationale for the existence of a divine, personal Creator, consider the following outstanding books. *I Don't Have Enough Faith to Be an Atheist* is an excellent, thorough, and compelling book detailing how just as much (in fact more) faith is required to believe atheism as to accept the tenets of orthodox Christianity.[45] Francis Schaeffer's *The God Who Is There* is a classic work of theology and apologetics, and can be read as the first in a trilogy of books in which Schaeffer argues thoroughly and convincingly that a personal, infinite Creator *must* exist.[46] *The Reason for God: Belief in an Age of Skepticism* is an accessible and compelling book that argues for the existence and character of the Judeo-Christian God.[47] Finally, Anthony Flew's *There Is a God*, though philosophically dense and not a light read, is a tour-de-force philosophical defense of the existence of an "outside agency" from a previously committed and widely regarded atheist and critic of religion.[48]

45. Geisler and Turek, *Faith to Be an Atheist*.
46. Schaefer, *God Who Is There*.
47. Keller, *Reason for God*.
48. Flew, *There Is a God*.

2

Science Has Proven That There Is No God

We routinely disqualify testimony that would plead for extenuation.
That is, we are so persuaded of the rightness of our judgment as
to invalidate evidence that does not confirm us in it. Nothing that
deserves to be called truth could ever be arrived at by such means.

—MARILYNNE ROBINSON[1]

"GOTT IST TOT," WROTE Friedrich Nietzsche in 1882.[2] In declaring God
dead Nietzsche did not believe that God had ever really existed, but that
man's dependence on or need for the divine had been exorcized. To religious people of the day the blasphemy of such a statement must have
been nothing short of breathtaking. Yet in the present day it is not only
increasingly acceptable to identify oneself as an atheist; in some circles it
is considered the height of intelligence and sophistication. In some fields,
including the sciences, there is a nearly universal expectation that one
rise above "foolish superstitions" such as the belief in a transcendent deity. We are taught in our classrooms, or it is at least implied, that science
has disproven what our forefathers thought of as miraculous, revealing
them to be chance occurrences and the unavoidable result of the natural

1. Robinson, *Death of Adam*, 27.
2. Nietzsche, *Gay Science*, 181.

workings of the laws of our clockwork universe. Rather than being the result of a creation event by a supernatural deity, the world came into being
as the result of a singularity, a "big bang" that occurred billions of years
ago. Throughout time and space, matter congealed and cooled. By shear
chance, along with the astronomically large universe providing seemingly endless substrate for chance occurrences to appear as organization and
design, order arose out of the disorder. Life on this earth evolved from
the simplest forms, which themselves arose on the early earth by chance,
and a fortuitous mixture of physical conditions and chemical ingredients.
All, we're confidently assured, can be sufficiently explained by the laws
of mathematics, physics, chemistry, and biology. We have been taught
that Darwin and Einstein, Watson and Crick, Miller and Urey, Bohr,
Heisenberg, Schrödinger, and many other of the great lights of science
have explained away much of what our foolish and superstitious ancestors thought was mysterious, unknown, and unknowable, dispelling any
need for a transcendent deity. But did they? Has science indeed made the
need for the God "hypothesis" obsolete?

I am proceeding here with some trepidation. I am acutely aware of
how contentious the subject matter in this chapter is. For many on both
sides, acceptance of one or another theory regarding origins is something
of a litmus test. For many evangelicals, acceptance of anything other than
a young earth and a literal reading of the Genesis account makes one a
heretic or (perhaps, in their eyes, worse) a liberal. Conversely, for many
atheists and agnostics anyone "ignorant" enough to even entertain any
part of the Old Testament accounts of creation, fall, and flood is not
worth being treated with seriousness or respect. Rather than further
alienating those who tolerated the claim in chapter 1 that scientific empiricism is not the only way to truth, and rather than losing conservative
religious readers who balk at the faintest whiff of accommodation, let me
stress that I am not here seeking to defend or refute the scientific theories
under discussion. In light of the fact that we cannot travel back in time to
witness events firsthand, we cannot say that any of the theories discussed
here are empirically proven, even though they may explain many of the
observations that can be made of our universe. If, as suggested in chapter
1, science deals with repeatable and testable phenomena, studying the beginnings of the universe or the origins of life should not be considered to
be science. As John Lennox has pointed out, such scientific pursuits rely

on the method of inference to the best explanation.[3] Perhaps we can at least agree that, just as an "incomplete" theory such as Newtonian physics (incomplete in light of general relativity) can still prove useful, so too can theories such as the big bang or Darwinian evolution provide useful frameworks for asking and answering additional scientific questions, even if you happen to believe that they are partly or wholly incorrect. My purpose is not to defend or refute these scientific theories. But even if entirely true, these theories neither disprove nor even obviate a Creator. We have been taught that there is no evidence that points to the existence of anything that could be called "God," but many believe (your author among them) that much of the scientific data can just as reasonably be interpreted to support the existence of the divine.

Neither am I seeking to insert God as an explanation where the science ends. This is not meant, as some will accuse, to be a "god of the gaps" argument. Such arguments have fallen in the past, as science has advanced to fill gaps in our knowledge. In pointing out logical discrepancies and shortcomings I am not trying to discredit these scientific theories, but rather to show that, with a different set of preconceptions (specifically, entertaining the possibility of a divine Creator, rather than accepting the non-scientific insistence on materialism and strict empiricism), much of the data can just as easily be seen to support the existence of God. As discussed in chapter 1, no empirical pursuit can ever prove or disprove a supernatural God. In this chapter I am trying to show that there remain logical inconsistencies in much of what is considered by many to be settled science, and that the materialist premises upon which common secular interpretations are based leave glaring and internally contradictory shortcomings that are too often ignored.

"In the Beginning"—Is There a Beginner?

Although Einstein's theories of general and special relativity garnered him great notoriety and fame, even Einstein himself did not fully comprehend all the implications of his hypotheses initially.[4] In 1927 Georges Henri Joseph Édouard Lemaître was among those who studied

3. Lennox, *God's Undertaker*, 32.

4. When asked in 1919 if it was really true that only three people in the world truly understood the theory of general relativity, British astronomer and physicist Arthur Eddington is said to have paused, then replied, "I'm trying to think who the third person is" (https://www.math.ttu.edu/~pearce/jokes1/joke-197.html).

and began to understand Einstein's theory and some of the implications. Lemaître was a Roman Catholic priest, an astronomer, and a professor of physics at the Catholic University of Louvain in Belgium. He began to consider the implications of the theory of relativity to see if and how it could explain observations of radiation from distant light sources (that is, stars). Astronomers had observed that radiation from distant stars had a *red shift*, a propensity to be shifted toward longer wavelengths on the electromagnetic spectrum (Text Box 3). The light from distant galaxies was shifted to longer (redder) wavelengths, suggesting that these galaxies were moving away from us. The farther away the light source, the more red-shifted the light, suggesting to Lemaître that the entire universe was expanding. As a result, he proposed what he called his "hypothesis of the primordial atom."[5] The initial theory proposed an expanding universe (a theory often erroneously attributed to Edwin Hubble, but actually proposed by Lemaître),[6] based on the presence of this red shift in observations of stars.

> **Text Box 3.** Light (electromagnetic radiation) can be thought to travel in waves, like sound or like waves of water on the ocean (except that, unlike water, electromagnetic radiation has no mass). Light has a wavelength—that is, there is a measurable distance between the crest of each wave of light that we register with our eyes, or that scientists register with their instruments. Light of different colors has different wavelengths, or different distances between the crest of each wave. Visible light with a shorter wavelength is registered by our eyes as violet, while the longest wavelengths of visible light are registered as red light. Just as the water in a swimming pool can bend light, and make a straight pole seem bent where the pole breaks the surface of the water, so tiny water droplets suspended in our atmosphere can bend (the process is called "refraction") the light from the sun into the colors of a rainbow. The colors of light—red, orange, yellow, green, blue, indigo, and violet—decrease in wavelength from the longest to the shortest.

5. Lemaître, "Univers homogène," 49–59.

6. In fact, in 1922 Russian scientist Alexander Friedman proposed a similar solution to Einstein's equations, suggesting that the radius of the universe (it's "curvature") increased over time. Friedman's work was largely unknown, as he lived and worked in the USSR and died in 1925 ("Über die Krümmung des Raumes," 377–86).

These are the visible wavelengths of light. Light with a shorter wavelength than violet light is called ultraviolet, light with a wavelength longer than visible light is called "infrared." The retinas in our eyes are organized such that they can respond to particular wavelengths of electromagnetic radiation—so-called visible light. A red shift would be expected to occur if the light source were moving away from the detector. Just as sound waves stretch as a fire truck or ambulance moves away, causing an apparent elongation (lowering of the pitch) of the sound of the siren, waves of light stretch as the light source moves away from us.

Lemaître realized that an expanding universe implied that at some point in the past the universe must have been very tiny: essentially a single point. That single point, which Lemaître called the "primordial atom" (and has since been called a "singularity"), would have expanded over the millennium, with the result being our present, still-expanding universe. In other words, the universe had a beginning. And if it had a beginning, it must have had a "Beginner," a Creator. Prior to this, the common hypothesis was of a static universe, that is, a universe of more or less its current size that had always existed. The idea that the universe had a beginning was anathema to many physicists of the time. It was considered almost heretical, a step backwards in the advances made since the Scientific Revolution to understand and explain our universe without resorting to the God "hypothesis." Einstein declared to Lemaître, "Your calculations are correct, but your physics is atrocious."[7] In so doing, Einstein was ignoring data in favor of his own preconceived ideas of the nature of the universe. This theory was later referred to dismissively as the "big bang" theory, a term of derision attributed to physicist Fred Hoyle, who was among many early opponents of the theory. Einstein's initial rejection of the work was actually a rejection of an expanding universe. But work by Edwin Hubble published two years after the initial publication of Lemaitre's theories put forth Hubble's velocity-distance relationship, which strongly supported an expanding universe (and, consequently, a beginning to the universe at the so-called big bang).[8]

7. Deprit, *Monsignor Georges Lemaître*, 370.
8. Hubble, "Relationship between Distance and Radial Velocity," 167.

Over the years there has been additional empirical evidence for an expanding universe. Evidence supporting an expanding universe is so widespread that few scientists believe anything else. It is, perhaps, ironic that a theory which, when it was first proposed, was criticized by the atheistic scientific elite in part as quasi-religious nonsense is now criticized by many religious people as a godless theory that goes against Holy Scripture. Whereas scientists once roundly criticized the theory because of its seemingly religious implications of a creative force at the beginning of all things, many scientists (and many science teachers) now assume and teach that the theory is a nail in the coffin of religious belief. But does a big bang theory, if true, fully explain creation as we now observe it? And does it disprove a creator God? The answer to both questions is no.

The essence of the big bang theory is that the universe, which can be observed to be expanding, must have been very much smaller in the distant past. Presently every star and celestial object observable to us is moving away from us. As the universe expands, all of the matter in the universe is growing farther and farther apart. Imagine a balloon with a number of dots drawn on it with a felt-tip pen, with one of the dots representing our solar system. Dots near our own represent other stars in our Milky Way galaxy, while dots farther away represent more distant stars or entire galaxies. As the balloon expands (as someone breathes into it and inflates it), two dots on opposite sides of the balloon will get farther apart relatively quickly. But even two dots drawn fairly near to one another will grow farther apart as the balloon expands. And no dot drawn on the surface of the balloon would get closer to "our" dot as long as the balloon continues to expand. As with the dots on the balloon, all of the stars and galaxies that we can observe are moving away from us. The farther away they are, the faster they are receding, and the more red-shifted is the light that we can see from them. If the universe is getting bigger and bigger, then if one could run time backward, it would get smaller and smaller, and all of the matter in the universe would be much closer together. If one were to wind the clock back far enough, at some point in the past the universe would have been a nearly infinitely dense, nearly infinitely small point. This singularity, or "primordial atom" as Lemaître called it, would have contained all of the matter and energy in our current universe in a very small area. Put simply, the big bang proposes that this extremely small, incredibly dense singularity expanded, giving rise to the universe as we now see it.

Returning to the two questions above, does the big bang "theory" fully explain the origins of the universe, and does it discount the need for a creator God? In response to the first question, allowing that the big bang happened, what (or who) caused it? The first law of thermodynamics states that energy cannot be either created or destroyed,[9] and the law of conservation of matter states that matter can be neither created nor destroyed.[10] There are few who would question these two fundamental laws. So where did all of the energy and matter in our cosmos come from? What was the source of the energy that exploded the primordial atom? What (or who) created the matter that apparently blinked into creation in the form of this singularity, and what (or who) provided the enormous amount of energy needed to oppose the massive gravity of the primordial atom to "inflate the balloon" upon which the "dots" of the galaxies were drawn and hurl them across space? Nobel Prize–winning physicist Arno Penzias has said, "Astronomy leads us to a unique event, a universe which was created out of nothing, one with the very delicate balance needed to provide exactly the right conditions required to permit life, one which has an underlying, one might say 'supernatural,' plan."[11] Certainly science can theorize about the nature of matter and energy and their transformations, but the two questions above are not answered by the big bang. God is not disproved.

Accepting the scientific evidence that supports the big bang not only does not disprove God; it doesn't even make a belief in God unnecessary, as some would have us believe. *Ex nihilo nihil fit*—"out of nothing, nothing comes." Neither does the big bang necessarily discount the biblical account of creation. The biblical account of creation, found in the first book of the Jewish and Christian scriptures, is attributed to Moses. Regardless of who wrote it or when, it can be agreed that it was written by a person who was not present at the initial creation. The writer either made it up, recorded an earlier myth or an earlier account that was passed down orally prior to that time, or "witnessed" it himself in

---

9. Clausius, "Über die bewegende Kraft der Wärme." 368–97.

10. In fact, although credited in chemistry textbooks to Antoine Lavosier, the "Father of Chemistry," this law was first demonstrated by Russian polymath Mikhail Lomonosov, and later "rediscovered" by Antoine Lavoisier. Lavoisier, the French nobleman and chemist, served on the French Gunpowder Commission and was influential in the formation of the DuPont gunpowder business, but was beheaded during the French Revolution (Pomper, "Lomonsov," 119).

11. Penzias, "Creation Is Supported by All the Data So Far," 83.

a dream or a vision or some other divine inspiration. If one accepts for a moment that the biblical account was given (via dream or vision) by inspiration from a supernatural Creator to a human being who wrote the Genesis account or who began the oral tradition that was eventually recorded in Genesis, could the account not be expected to be rather short on scientific detail, while still being true? Bear in mind that the purpose of the Genesis creation account is Who created, not how He created. Robert Jastrow (former director of NASA's Goddard Institute for Space Studies) has said, "the details differ, but the essential elements in the astronomical and biblical accounts of Genesis are the same."[12] Bear in mind that this would have been thousands of years ago, prior to organized education, the development of chemistry and physics, and even the most basic knowledge of how things work. Furthermore, the vision would have been vastly abbreviated, with much detail removed. The human witness to this dream or vision would have been ill prepared to understand what he was seeing, and would have tried to couch it in terms that he and his peers could comprehend. Just as primitive tribes observing contrails formed by airplanes flying overhead describe birds with very long tails, so the author of the creation account in Genesis may have recorded a faithful narrative of what he observed in a dream or vision while lacking the proper scientific vocabulary. Thus, the Genesis account talks of a "vault" (the sky) to separate "the water under the vault from the water above it."[13] It was common belief in ancient times that rain came from the heavens, from water that existed above the "firmament" (the sky), when the sky "opened." I must stress that I am not saying that the possible interpretation above is truth. I am not a Bible scholar and I do not lightly propose any interpretation of the Bible. If the Scriptures are to be taken seriously, interpreting them in this way may be inherently dangerous, and not something to be taken lightly. But it is important to remember that the purpose of the creation account in Genesis 1 is not to provide a detailed scientific understanding of how God created everything. It is meant to state Who created the universe and the earth. A secondary purpose is to affirm that the culmination of the creation event was the creation of humans "in God's image." Regardless of your view of the Christian scriptures, the data in support of the big bang does

12. Jastrow, *God and the Astronomers*, 105.
13. Gen 1:7 (NIV).

not disprove the existence of a supernatural Creator or nullify the biblical account of creation.

If the statements excerpted above from the Bible seem contradictory and obviously wrong, consider for a moment the alternatives. In a world-view that accepts that the big bang happened without the intervention of an astonishingly powerful Creator, then one must accept that at a particular moment about 13.8 billion years ago nothing blew up into everything. In an "explosion" of unimaginable power every bit of energy and matter in the universe today blinked into existence. The singularity at the beginning of our universe was a nearly infinitely dense object, and it had to have come from somewhere. The first law of thermodynamics states that "the total energy of an isolated system is constant," and that "energy can be transformed from one form to another but can be neither created nor destroyed."[14] The law of conservation of matter states that matter can neither be created nor destroyed.[15] Einstein's theory of special relativity famously describes how energy and mass may be interchangeable,[16] but these theories in no way provide for the creation of either mass or energy from nothing. Where then did all of the matter, and the energy to spread it across the heavens, come from? Indeed, this is not a new "problem" with any account of origins. In the Bhagavad Gita (ca. first century BC) Krishna identifies the eternal Brahmin as "That which is immutable, and independent of any cause but itself."[17] Even earlier, in the sixth century before Christ the pre-Socratic Greek philosopher Anaximander proposed the existence of the *apeiron*, literally "that which is boundless or without limit," as the source from which everything else is derived. Although Anaximander never ascribed personality to the *apeiron*[18] (God did not reveal Himself to the ancient Greeks), he apparently recognized the need for what he and other Greek philosophers of the era referred to

14. Clausius, "Über die bewegende Kraft der Wärme," 500–524

15. Lavoisier, *Traité Élémentaire de Chimie.*

16. Einstein, "Zur Elektrodynamik bewegter Körper." Although it is a vast over-simplification, the famous equation $E = m{\cdot}c^2$ essentially shows that the energy of an object is equal to its mass times the square of the speed of light. Werner Heisenberg wrote "mass and energy are, according to the theory of relativity, essentially the same concepts. We may say that all elementary particles consist of energy," and "Perhaps the most important consequence of the principle of relativity is the inertia of energy, or the equivalence of mass and energy" (*Physics and Philosophy*, 44 and 91).

17. Bhagavad Gita 8.3, 74.

18. Most of Anaximander's work is lost. Only a few fragments remain, and these are many years removed from the original manuscripts.

as the "first cause" or the "prime mover." The ancients recognized that every effect has a cause, but this could not go back forever into eternity. Instead, they postulated a first uncaused cause.[19]

Furthermore, if one believes that no divine hand guided the creation of all that we see today, then one must also accept that after nothing blew up into everything 13.8 billion years ago, all of this matter somehow congealed and, against all odds and against another primary law of physics, formed, by a mistake of chance, the highly ordered world we now see. The second law of thermodynamics states that systems go from a state of order to a state of disorder (called "entropy," a measure of disorder). As stated in the nineteenth century by Rudolf Clausius, German physicist and one of the founders of the field of thermodynamics, "The entropy of the universe tends to a maximum."[20] But creation without a divine intelligence would require us to believe that this unfathomably large explosion occurred from nothing, and that against all experience you or I have with explosions, instead of destruction and ruin, structure and order emerged. This would be as if, for example, instead of a natural gas explosion destroying a home and leaving behind rubble and waste, the explosion resulted in the creation of a complete set of the *Encyclopedia Britannica* ordered neatly on a bookshelf where there had previously been no such book collection. But the order that we are to believe occurred by accident in the absence of supernatural intervention is *much more* unlikely. In a vast sea of nothing a giant explosion (one wonders, "of what?") caused everything to blink into existence, out from which arose (we are to believe by random chance) the human genome and countless other examples of inconceivable complexity and organization. Philosophy professor Peter Kreeft has written:

> Someone once said that if you sat a million monkeys at a million typewriters for a million years, one of them would eventually type out all of Hamlet by chance. But when we find the text of Hamlet, we don't wonder whether it came from chance and monkeys. Why then does the atheist use that incredibly improbable explanation for the universe? Clearly, because it is his only chance of remaining an atheist. At this point we need

19. Aristotle, *Metaphysics*, xii (referenced in Clouser, *Myth of Religious Neutrality*, 11). Being educated in Greek philosophy, the apostle Paul was attributing the uncaused cause to the Judeo-Christian God when he argued at the Areopagus in Athens (Acts 17:28) that "in him we live and move and have our being."

20. Clausius, "Über die bewegende Kraft der Wärme."

a psychological explanation of the atheist rather than a logical explanation of the universe"[21]

Even this comical example of monkeys at typewriters vastly understates the problem. The universe contains immeasurably more information than is present in the collected works of Shakespeare, and one must assume not only that all these hypothetical monkeys are typing away, but that they can repair the typewriters when they break (remember that the second law of thermodynamics implies that the typewriters will break—entropy, or disorder, tends to a maximum), and that the monkeys could have built the typewriters in the first place. Although it seems easy to look at the Genesis account of creation in light of current scientific theory and find apparent discrepancies, it is just as easy to look at the materialist theories of the origin of the universe and find far more gaping problems that require a willing suspension of disbelief, the argument of personal credulity notwithstanding.[22]

The Anthropic Principle: The Impression of Design

Although it is difficult to calculate the odds against the astonishing order in our universe developing purely by chance following a massive explosion in which all known matter was flung out into the far reaches of space, it is possible to comment on and marvel at the precision with which our universe is organized. This precision runs counter to chance occurrence and impersonal probability—it appears as if the universe is deliberately organized to support the existence of intelligent life. This concept was first given a name—the anthropic principle—by physicist Brandon Carter in 1973, while presenting at a symposium honoring the five-hundredth anniversary of the birth of Nicolaus Copernicus.[23] In short, the anthropic principle holds that, contrary to some interpretations of the enormity

---

21. Kreeft, "Argument from Design."

22. In his book *The Blind Watchmaker*, Richard Dawkins rightly points out that what he calls the "argument against personal *incredulity*" is not a valid argument against a scientific theory (p. 55). When educated persons (Dawkins limits his critique to Christians) say or write, "I simply cannot believe that . . . ," their incredulity in spite of scientific evidence is no legitimate argument. I agree (provided the evidence in question is valid). However, the credulity of some educated atheists to accept entirely ridiculous hypotheses is no legitimate argument supporting these arguments, no matter how distinguished the individual who is espousing the illogical hypothesis.

23. Carter, *Large Number Coincidences*, 291–98.

and age of the cosmos, humanity appears to hold a special place in the universe. That is, in order for the universe to support life, the laws of nature, physical constants, and other parameters of the universe must have values that are consistent with conditions for life, and those values appear to be finely tuned to allow life.[24] The four fundamental forces of nature (gravity, electromagnetism, and the strong and weak nuclear forces) and the various physical constants (e.g., the speed of light in a vacuum, the masses and charges of protons, electrons, and neutrons, etc.) have very precise values; values that, if changed even a tiny bit, would render life (and in many cases, the universe itself) impossible. For example, Nobel Prize–winning physicist and avowed atheist Steven Weinberg commented that the cosmological constant (just one among many physical constants that, if only infinitesimally different from its actual value, would render life in our universe impossible) is "remarkably well adjusted in our favor."[25] Stephen Hawking wrote that if the expansion rate of the very early universe "had been smaller by even one part in a hundred thousand million million, the universe would have re-collapsed before it ever reached its present size."[26] Carl Sagan noted that "only a very restricted range of laws of nature are consistent with galaxies and stars, planets, life and intelligence."[27] None of these critical values appears to rely on the others; that is, they are in most cases independent of one another—each one could have had virtually any value—yet they all have exceptionally fine-tuned values for a universe that supports life. Richard Dawkins defines science as "the study of complicated things that give the appearance of having been designed for a purpose," though he maintains that there is no Creator and we are here by chance.[28] Nobel laureate Francis Crick reminds scientists that they "must constantly keep in mind that what they see was not designed, but rather evolved."[29] Hawking wrote that "these numbers seem to have been very finely adjusted to make possible the development of life,"[30] yet physicist John Barrow has noted that "we have never explained the numerical value of any of the constants of nature . . .

---

24. Gonzalez and Richards, *Privileged Planet*, 195–208.

25. Weinberg, "Designer Universe?"

26. Hawking, *Brief History of Time*, 121.

27. Quoted in Heeren, *Show Me God*, 201.

28. Dawkins, *Blind Watchmaker*, 4.

29. Crick, quoted in Geisler and Turek, *Faith to Be an Atheist*, 119.

30. Hawking, *Brief History of Time*, 125.

the reason for their values remains a deeply hidden secret."[31] Faced with obvious evidence of design, these men of science cannot put aside their materialist presupposition. They refuse to see what is clearly evidence in support of a Creator.

Other noted physicists have commented on the apparent fine-tuning of the universe and been led to entertain heretical (to the atheist scientific community) possibilities. Fred Hoyle, the same physicist who originally dismissively termed Lemaître's theory of the primordial atom the "big bang," commented that it appeared as if "a super-intellect had monkeyed with physics, as well as with chemistry and biology,"[32] while physicist Paul Davies has noted that "the impression of design is overwhelming."[33] Princeton physicist Freeman Dyson has noted that the more he studies the universe, the more he finds evidence that "the universe in some sense must have known that we were coming."[34] Stephen Hawking wrote that it would be very difficult to explain why the universe should have many of the characteristics it does "except as an act of a God who intended to create beings like us."[35] Oxford physicist Roger Penrose, commenting on a single parameter (called the "original phase-space volume") that demonstrates how unique the big bang was, says, "this now tells us how precise the Creator's aim must have been: namely to an accuracy of one part in ten raised to the power of ten raised to the power of 123."[36] Penrose goes on to write that "this is an extraordinary figure. One could not possibly even write the number down in full." It would be one followed by a successive number of zeroes too large to write out. Penrose notes that if we wished to count that number out on protons (rather than pieces of paper), we would fall far short of enough matter in the entire universe to write down the figure.

The so-called weak anthropic principle holds that only in a universe that is capable of supporting life will there be living beings present to observe any such fine-tuning. This is sometimes called a "selection effect." In other words, to us within our present universe it may seem astonishing that all of the physical constants in the universe appear to be so fine-tuned

31. Barrow, *Constants of Nature*, xiii.

32. Hoyle, "Universe," 12.

33. Davies, *Cosmic Blueprint*, 203.

34. Dyson, quoted in Lutzer, *Seven Reasons*, 127.

35. Hawking, *Brief History of Time*, 131.

36. Penrose, *Emperor's New Mind*, 344.

as to make our existence possible, but we only think that because we do not (in fact could not) exist in the vast number of other possible universes in which life is not possible. But this does nothing to address or dispel the astonishing improbability of creation. Faced with these astronomical odds against the possibility of our existence, some have put forward the multiverse "theory," in which a sort of vast cosmic soup of energy and subatomic particles is continuously burping up new universes all the time. Although the vast majority would not support life (most would not, in fact, even result in an expanding universe), given an infinite number of such new universes, and an infinite amount of time (this hypothetical universe generator would have been around well before our universe popped into existence), even the extremely statistically improbable circumstances of our universe would eventually occur. Those who entertain such theories have neatly discounted the fact of our fine-tuned universe by referring to other universes, none of which have been found or proven, none of which ever could be found or proven using empirical means, and for which there is no supporting data. In fact, other than as a denial of a divine Creator as the cause of our fine-tuned universe, there is no reason to even speculate such a preposterous notion.[37] The hypothesis is entirely untestable and is therefore not science by any standard of science. Now who is believing "in spite of, even perhaps because of, the lack of evidence"? Dinesh D'Souza rightly points out that "In order to abolish one invisible God, [they] have to conjure up an infinity of invisible universes."[38] Physicist Lee Smolin has said of the multiverse theory that "it makes it possible to explain almost anything," and "to argue this way is not to reason, it is simply to give up looking for a rational explanation."[39]

Although a more thorough treatment of the physics behind this evidence is complicated and beyond the purview of this book,[40] the fact remains that the values of the various fundamental forces and physical constants that make life possible are so finely tuned with respect to each other, and to all of the possible values that they could have had, that it is statistically impossible that it happened by chance. If I were to bet you one

37. The genesis of the idea of a multiverse appears to be a statement by Erwin Schrödinger in which he stated that his equations appeared to describe several different, parallel, and simultaneous histories.

38. D'Souza, *Godforsaken*, 174.

39. Smolin, *Life of the Cosmos*, 45.

40. For a more thorough detailing of some of the physics behind the anthropic principle, see for example Rees, *Just Six Numbers*; and Davies, *Cosmic Jackpot*.

million dollars that I could roll a single six-sided die ten times in a row and get a one each time, and then proceeded to do it, you would likely not pay me. You would be certain that the die must have been loaded. Even without knowing the odds against my having rolled ten ones in a row (the odds are about one in sixty million), you would *know* that it could not have happened simply by chance. Yet atheists routinely accept more astronomically unlikely odds that our universe arose by chance. One day, we are assured optimistically, humans will advance sufficiently in their scientific understanding to make sense of this evidence—God need not apply.

Darwinian Evolution—Survival of the Fittest

There is implicit in today's science curricula the implication that the Darwinian theory of evolution has explained the origins of life sufficiently, that we no longer need the idea of a divine Creator. Richard Dawkins states that "Darwin made it possible to be an intellectually fulfilled atheist."[41] Because of the controversy surrounding Darwinian evolution, "evolution" has become a philosophically freighted word. The fact is that things—*living* things—evolve. Drug-resistant bacteria are an increasingly challenging problem in the medical profession. There are strains of the bacterium *Staphylococcus aureus* that have developed resistance to the drugs (like penicillin) used to kill them. These "methicillin-resistant" (or multidrug-resistant) *Staphylococcus aureus* (MRSA) strains have evolved to be resistant to antimicrobial and antibacterial drugs. In some cases, this drug resistance is genetically based; that is, it is mediated by the acquisition of mutations resulting in the regulation of drug-resistance genes, or even in the acquisition of an entire new drug-resistance gene from a resistant strain. The defining characteristic of MRSA is its ability to thrive in the presence of antibiotics such as penicillin, which usually prevent bacterial growth by inhibiting synthesis of the bacterium's cell wall. These MRSA strains are not new species, but they are an example of the acquisition and propagation of a beneficial genetic change. However, perhaps a step back is in order to explain a bit more about DNA and genetics in general for non-scientists.

DNA, which stands for deoxyribonucleic acid, is a *biopolymer*, or a long chain comprised of repeating subunits (monomers). The subunits

---

41. Dawkins, *Blind Watchmaker*, 10.

(called "nucleotides") that make up DNA are comprised of three parts: a nitrogenous base, a pentose sugar, and a phosphate group.

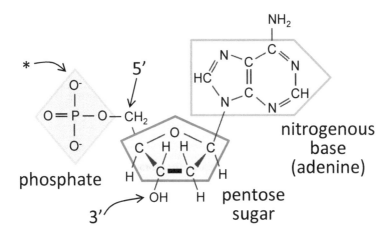

Figure 1. The Parts of a Nucleotide. Deoxyribonucleic acid (DNA) is a biopolymer (a naturally occurring polymer) for which the monomer (the basic building block) is a nucleotide. Each nucleotide is comprised of a phosphate group, a pentose sugar (deoxyribose in DNA), and one of four nitrogenous bases (adenine is shown). The asterisk shows where the 3' hydroxyl group of the next nucleotide attaches.

Each nucleotide in DNA contains one of four nitrogenous bases. Each individual nitrogenous base is attached to a pentose (meaning "five-carbon") sugar called "deoxyribose," which is then connected to a phosphate group. Individual nucleotides are linked together to form a DNA strand. Each nucleotide is joined together by a linkage between the deoxyribose (sugar) of one nucleotide and the phosphate group of the next, forming what is referred to as the DNA "backbone." The DNA molecule consists of two complementary strands that are joined together much like the two sides of a zipper. The nitrogenous bases (abbreviated as A, C, G, and T from their names, adenosine, cytosine, guanine, and thymidine) are like the teeth of the zipper, interacting preferentially with each other. That is, in the two complementary strands the nitrogenous bases on the first strand interact preferentially with bases on the complementary second strand.

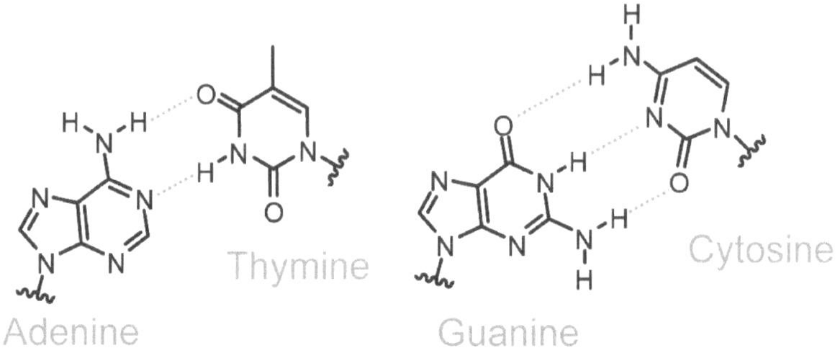

Figure 2. Base-Pairing in DNA. The four nitrogenous bases pair preferentially with the bases on the adjacent DNA strand via formation of intermolecular hydrogen bonds. Adenine and thymine pair up by forming two H-bonds, while cytosine and guanine pair via the formation of three H-bonds.

Each A interacts preferentially with a T on the complementary DNA strand while each C bonds preferentially with a G on the complementary strand. For the sake of ease, imagine a numeric value for each nitrogenous base: A=1, C=2, G=3 and T=4. The two bases on the complementary strands must add up to five. When one strand has an A, the complementary strand must have a T; when one strand has a G, the complementary strand must have a C. The arrangement of bases on the DNA strand contains coded information, much like the order of dots and dashes in Morse code contains information.

Our DNA is organized into genes (much like words in a sentence), with most genes encoding a protein or protein subunit. A set of three nitrogenous bases (called a "codon") can be translated by the cellular machinery into a single amino acid, the building block of proteins. Proteins are the machinery of the cell. Just as DNA is a long chain of repeating nucleotide subunits arranged in a specific order, so proteins are long chains of amino acids. While there are only four naturally occurring nitrogenous bases present in DNA, there are twenty naturally occurring amino acids present in proteins that are encoded by DNA. These twenty amino acids are much like the letters of our alphabet—the order in which they appear spells out information (in this case, a protein). The sequence of nitrogenous bases in DNA encodes the sequence of amino acids in a protein, with each set of three nitrogenous bases (each codon) "translated" by the cellular machinery into an amino acid. Proteins serve many useful functions within the cells that make up our body. They can serve in a structural capacity (such as actin and myosin in skeletal muscle), they can serve as carriers (e.g., hemoglobin carries oxygen in the blood, lipoproteins carry fats and cholesterol), and they can perform or facilitate chemical reactions (such proteins are called "enzymes"). The translation of DNA into proteins is performed in concert by dozens of enzymes (themselves encoded in the organism's DNA).

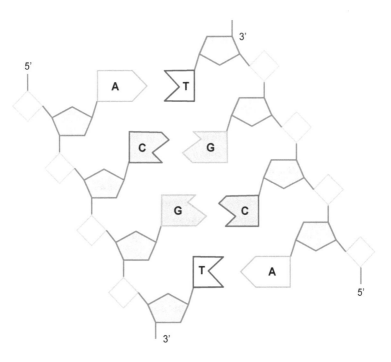

Figure 3. Double-Stranded DNA. The phosphate group attached to the fifth carbon of the deoxyribose sugar forms a linkage with the third carbon on an adjacent nucleotide. This forms the DNA backbone (e.g., repeating sugar-phosphate-sugar-phosphate, etc.), leaving the nitrogenous bases free to pair with their counterparts on the adjacent second strand. DNA is double-stranded; across from every A is a T, across from every C is a G, and so on.

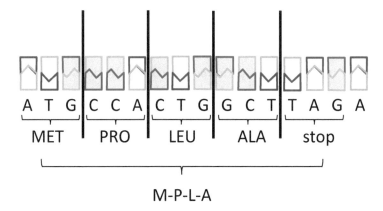

ATG CCA CTG GCT TAGA

MET   PRO   LEU   ALA   stop

M-P-L-A

Figure 4. DNA to Protein. Within the regions of DNA that encode proteins, a group of three bases (called a "codon") are translated into one of the twenty amino acids that are incorporated into proteins. For example, an A-T-G on DNA encodes the amino acid methionine, whereas a T-A-G (or T-A-A or T-G-A) signals the cellular machinery to stop adding amino acids to the nascent protein. The sequence of amino acids in a protein determines its three-dimensional structure and its physical and chemical properties.

Each cell in your body contains the instructions for every protein that you'll need to live, plus information on when and where to make those proteins. In this way, an organism's genome (its complete complement of DNA) is similar to a library containing instructions for how to make a fully functioning copy of that organism. Not every gene is expressed or turned on in every cell, but every cell contains all of the DNA needed to make every sub-cellular structure or protein in the entire organism. For example, the genes encoding proteins involved in lactation are expressed only in the breast of a lactating woman, though the genes for these proteins are present in the DNA of every cell in women as well as men. The amount of information present in the human genome, or in the genome of even the simplest bacterium, is enormous. Printing the human genome on paper would take about two thousand books the size of this one.

Although the amount of information, the amount of order represented by the genome of even an apparently simple single-celled organism is remarkable, because of the relatively high natural mutation rate and the very high reproduction rate of bacteria, new genetic variations can happen with great frequency simply by chance. The high reproduction rate effectively selects against any chance mutation that provides a disadvantage, since a healthier bacterium will out-compete (e.g., grow more quickly, or reproduce more successfully) one with an unhealthy mutation, quickly overwhelming any with deleterious mutations. And because of this high mutation rate and rapid reproduction rate, evolution within many bacterial species can be studied effectively. In a classical example of "survival of the fittest," individual bacterium in a population exposed to a drug may contain chance mutations. Many of these mutations make them less fit, and these individuals fail to thrive and reproduce. Other mutations may impart no benefit at all, and given the absence of a selective advantage, these mutations would most likely not persist. However, a small number of mutations may provide a selective advantage—perhaps an increased ability to pump out and thus resist a particular class of antibiotics. Given a population of billions of individual bacteria, the comparatively high mutation rate and very short doubling time suggests that it is not unlikely that there may exist individuals within the population that have a chance mutation that provides such resistance. An individual bacterium that carries a beneficial mutation may reproduce, while its peers die or fail to thrive when exposed to the antibiotic. With a doubling time of twenty minutes, for example, that one bacterium would produce two daughter cells in twenty minutes, eight in one hour, and about one billion individual bacteria in ten hours—all carrying the advantageous mutation.[42]

If the theory of evolution can thus be demonstrated experimentally, why is there still so much argument around it? Put simply, the disagreements revolve around how far we can extrapolate to say that these molecular mechanisms, which can be demonstrated in the laboratory to explain variations such as drug resistance within asexual bacterial species, can be said to explain the origins of life on our planet. In short, they cannot. Darwinian evolution is not a theory of the origins of life. It has never claimed to be. It is a theory of adaptive complexity, an attempt at explaining the development of diversity in biological systems, but it does not describe how life arose from inanimate materials. The theory of

---

42. Note that a doubling time of twenty minutes is very optimistic and assumes perfect conditions and unlimited energy resources upon which the bacteria can feed. The specifics in this example are given only as an ideal case demonstrating that an advantageous mutation could be incorporated in a population of bacteria is a short enough timeframe to be studied in the laboratory.

evolution as put forward by Darwin[43] and as understood by its advocates requires the presence of life. If there is no life, there can be no survival, and therefore survival of the fittest is a meaningless concept. If there is no life, there is no replication, and thus no genetic material to be mutated and no way for the mutation to be fixed into an organism's offspring. To the scientist reading this chapter, this may come as no surprise. But to the non-scientist, both the Christian and the atheist or agnostic, the implications of Darwinian evolution are so politically and philosophically fraught that few seem to have taken the time to distinguish what the theory actually does and does not claim. In short, something must be alive to adapt and survive in the sense Darwin intended, and it must reproduce in order to pass on that adaptation. Non-living matter does not adapt to the environment, nor does it pass on those adaptations to any progeny. Darwinian evolution does not explain the origins of life.

That Darwin's theory does not explain the origins of life does not dispel the real scientific issues and disagreements surrounding the theory. The real point at issue relates to what some have called "macroevolution" vs. "microevolution." Molecular evolution is a critical premise in the study of medicine, epidemiology, pharmacology (the study of how the body works and how it interacts with foreign agents such as drugs and nutrients), genetics, and biotechnology. The rapid response to the COVID-19 pandemic impacting the world as I write this was enabled in part by premises underlying Darwin's theory, and our ongoing response to the virus will likely be benefitted by some of the assumptions of the theory of evolution.[44] Everyone ought to acknowledge and understand microevolution. It explains the basic mechanisms by which organisms may adapt genetically to their environment, and it provides an explanation for how some disease genes have persisted in human populations (see Text Box 4). What it does not do, however, is prove or disprove any aspect of the Bible.

Text Box 4. Cystic fibrosis (CF) is among the more common lethal genetic disorders. It is caused by a mutation in the CFTR (cystic fibrosis transmembrane conductance regulator) gene, which affects the cells that produce mucus and digestive fluids. Approximately one in every 2,500 children are born

43. Darwin, *Origin of Species.*
44. See for example Callaway, "Coronavirus Is Mutating."

with CF, and about one in twenty-five Caucasians are carriers of a mutation that causes the disease. We each carry two copies of every gene in our genome, one copy from our mother, and one from our father. If both copies of a particular disease gene are non-functioning, we have the disease. If one copy is non-functioning, we are said to be a heterozygote. Depending on the gene itself and the nature of the mutation, a heterozygote may see very little functional effect of the mutation in one copy of the gene—the single remaining functional copy can often accommodate for the absence of the second copy. However, heterozygotes are carriers, and can pass the mutation on to their offspring. If two people who are heterozygotes for the same disease gene reproduce, there is a one in four chance that their offspring will get two non-functioning copies of the gene and will have the disease. Initially the persistence in human populations of disease genes such as mutations causing CF (which clearly cause a competitive disadvantage) was considered a possible refutation of Darwinian "survival of the fittest." However, it has been demonstrated that heterozygotes (those with one non-functioning copy of the gene) may survive better upon infection with cholera,[45] and they may be resistant to typhoid fever,[46] demonstrating a clear survival advantage to carriers, and explaining why a seemingly disadvantageous disease gene has persisted.

In between theories on the origins of life and what has been referred to as microevolution, there is another level of Darwin's theory. Specifically, Darwin proposed that speciation (the emergence of a new species) can be explained by the fixation of advantageous mutations over an extended period of time. That is, as two geographically separate populations of the same species diverge (as they accumulate mutations that are advantageous to survival in their particular habitat), they could eventually become two separate species. For higher organisms, a species can be thought of most simply as the largest group of organisms capable of

45. Gabriel et al., "Cystic Fibrosis," 107–9.
46. Pier et al., "Salmonella."

interbreeding and producing fertile offspring.[47] For example, a horse and a donkey, which are two different species, can produce offspring (either a mule or a hinny), but the offspring is typically not fertile, while two different breeds of dog (species *Canis lupus familiaris*), even two breeds that look much more different than a horse and donkey, can produce fertile offspring. According to Darwin, as mutations accumulate and are fixed over time, and assuming that the populations do not continue to interbreed (if they are geographically separated), they will eventually lose the ability to interbreed—they will become two different species. The proposal that all species originally evolved from a common ancestor is the contentious part of the Darwin's theory. This is what provoked what has come to be known as the "Scopes Monkey Trial," more formally known as *The State of Tennessee v. John Thomas Scopes*.[48] In 1925 John Scopes, a substitute high school teacher, was accused of violating Tennessee's law (known as the Butler Act) that made it illegal to teach human evolution in a state-funded school. Although the typical narrative around this trial is routinely simplified and distorted,[49] it is not my purpose in this chapter to go into exacting detail regarding the truth or inaccuracies. However, it is important to note that this aspect of Darwin's theory (descent of all species from a common ancestor) has not been proven empirically. This is not to say that it has been disproven either, but rather that there has not been an example where a single species was studied in detail over the time necessary to track the accumulation and fixation of numerous mutations that eventually resulted in two distinct species. Simple organisms such as bacteria, which have a high enough reproduction rate to allow for empirical study, do not reproduce via sexual reproduction, so they are imperfect models for such studies. And because of the number of mutations and the time necessarily involved in such a process, it is simply not feasible to have observed the complete process of speciation firsthand.

As with so many scientific theories, the fact that it has not been proven with empirical vigor does not preclude the theory from being useful. There are many observations that Darwin's theory, and the numerous corollaries that have arisen more recently, appear to explain. The entire

47. This is a definition of convenience for the point being made here. It should not be construed as a textbook definition of "species" in that it does not account for organisms that reproduce asexually.

48. *The State of Tennessee v. John Thomas Scopes*, Supreme Court of Tennessee, December term, 1926; opinion filed January 17, 1927.

49. Perry and Olasky, *Monkey Business*.

field of nonclinical science—that is, the study of candidate pharmaceutical agents prior to advancement into studies in humans—relies on the idea that these nonclinical species can predict what will happen in humans. It is a fact that, by most methods of reckoning similarity, the human genome is very similar to that of the chimpanzee.[50] Even the mouse genome (and in some ways the genome of the fruit fly) is remarkably similar to the human genome. This is well, because it means that much very useful genetic and biochemistry research can be done in nonclinical models. However, it is not empirical proof that humans arose from a common ancestor to the mouse or the fruit fly, or even from an earlier primate precursor to *Homo sapiens* and *Pan troglodytes* (the chimpanzee). Simply because some of the mechanisms of Darwinian theory have been demonstrated (e.g., the accumulation of beneficial mutations in a population of bacteria) does not mean that the entire theory must be accepted. The fact remains that the theory does not explain speciation very well. That is, the mechanisms are lacking in detail (understandably, in light of the fact that Darwin's theory came out well before the structure of DNA and in the absence of a general appreciation of Mendelian genetics[51]). Although these shortcomings do not disprove the theory, it does not follow that, absent more mechanistic detail and more vigorous scientific proof, only very stupid or hopelessly doctrinaire individuals would doubt aspects of the theory.

Similarity in DNA sequences in no way proves a common ancestor for all living organisms. It is simply data that can be verified empirically and that advocates have interpreted to support Darwinian evolution in its entirety. Similarity in DNA sequences could just as reasonably be seen to reflect similarity in purpose, and the hand of a single Creator. Furthermore, there are a number of issues with the theory's ability to explain how speciation actually works. One such issue is with syntenic regions within the genome of different species. The genomes of even closely related species have been scrambled. Although the genes—regions encoding specific proteins—tend to be well conserved, the order of the genes has been mixed. Imagine the human genome as an encyclopedia in twenty-three volumes,[52] organized alphabetically by the first letter in the topic.

50. Varki and Altheide, "Comparing the Human and Chimpanzee Genomes."

51. Mendel, "Versuche über Pflanzenhybriden."

52. The human genome contains twenty-two pairs of autosomes, and a twenty-third pair of so-called sex chromosomes. The female contains a pair of X chromosomes while the male contains one X and one Y chromosome. The human genome contains ~3,096,649,726 base pairs and ~20,465 coding genes. It is ~96 percent identical to

Articles on "atheism" and "Anabaptists" appear in volume 1, under the letter A, while articles on the "xenobiotic" and the "zoographic" appear in the final volume. The various articles (the genes in this analogy) are well conserved in species closely related to humans, but their order on the chromosomes is scrambled. It is as if in even a closely related species a portion of the topics in volume 1 were chopped out and placed in volume 7, and a portion of volume 15 was moved to volume 4 and the alphabetical order reversed in that block of articles. So, the article on "Graves' disease" in volume 7 of the chimpanzee version of the encyclopedia (the chimp's genome) is followed by the article on "agnosticism" instead of the article on "gravity." These relocations are called chromosomal rearrangements, and with the advent of whole genome sequencing, hundreds of them have been identified between even closely related species. Within a species chromosomal rearrangements (translocations) are associated with genetic disorders (e.g., Downs syndrome, in which there are three copies of chromosome 21 instead of the usual two copies, and activation of the MYC oncogene by a translocation in Burkitt's lymphoma), and are characterized by adverse consequences such as metabolic disorders, learning disabilities, developmental delays, infertility, and/or increased risk of cancer.[53] One must wonder, then, how did the introduction of chromosomal rearrangements (presumably by aberrant crossover during meiosis) result in a competitive advantage during speciation? That is, how did the presumed first ancestor of a new species survive, given the chromosomal translocation(s) that must have happened? Furthermore, how did an individual chromosomal rearrangement persist? If a particular rearrangement occurred in one individual (e.g., articles in our hypothetical encyclopedia from "deism" to "dogma" were moved to volume thirteen between articles on "methodological materialism" and "methadone"), this would be present initially on only one copy of the genome (recall that we carry two copies in nearly every cell in our body). The affected individual would only be able to transmit the rearranged genome to half of its offspring. Even assuming that the offspring were viable, and that the rearrangement did not result in infertility or an adaptive disadvantage, it would instead have had to cause a marked selective advantage. That is, offspring with initially only one copy of the mutation would have been so advantaged by that mutation that they would have been able to

chimps and bonobos. Approximately 98 percent of the human genome does not encode proteins or protein subunits (Human Whole Genome, GRCh38.p13).

53. O'Connor, "Human Chromosome Translocations and Cancer."

out-compete individuals without the mutation and pass along their one mutant copy of the genome more successfully, until it became abundant enough in the population that multiple individuals in later generations shared the identical rearranged genome. This is not, as some will charge, a "god of the gaps" argument. Although it is not possible to reliably calculate the odds against such a fortuitous combination of occurrences, in light of the apparently short time (based on the fossil record) in which most of the species and genus arose,[54] the odds are stacked against the Darwinian notion of evolution from a common ancestor. There are other issues with the theory of evolution, and it is beyond the scope or length of this book to deal with these. Many have been described elsewhere.[55] Many, including prominent scientists and those who do not claim to be Christians or even theists, believe the evidence shows that Darwinism is not as ironclad as its most outspoken advocates would have you believe.

Finally, even if all of the mechanisms necessary for macroevolution were to be demonstrated, this is not empirical proof of a common ancestor. Nor does it definitively disprove the existence of God. It might be accepted as the mechanism by which God created the diversity of life on earth, but it still does not explain consciousness. On the other hand, even if one accepts only those parts of Darwinian evolution that have been demonstrated empirically, it does not mean that the theory is not scientifically useful—just as Newtonian physics is useful though incomplete. But the idea that a Christian who rejects some aspects of evolutionary theory must therefore not be a good scientist or a good medical doctor must be discarded, particularly when atheists use the same lack of empirical evidence as their primary reason for rejecting the existence of God. Such faulty notions should be dismissed; they do no service to either side of the debate on the existence of God.

The Origins of Life

Since Darwinian evolution cannot explain the origins of life from inanimate chemicals, a theory on the origins of life is needed if one wishes to be an intellectually fulfilled atheist. Many science textbooks

54. Nearly all of the major animal phyla that exist today appear to have arisen in the fossil record in a relatively short time about 540 million years ago. This is called the "Cambrian radiation."

55. See for example Eden, "Heresy in the Halls of Biology;" Eden, "Inadequacies of Neo-Darwinian Evolution;" and Behe, *Darwin's Black Box*.

today describe experiments performed under conditions that purported to mimic those present on the early earth. In these experiments, scientists first speculate on the conditions present in the early earth—temperature, pressure, the chemical compounds that might have been present, and at what concentrations. They then try to recreate these conditions in the laboratory, adding an energy source to mimic a lightning strike or energy from a thermal vent at the bottom of the ocean. Under the controlled circumstances of these experiments, some have shown that a few of the basic building blocks of life have been created. Some of the earliest and most famous experiments, performed by Stanley Miller and Harold Urey demonstrated the formation of several amino acids (recall that there are twenty amino acids that comprise the building blocks of proteins).[56] Speculating on the hypothetical conditions of the early earth is not empirical science, and the current consensus among geochemists is that the conditions that Miller-Urey recreated in the laboratory were incorrect.[57] Regardless, results of Miller's original experiment, and similar experiments performed over the years, are often presented as evidence supporting the possibility of the beginnings of life on earth by chance.[58] If these experiments show anything, it is that life did not simply spring into being under the conditions on the early earth. Claiming that the results of limited experiments under controlled conditions performed by an intelligent being disprove the existence of an intelligent Creator of something as complex as biological life is not sensible.

Allowing for a moment that the conditions were predictive, there remain numerous issues related to the nature, identity, and concentration of the products, as well as the likelihood of these products persisting long enough to be incorporated into anything resembling the macromolecules required for life. In the original reports, Miller included an image of a thin-layer chromatography analysis of the results. This includes five identified spots, and two that were unidentified. Of the five spots that were identified, three were amino acids among the twenty that occur naturally in proteins. One of the other spots (proposed to be α-amino-n-butyric acid) is an *alpha amino acid* (like those found naturally in proteins) that

---

56. For example: Miller, "Production of Amino Acids"; Miller and Urey, "Organic Compound Synthesis"; and Johnson et al., "Miller Volcanic Spark Discharge Experiment."

57. Lennox, *God's Undertaker*, 126.

58. Bada, "New Insights into Prebiotic Chemistry."

is not one of the twenty found in proteins, while the other is a *beta amino acid*, also not incorporated into proteins in nature.

Although the two darkest spots were glycine and alanine, these are not the two amino acids (AAs) found most often in proteins. If all twenty AAs were used randomly in equal proportion, one might expect each to represent 5 percent (one-twentieth) of the amino acids found in nature, but some AAs are incorporated into proteins quite a bit more often than others. If proteins were made simply by chance combination of AAs, one might anticipate that the amino acids found most frequently in proteins would be those produced in the greatest abundance in these experiments, but this is also not the case. Although glycine and alanine are among the more frequently used amino acids in naturally occurring proteins, they are not the most common. The amino acids most commonly incorporated into proteins, leucine and serine, were apparently not made in comparative amounts. Similarly, the alpha amino acid α-amino-*n*-butyric acid (also called "homoalanine") was produced, but this amino acid is not present in proteins found in nature. There is no obvious reason why this should be. As shown in Figure 5 (panel A), all alpha amino acids have a variable group on their *alpha carbon*. In glycine (Fig. 5, panel B), the variable group, sometimes called an "R-group," is a hydrogen. For alanine, the R-group is a single carbon with three hydrogens bonded to it (called a "methyl group" and denoted CH_3). For valine, the R-group contains three carbons. The amino acid with the intermediately sized R-group comprised of two carbons, namely α-amino-*n*-butyric acid, is not found in proteins in nature, yet this amino acid was present in Miller's experiment. There is no reason why this amino acid, since it was made in the supposed prebiotic soup that Miller and Urey allegedly reproduced, should not be used in proteins, as the peptide linkage used to form proteins does not involve the R-group at all.

Also shown in Figure 5 (panel B) is beta-alanine, a typical beta amino acid. Unlike the alpha amino acids that occur naturally in proteins, the beta amino acids have two carbons between the nitrogen (N) and the carboxylic acid carbon. In spite of the relative abundance of this chemical in Miller's experiments, this compound is never incorporated into any natural proteins, although it shares similar reactivity and bonding capacity to the alpha amino acids. The spots shown in Miller's report were visualized with a compound called "ninhydrin," which is used to visualize certain types of compounds (such as amino acids). If one speculates (as Miller did) that the other naturally occurring amino acids may have been present but at concentrations too low to visualize, then most certainly other beta amino acids as well as other amines may well have been present. And there may also have been non-amine compounds present at very high levels that would not have been seen at all upon visualization with ninhydrin. In fact, in none of the related experiments have all twenty of the "natural" amino acids been detected,[59] while the presence of numerous side products has been confirmed in more recent analyses of Miller's results and in more recent repeats of the experiments.[60] The absence of some essential amino acids, along with the presence of all of these side-products, capable of forming similar and competing chemical bonds as the alpha amino acids, adds to the unlikelihood of proteins containing only the twenty "natural" alpha amino acids arising by chance.

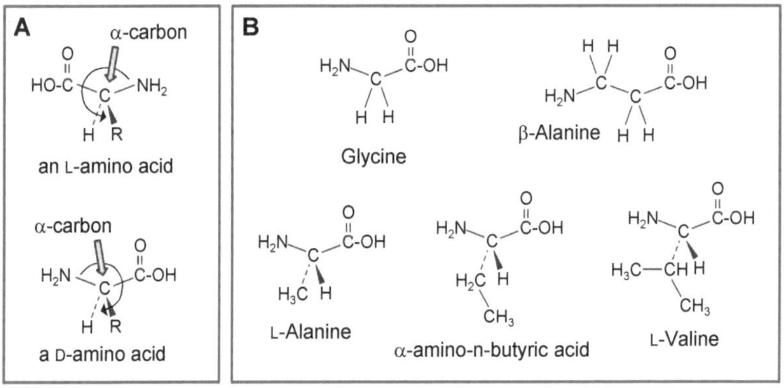

Figure 5. Amino Acids: The Building Blocks of Proteins.

Panel A. All alpha amino acids have a variable group (called an "R-group") on their alpha carbon (indicated by the arrow) between the nitrogen (N) and the carboxylic acid carbon. Many of the amino acids incorporated into proteins are chiral (they exist as one of two non-superimposable mirror images; see Fig. 6).

Panel B. Among the twenty amino acids encoded by DNA and incorporated into proteins, glycine in the simplest. It's R-group is a second hydrogen, and it is not chiral. Alanine and valine have 1 and 3 carbons, respectively, in their R-group. Intermediate to these two naturally incorporated amino acids is the amino acid α-amino-n-butyric acid. It has two carbons in its R-group and was made in the Miller-Urey experiments, but it is not incorporated into proteins. Also present in the Miller-Urey experiment was β-Alanine, a beta amino acid that is not found naturally in proteins.

59. Gishlick, "Icons of Evolution?" 4.

60. Bada, "New Insights into Prebiotic Chemistry."

In addition, it is important to note that compounds such as amino acids, and the proteins they make, are "handed." That is, each amino acid (except glycine) has what is called a "chiral center" and can exist as one of two non-superimposable mirror images (Fig. 6). These compounds have the same molecular formula, the same bond connectivity, and the same basic chemical reactivity, yet the proteins in nature contain only one of the two possible chiral isomers. In nature, only the l-isomers (also called "S isomers"), and not the d-isomers are incorporated into the proteins of living organisms.[61] In a non-chiral environment such as that used in Miller's experiment, there is no reason why both chiral isomers would not have been formed (they would appear in the exact same spots on the thin-layer chromatography analysis). The presence of the "non-natural" chiral isomers would more than double the number of "non-natural" building blocks that could inadvertently have been incorporated into nascent proteins if these formed purely by chance. The presence of these "right-handed" or d-isomers in concentrations similar to the "left-handed" ones also cannot explain why random chance resulted only in the "left-handed" l-isomers being incorporated into living organisms.

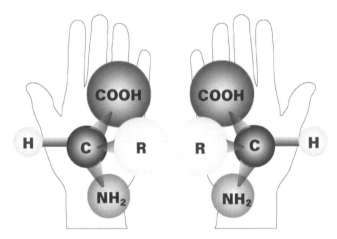

Figure 6. Chirality (Handedness). Chiral molecules, such as amino acids, exist as one of two non-superimposable mirror images. Although they share identical physical and chemical properties in a non-chiral environment, only one chiral isomer of each amino acid is incorporated into proteins in nature.

61. Note that of the twenty amino acids typically incorporated into protein, glycine is not chiral. In addition, cysteine occurs in natural biomolecules as the right-handed or R isomer, though this is an artifact of the nomenclature rules and the fact that its R-group contains a sulfhydryl moiety.

The odds of even a modestly sized (perhaps seventy-five to one hundred amino acids in length) protein forming simply by chance are remarkably small. Taking into account the very low concentrations of each amino acid in a prebiotic soup, along with the presence of all of the incorrect right-handed amino acids and myriad other compounds (α-amino-*n*-butyric acid, beta amino acids, etc.) that could contribute to inappropriate chemical linkages, the chances of the proper chemical bonds (and *only* the proper chemical bonds) forming between the appropriate amino acids in the appropriate order are astonishingly small (one in a number equal to 10 with 125 zeroes after, it by one estimate[62]). This is for the formation of only a single protein. Even the simplest single-celled organism would need hundreds of different proteins in order to live and reproduce. The odds against this occurring even in the time the universe has existed are remarkably miniscule, but considering how much shorter the time between the proposed cooling of the earth after its formation and the appearance of fossil evidence for microscopic life (approximately 100 million years), the possibility that life arose by chance without the involvement of some sort of outside agency seems preposterous. In addition, as noted above, there is no "fitness" that would support the accidental orientation of amino acids in an inanimate soup of building blocks into a "useful" protein if there were no living, reproducing organism to enjoy the advantages that the useful protein might provide.

These analyses have left out another important consideration, that of thermodynamics. The chemical bonds that hold the atoms together in compounds contain potential energy. It takes energy to break bonds, and energy can be generated by forming new chemical bonds. Burning wood, for example, breaks bonds in the compounds that make up the wood while forming new bonds in the carbon dioxide and water vapor produced, resulting in a net release of energy. The products—carbon dioxide, water vapor, heat, light, and ashes—have the same overall amount of mass and energy as the reactants (wood and oxygen) had. This exemplifies the first law of thermodynamics mentioned previously, the law that states that total energy is conserved, and the law of conservation of matter, which states that in a chemical reaction matter and mass are conserved. Energy is neither created nor destroyed; some of it simply changes form from the chemical energy of the bonds in the wood to the heat energy and light energy produced by burning. The burning of

62. Strobel, *Case for a Creator*, 229.

wood is called an exothermic reaction, in that energy is released from the system. Conversely, an endothermic reaction is one in which energy must be added to the system in order to produce a product with greater bond energy than the starting materials. To use the example of wood, a tree as it grows converts water and carbon dioxide into wood. It does not do this without an input of energy, it uses light energy from the sun in a process called photosynthesis to synthesize cellulose and the other compounds present in the wood.

Not all chemical reactions occur spontaneously. Even many exothermic reactions need a kick start. Wood does not spontaneously catch fire simply because the reaction is exothermic. One must start a fire, either by striking a match, or by a lightning strike. The energy required to initiate a chemical reaction is called activation energy. Essentially every chemical reaction has an activation energy associated with it, even exothermic reactions (an unstable compound is one for which the activation energy is very small). This is a fortunate thing for the on-going existence of life. Without activation energy, all of the chemical compounds in our body might just spontaneously react in a manner that increases disorder and decreases free energy. Going back to the "primordial earth" experiments, these experiments assume a source of energy (lightning or heat from a thermal vent) to produce products that are among the simple building blocks of life. Somehow, these building blocks are thought to have combined to form more complicated "macromolecules" (such as proteins, DNA and RNA). However, lightning is an imprecise source of activation energy, and could provide just as much activation energy to break chemical bonds as to form them. Furthermore, the formation of even a single peptide bond is thermodynamically unfavorable at any temperature (see Text Box 5). All of this is a vast simplification, but the principal remains that thermodynamically unfavorable chemical reactions do not simply occur by chance and predominate under conditions that might also cause (and may in fact favor) the reverse reactions. In other words, if heat from a hot vent can provide energy to combine amino acids to form proteins, it is just as likely (in fact more likely) to provide energy to break peptide bonds that may have formed between amino acids, or to break phosphodiester bonds that formed between nucleotides to make DNA. Chemists in the laboratory experiment to find ways to perform reactions that result in high yields of specific, desired end-products. They must carefully control the inputs of reactants and activation energy to shift the equilibrium in the desired direction and to avoid destroying the products as quickly as they form them. Yet we are to believe that in the greatest experiment of all, the creation of an astonishing array of chemical precursors, and then increasingly complex biomolecules, and then life itself from inanimate matter, there was no expert chemist controlling the reaction conditions. Is it more credulous to believe that the complexity of the products and the fine-tuning required to achieve them suggests the presence of an external agency, or that all of this could have happened by mere chance?

Text Box 5. One of the assumptions made in accepting results such as those of the Urey-Miller experiments is that given the proper conditions and sufficient time, even unlikely events may occur. Thermodynamics does not support this. The formation of a dipeptide from two amino acids is an endothermic reaction—that is, it requires the input of energy. In thermodynamics, we say that its ΔH (enthalpy of reaction) is positive. For a reaction to be spontaneous, the ΔG (Gibb's free energy) must be negative. The relevant equation is $\Delta G = \Delta H - T \cdot \Delta S$, where T is temperature and ΔS is a measure of randomness or disorder (called "entropy"). But notice that the $T \cdot \Delta S$ term is subtracted. Joining two amino acids to make a simple dipeptide reduces disorder (that is, ΔS is negative). Subtracting a negative (adding a positive) to the positive ΔH term makes ΔG more positive—this reaction is not spontaneous at any temperature. Notice too that increasing the temperature makes the $T \cdot \Delta S$ term bigger. At higher temperatures we're subtracting a bigger negative number, making ΔG even more positive, and the reaction even less thermodynamically favorable. A positive Gibb's free energy translates to a very small equilibrium constant. In the presence of low concentrations of the reactants (two amino acids), a very small equilibrium constant translates to very low concentrations of product. And since the dipeptide product of this reaction in turn becomes a reactant for the formation of a tripeptide, the theoretical concentration of a randomly formed polypeptide of any useful length becomes vanishingly small.[63]

63. On the 2017 AP Chemistry Practice Exam, multiple choice question 36 shows an example of this, providing Gibbs Free Energy, enthalpy, and entropy values for the formation of a peptide bond between two glycine molecules. The correct answer is that the reaction is not favored at any temperature. Moreover, the calculated value for K_c resulting from the Free Energy, enthalpy, and entropy values is 2.35×10^{-13}. Assuming

Finally, the fact that controlled experiments under theoretically relevant conditions result in small amounts of a small subset of the chemicals needed to form the macromolecules necessary for life proves nothing. It does not explain how amino acids formed and collided in just the right proportions to produce proteins. It does not explain how nitrogenous bases, pentose sugars, and phosphates combined to form nucleotides, or how thousands of these nucleotides combined to form a nascent strand of RNA or DNA that could survive under highly unfavorable conditions. Nor does it provide any mechanism by which this hypothetical DNA strand came to encode information for encoding a functional protein, and how that specific sequence persisted in the presence of the countless hypothetical nonsense sequences. It has been estimated that the very simplest living organism would need ~250 genes[64] (there are ~20,465 genes in the human genome, encoding many more proteins). Many of the proteins encoded by these genes contain several hundred amino acids and all are organized in a specific sequence. In comparison, the number of possible proteins of only twenty amino acids in length (assuming random incorporation of only the twenty naturally occurring amino acids, and none of the possible "contaminants" described above) is equal to approximately ten with twenty-six zeroes behind it. The number of possible proteins containing a hundred amino acids is too large for most handheld calculators to calculate, yet a DNA mutation changing a single amino acid in a single protein can impact the protein's function and even its shape, suggesting that the number of "useful" proteins is vastly smaller than the number of possible proteins. Are we then to believe that the ~250 genes specifying at least as many highly selective protein sequences arose simply by chance under conditions in which the DNA and proteins themselves would be denatured and destroyed? Even the debatable possibility that a subset of the building blocks of life could have been formed by chance on a theoretical primordial earth does not explain how the information contained in DNA and proteins came to be, or how that information might have been "translated" in any

---

even a very generous initial concentration of glycine of 10 mM (0.01 M—the concentration of salt in sea water is around 0.6 M), this gives an equilibrium concentration of diglycine of 0.325 μM (0.000000325 moles, or ~0.000043 grams, of diglycine per liter of sea water). That very small concentration equates to an equilibrium concentration for a tripeptide that is markedly smaller. Chance formation of even a short polypeptide under such conditions quickly becomes remarkably unlikely.

64. Maniloff, "Minimal Cell Genome."

meaningful way to sustain its existence, or how (or why) they could have grown and/or replicated in the absence of a living organism with a full complement of proteins necessary for growth and replication. There are those who would say that given sufficient time and the right conditions, chance could allow for the creation of such a system, but the odds of this occurring are so astronomically small as to be ludicrous. Furthermore, for a thermodynamically unfavorable reaction, such as the formation of a single peptide bond between two amino acids, great lengths of time would decrease the formation and persistence of the products.[65] The fact that a handful of experiments planned and carried out by intelligent beings have demonstrated the formation of a small subset of chemical compounds that are the very simplest precursors to the macromolecules present in life is no evidence for the serendipitous chance formation of life, the argument of personal credulity notwithstanding. In fact, to those who are willing to question their materialist preconceptions, it can be seen as evidence demanding the intervention of an external agency with intelligence and will who in some way overcame the hostile conditions to create immense complexity from disorder, life from inanimate matter.

Additional Reading

For additional reading on the scientific evidence in support of the existence of a divine, intelligent Creator, consider the following outstanding books. *God's Undertaker* by John C. Lennox, though somewhat technical, is an excellent, thorough, and compelling book describing how science and mathematics, rather than refuting His existence, actually point to the existence of God.[66] *The Privileged Planet* by Guillermo Gonzalez and Jay W. Richards provides exhaustive evidence that planet earth is unique among the billions of planets in the universe, and uniquely situated to

65. As noted in Text Box 5, the formation of a protein comprised of two amino acids joined by a peptide bond represents a decrease in disorder (entropy), but the second law of thermodynamics states that disorder in the universe is increasing. Without a living organism, which (though we know not how) can extract "a stream of negative entropy upon itself, to compensate the entropy increase it produces by living" (Schrödinger, *What Is Life?*, 73), a randomly formed dipeptide would fall apart. The excessive heat of a thermal vent, rather than catalyzing the forward reaction, would speed up the reverse reaction.

66. Lennox, *God's Undertaker*.

allow for scientific discovery.[67] *Darwin's Black Box* by Michael J. Behe provides a thorough scientific challenge to macroevolution.[68]

67. Gonzalez and Richards, *Privileged Planet*.

68. Behe, *Darwin's Black Box*.

3

God Can Not Be Known

Coincidence is God's way of remaining anonymous

—ALBERT EINSTEIN[1]

ON FRIDAY, DECEMBER 14, 2012, Adam Lanza walked into Sandy Hook Elementary School in Newtown, Connecticut, and opened fire, murdering twenty children (ages five and six) and six adults (having murdered his own mother earlier), and then took his own life. Although out of the news as I write this many years later, I can only imagine that the pain and loss felt by the affected families is still very real. On October 2, 2006, Charles Carl Roberts IV entered a one-room Amish schoolhouse in the village of Nickel Mines in Lancaster County, Pennsylvania, and shot ten little girls ages six to thirteen (killing five), before committing suicide. Between 2002 and 2004 Ariel Castro kidnapped three women between the ages of fourteen and twenty-one. The three remained in captivity until May 6, 2013, when they were discovered and rescued, and Castro was subsequently charged with (and pled guilty to) 937 criminal counts of rape, kidnapping, and aggravated murder. Where was God? Is there no divine justice? Following such terrible events as the terrorist attacks on September 11, 2001, many asked, "Where was God?" How can God allow

1. Attributed to Albert Einstein.

such evil? Even in people's daily lives, many complain of the apparent silence of God. When we pray, does anyone hear us? Does anyone care? Where is God, alleged by Christianity to be a loving Father, when we hurt? If there is indeed a God, is He worthy of our gratitude, obedience, and service? What is the nature of this God, and how are we to know about His characteristics? Assuming that you believe that there may indeed exist a transcendent deity, perhaps the most pressing question that can be asked is, "What is God like?" Is it an impersonal force or a personal entity with mind, will, and emotions? If God is a person (rather than an impersonal force), is He a loving Father, an angry Judge, or an absentee Landlord? How can we come to know anything about a being whose very existence is open for debate?

What Is God Like?

Richard Dawkins has commented, "We are all atheists about most of the gods that humanity has ever believed in. Some of us just go one god further."[2] Dawkins's statement was made in defense of his atheism, but the implication is that all belief in the divine is equally foolish, and that all religions are the same. This argument is silly—it is tantamount to an anarchist stating that someone is almost an anarchist because he rejects every form of government (e.g., monarchy, dictatorship, theocracy) *other* than the one that he believes to be best (e.g., democracy). All forms of government are not the same, at least not to anyone who thinks about it for more than a moment, and saying that a person who favors democracy is almost an anarchist because he rejects every other form of government is ridiculous. If in the process of dating I reject every possible spouse but one, that most certainly does not mean that I almost disbelieve in the sanctity of marriage; to the contrary, it likely means that I take the marriage covenant very seriously. I think you'll agree that the nature of one's spouse is of critical importance—how much more the nature of God?

Belief in a supreme being leads to some logical conclusions regarding the nature of the world based on the nature of that divinity. Conversely, the nature of creation can lead to knowledge of its Creator. As noted in chapters 1 and 2, the Scientific Revolution was started by men who were convinced that a God of order and reason would have imposed rational order upon His creation. The discovery of this rational order also tells

2. Dawkins, *God Delusion*, 24.

us something about God. It is worth considering what sort of world we might expect if there is a particular kind of deity, or if there is none at all. The Christian scriptures support the idea that we can draw conclusions about God based on our observations of creation, stating that "Ever since the creation of the world His invisible nature, namely, His eternal power and deity, has been clearly perceived in the things that have been made."[3] As noted earlier, the ancient Greeks recognized the need for what they referred to as the "first cause" or "prime mover." Studying creation is one way to know more about this Creator, but in so doing we must take care to understand our own preconceptions, and our own limits. If there is indeed a transcendent divinity, it is by definition greater than us. We risk misunderstanding motives, misinterpreting evidence, and drawing wrong conclusions. When a parent takes their child to the doctor for an inoculation, the child, who lacks an understanding of the benefits of the shot and the harm caused by the disease it seeks to protect against, may cry in fear at the pain of the needle. The child could conceivably even question the parent's character for allowing such a "bad" thing to happen. It is possible that we humans, bounded by time, mortality, and incomplete knowledge, may draw incorrect assumptions regarding the character of God. We are *not* God. Our intellect and understanding are incomplete, and our preconceptions and limitations can color our interpretation of what is to be learned of God through the study of His creation. With these caveats in mind, it is still worth investigating the nature of God.

Everything in the universe is derivative. That is, everything depends upon something else for its existence, something that came before it. Every effect has a cause. But there had to have been something that was first—an uncaused cause. For both logical and scientific reasons, our universe cannot be infinitely old (see Text Box 6). The ancient Greeks, as well as many other ancient cultures, realized that there must have been a first cause. It is this uncaused cause in which the Greek poet Aratus claimed that "we live and move and have our being."[4] First and foremost, this uncaused cause is not derivative. Roy Clouser has argued that all religious traditions include a belief in the divine, defined as something with unconditional, non-dependent reality.[5] It is worth noting that a belief in an eternal multiverse is by this definition a religious belief—the

3. Rom 1:20.

4. The quote is taken from the fifth line of Aratus's *Phenomena* and was quoted by Paul in his speech to the men of Athens at the Areopagus, as recorded in Acts 17:28.

5. Clouser, *Myth of Religious Neutrality*, 17–24.

multiverse itself, having non-dependent reality, is eternal, divine. In the ontological argument for the existence of God, first put forward in the eleventh century by Anselm of Canterbury, God is defined as "that than which nothing greater can be conceived."[6] From this we can conclude that God is great. To have created matter, the first cause would need to have preceded it, and is therefore not likely to be, or is at least not primarily, a physical being. That is, the divinity for which we seek cannot be made of matter (although in theory the Creator might conceivably take physical form), else matter preceded it and is therefore divine. So, we can conclude that the Creator is a non-corporeal (spirit) being. Furthermore, although it is possible that the Creator is presently residing at a physical location that we have yet to discover given the vastness of the universe, it seems most likely that, being a spirit, the Creator need not limit itself to a single locale in the created order. If the Creator was present at the creation and is still living now, that being would need to be very old. It can also be concluded that the uncaused cause that created everything is incredibly powerful. Although one can quibble about whether or not this being is omnipotent (that is all-powerful, capable of doing anything), it is certainly true that any being capable of setting into motion our vast universe would have to possess staggering power. Faced with this Creator, there is little doubt that one would be awestruck, if one could even comprehend such a being. The amount of order in the creation bespeaks a Creator of logic and rationality. The complexity of creation suggests a remarkably creative and intelligent God, and the very finely tuned nature of our universe suggests that in some way this Creator intended for us to be here. This intentionality certainly suggests a purpose for our being here as well. Finally, the existence of personality in creation certainly suggests a personal Creator, unless we conclude, as many Eastern religions suppose, that our personality is either a myth or an aberration.

> **Text Box 6.** As noted in chapter 2, the first law of thermodynamics and the law of conservation of matter state that energy and matter are conserved. That is, the total amount of energy and matter in the universe is unchanging. The second law of thermodynamics says that disorder in a system can never decrease (though it can remain constant in certain ideal cases of thermodynamic equilibrium). The offshoot of this is that the

6. Logan, *Reading Anselm's Proslogion*, 85.

disorder of the universe is always increasing. In an infinitely old universe, with randomness increasing for an infinite time, there could be no order remaining. But there is clearly order in the universe. For this reason, we can conclude that the universe cannot possibly be infinitely old. Furthermore, as William Lane Craig has argued, an actual infinity is a metaphysical impossibility. This argument, referred to as the "Kalām cosmological argument" and based upon the work of eleventh-century Persian philosopher Al-Ghazali, has been described in detail in Craig's book *The Kalām Cosmological Argument*.[7]

In summary, at the very least, this divine Creator would have to be powerful and ancient, as well as rational, personal, and intentional. Thus far we have only touched on what the apostle Paul called God's "invisible nature . . . His eternal power and deity." We have dealt only with the characteristics and properties of this uncaused cause, but nothing about its personal attributes (if any). Knowing about someone is not the same as knowing that person. The Judeo-Christian tradition speaks of being in relationship with God and God wanting to be in relationship with us. Before we can be in any sort of meaningful relationship with God (or with anyone), we may wish to know more about His character. Therein lies an issue. In some religious traditions god is not a person at all. Can an impersonal force be known? Before delving into God's character or considering God's purposes, it may be worthwhile to broadly review the kinds of deity we might believe in.

Three Different Gods

Every culture, tribe, and people throughout history has had a concept of the divine. An evaluation of the kinds of divinity that humans have believed in may demonstrate that some beliefs do a better job than others of describing the world that we experience every day. In order to be successful, any system of beliefs must deal with four big questions in an internally consistent manner.[8] These four questions deal with origins

7. Craig, *Kalām Cosmological Argument*.
8. Zacharias, *End of Reason*, 31.

(where do we come from?), meaning (is there meaning or purpose, and how is it derived?), morality (what is good/right and what is evil/wrong?), and destiny (where are we going?). The variety of religious beliefs among cultures and individuals is significantly greater than could be dealt with in any number of books, but some generalizations can be made for the purposes of evaluating how well a particular belief system explains our world, and if it can address these four questions in a logical and internally consistent manner. Although not empirical proof, this inference to the best explanation can identify issues with particular beliefs that do not describe or explain the world and the universe as we know them to be. Putting aside atheism for a moment (which Clouser argues is a religion in that it believes in a non-derivative absolute, and could be grouped with pantheism),[9] the kinds of God or gods that people have believed in can be placed into three broad categories. These are: pantheism (the belief that the universe, or nature, is identical with divinity, or that everything comprises an all-encompassing divinity), polytheism (the belief in a pantheon of multiple gods), and monotheism (the belief that there is only one God). Some systems of belief (such as ancestor worship, a belief that dead ancestors take on some supernatural ability to answer prayers and influence the natural world) cannot be neatly fit into these three categories; but then the example of ancestor worship, if that were the only kind of divinity, does not begin to explain the origins of creation. Cultural traditions that include ancestor worship must also include elements of one of the three categories above to explain origins—the ancestors had to have come from something or somewhere.

Pantheism

Many ancient people and many people today have pantheistic belief systems. Generally stated, pantheism is the belief that the universe (or nature) is identical with divinity, or that everything composes an all-encompassing divinity. This all-encompassing divinity is not very different than "the force" in the Star Wars movies:[10] an energy field created by and residing within all living things, and into which we all dissolve when we die. A modern version of pantheism is found in the Gaia theory,

9. Clouser, *Myth of Religious Neutrality*, 17–24.

10. See for example *Star Wars: Episode IV—A New Hope*, directed by George Lucas (Lucasfilm, 1977).

permutations of which take on a religious bent. Named for the Greek mother goddess of the same name, Gaia theory proposes that all of the organisms on the earth interact with one another and with their inorganic surroundings to form an essentially self-regulating complex system that maintains conditions of habitability on our planet.[11] Although the initial hypothesis was meant to address scientific questions, the more religious off-shoots posit that the Gaian earth mother has evolved to the level of consciousness and sentience. Even contemporary atheism must include something divine—that is, something with non-contingent, non-derivative reality. A god need not be sentient to be divine, so atheism is itself a form of pantheism; atheists simply don't worship that which they believe to be the non-contingent, uncreated reality.

As a worldview pantheism has two immediate problems in its ability to explain the natural world as we know it. First, as already noted, if one believes in an impersonal force comprised of the combined spirit of all of creation, how could this life force have existed before the creation of everything that underlies its existence? An impersonal pantheistic deity, existing in and derived from all of the created order, cannot explain how the created order came about, since such an entity (if it can be called an "entity" at all) would not exist without the created order. The sum cannot exist without any parts. Even if, as a materialist would propose, the universe sprang into being from nothing (in opposition to the laws of logic and science), whatever it is that has non-dependent existence (in this case, the entire universe itself) is "divine," in the sense of depending on nothing for its existence.

A second issue with pantheism is its inability to explain consciousness and individuality. If this divine spirit being is an impersonal force, how would individual personality and consciousness arise? There is uniqueness in nature. It is said that no two snowflakes are the same, but this is not the same as individuality. Even amongst higher organisms there may be traits that make one member of the species different from all others (for example, you may maintain that your pet dog is a unique "individual"), but this is not the same as being a truly sentient, conscious individual. The idea that a human being is a unity of soul, mind, and body as distinct parts of an individual whole is a very old concept. Assuming for a moment that the mind is separate from (though clearly

---

11. Lovelock, "Gaia as Seen through the Atmosphere," 579–80.

connected in some way to) the brain, how does consciousness arise from and transcend its inanimate precursors?

Finally, were such a pantheistic deity to exist, among its primary functions would appear to be quelling the individuality of some of its component organisms (humans) in favor of the collective whole, because the inexorable sense of self possessed by human beings can only be considered to be an aberration. How does one explain the sense of individuality that has arisen amongst humans? One is left to wonder, how did this individuality arise, and why is it so much more highly developed in humanity (the creation) than in the life force (the Creator)? Why would humanity, so intent upon expressing individuality, have been created by or worship an entity whose highest concept of paradise is apparently the merging and loss of individuality?

Polytheism

Polytheism was the primary form of religious belief in many ancient cultures and is most simply defined as a belief in multiple individual gods. Each god is an individual with specific attributes and particular realms of authority or responsibility. In the case of many ancient cultures, the gods lived in a physical location (Mount Olympus in the Greek mythology) that could conceivably be travelled to by humans, and they routinely interacted with humans within the physical world. Perseus slew the Medusa, with guidance from the goddess Athena; Heracles, driven mad by the goddess Hera, slew his own children; and numerous human women were the object of the desires and sexual advances of male gods, resulting in several half-human, half-god heroes. These gods were fallible, capricious, spiteful, and petty. Although they were knowable, they were neither all-powerful nor very good in any meaningful sense of the word. The gods of these polytheistic pantheons were themselves physical beings. In fact, many ancient polytheistic mythologies contain theogonies, accounts of the generation of the gods from primeval matter, making them little different than pantheism in their ultimate deification of the material universe. Aside from the issues this creates (how could the first god in the pantheon, himself a physical being, create the physical universe?), these gods were limited. They were not all-powerful (if they were, why was there more than one?); their plans could be thwarted by mere mortals, and they could even be defeated. Furthermore, it was often believed that the gods themselves gained something from the act of human worship and service. Gods or goddesses set tasks for mortals that benefitted the deity; and in some traditions, the greater the number of worshippers, the greater the god's personal power. In general, as polytheistic religions evolved the lesser deities diminished in stature or vanished entirely, while their attributes were assigned to other gods. For example, Zeus, though initially a sky god in the Greek mythology, became the most powerful ruler of all of the gods, while the Indian Vedic gods (initially numbering in the thousands) were gradually displaced by Vishnu, Shiva, and Brahma. But regardless of the number of such gods or their attributes, they were neither all-powerful nor particularly good.

Monotheism

Monotheism posits a single eternal and supernatural creator God. In monotheism as understood throughout history, God transcends and exists outside of the created realm, and is believed to have existed before the creation of anything in the material universe. God is therefore the author of all of creation, the first or uncaused cause. In monotheistic belief systems God is also typically understood to be eternal, existing outside of the bounds of time. God always has been and always will be. To be sure, this strains the human imagination; but if an eternal God exists, it seems likely that He is far superior to humans, and we might not expect to understand everything about him. So far this concept of God is little different than Anaximander's *apeiron* (chapter 2). But the monotheistic God is a personal being imbued with mind, will, and emotions, and has, in the major monotheistic traditions, revealed Himself to humanity both through the created order (general revelation) and through chosen prophets (including written scriptures).

There exist several major monotheistic religious traditions, including the so-called Abrahamic religions: Judaism, Christianity, and Islam. These three religions all claim a direct lineage to Abraham, details of whose life appear in the first book of the Jewish and Christian scriptures. These religions share a belief in a transcendent supreme being who is both eternal and omnipotent. Although these three account for over 50 percent of the world's population and are the primary forms of monotheism practiced in human history, there are distinct differences between them. In spite of these differences, many, including the author, have used the term "Judeo-Christian" when referring to the Bible and the shared religious traditions of the Judaism and Christianity. The earliest traditions of these two religions are the same, with the Jewish scriptures, being the Old Testament in the Christian Bible, and the entire history of the Christian Messiah (Himself a Jew) having occurred against a backdrop of Judaism. This is not intended to suggest that the two religions are the same, nor is any affront intended to Jews (who would not likely use the term "Judeo-Christian"). Although the differences between Christianity in all of its forms and Judaism are profound, the Judeo-Christian tradition in general is unique in that it speaks of our being in relationship with God and of the creator God wanting to be in relationship with us. The Judeo-Christian tradition is unique in having provided the world with the earliest account of creation by a single personal, intentional, and loving God, and in giving the first testimony to the linearity of time.[12]

Other monotheistic religions exist or have existed that may be considered as well. Religions such as the Church of Jesus Christ of Latter-Day Saints (commonly called "Mormons"), and the Jehovah's Witnesses are other common examples of monotheistic religions. Within monotheism there have been several views of God that spring from different understandings of, and result in different perspectives on, the nature of God and of creation. Although in most cases monotheism entails a personal God who interacts in some ways with His creation, one type of monotheism is decidedly different and worth distinction; that is, deism.

Deism

Deism is the belief that an all-powerful creator God exists and that the primary way to know about this God is through human reason (and not revelation). Deism is not a specific religion or religious denomination but is rather a particular perspective on the nature of the Creator. Although deists believe that a creator God exists, they believe that having set creation in motion and established universal laws by which everything is ordered, the Creator has had no further interactions with the created order or the beings living within it. From this belief come terms like "absentee landlord." The deist God does not interact with or intervene in creation. Everything therefore follows the natural laws set in motion at the beginning, and the possibility of any supernatural events is discounted.

12. Guinness, *Carpe Diem Redeemed*, 17.

Since the deist God is no longer involved in creation, special revelation (such as Scripture) and personal revelation (such as the idea that God "spoke to" an individual to reveal his will) are discounted as sources of authority or truth. Similarly, miracles, which defy the natural laws of the created order (e.g., the biblical account of Jesus turning water into wine), are discounted and considered either to be myth or to have some perhaps as-yet-unknown naturalistic explanation. It may be no surprise that deism increased as the enlightenment progressed, as scientists increasingly defined physical and natural laws. There has been much debate as to whether the earliest religious influences of the founding fathers of the United States were in fact deist (rather than Christian). Although beyond the scope of this book, given the prevalence of deism throughout Europe just a generation earlier,[13] it seems certain that some of the founding fathers (notably Thomas Jefferson and Thomas Paine) were familiar with and even influenced by deism. However, careful investigation into the beliefs of the founding fathers themselves demonstrates that the majority were in fact Christians,[14] albeit with a healthy respect for both science and human reason. In one exhaustive study, analysis of about fifteen thousand documents written by the US founding fathers determined that 34 percent of the quotations came from the Bible. The three next most cited sources—French political philosopher Montesquieu (8.3 percent), English legal scholar William Blackstone (7.9 percent), and John Locke (2.9 percent)—add up to just over half that number of quotations.[15]

With deism, one immediate response that can be raised is that discussing God at all is somewhat pointless. Although we may still conclude that God is powerful and ancient, we might also conclude that he is not relevant. He does not appear to have any regard for creation or creatures—He neither gives us anything (beyond the initial act of setting the universe in motion), nor apparently does He expect anything of us. Mike Bryan writes:

> People have bought into the philosophical naturalism, but they also want the warm fuzzy. So they're deists . . . [but] Deism is a non-answer, an emotion more than anything else, not really a belief. Nor does it hold up well under scrutiny because an uninvolved God is really a malevolent God, given the way

13. See for example Gay, *Deism*.

14. Medved, *10 Big Lies*, 72–94.

15. Lutz, *Origins of American Constitutionalism*, 136–49.

matters have turned out. But deists don't have a malevolent God in mind. Most of them have little at all in mind.[16]

The deist concept of God is really just a cosmic "get out of jail free" card. One can invoke such a God when science fails to explain the origin of matter and the big bang, but then ignore him in trying to create standards of morality. In contrast, other forms of monotheism posit a God who is involved in creation in an ongoing way. Although deism as an organized movement was short-lived and is largely a thing of the past, it was influential as a stepping stone to modern atheism. Furthermore, there remain aspects of deism (e.g., the rejection of the miracles) in the beliefs of many theologically liberal Christian denominations. But as will be shown below, neither deism, pantheism, nor polytheism adequately address many of the issues surrounding meaning, morality, and destiny.

A "Personal God"

If the monotheistic Creator is a personal being, with mind, will, and emotions, is it possible not just to know about Him, but also to know Him? The Judeo-Christian tradition, unique among other religions, speaks of being in relationship with God as our heavenly Father. This leads to at least one additional question that other religions may not need to answer—how?[17] What does it mean to be in relationship with God, and how is this achieved? Although we have seen that religious texts, the study of creation, and reason can all tell us about God, in what way can we know Him in a personal sense? Being a spirit, we cannot interact with Him in the usual ways that we interact with one another. The mythical gods of polytheistic belief systems were physical beings with whom one could interact directly, but how can we physical beings be in relationship with a spirit God who is outside of time and the physical world? If such a being were to manifest Himself in all of His glory, we would be so completely cowed as to be unable to respond to Him in anything other than abject fear and awe. He has only revealed a portion of Himself. God is so much more than we can fathom—for Him it must be like humans trying to be in a relationship with an ant. Humans can certainly interact

16. Bryan, *Chapter and Verse*, 83.

17. The short answer is "prayer," though in truth this answer too is not without some difficulties and has engendered numerous books. See for example Yancey, *Prayer*; and Yancey, *Reaching for the Invisible God*.

with ants, even though a human being is far superior to the ant with respect to power, consciousness, longevity, and intellect. If we put a pebble in front of the ant, it can turn and go around it. We can try carefully to pick it up and move it or change the direction it is traveling. Certainly, the ant responds to our presence, or at least to the impediments we place in its way, but is it at any level "aware" of our presence? Even if it is aware of our presence, this can hardly be said to be a relationship. But a God who is spirit, a transcendent, all-powerful God, is far greater than us than we are greater than an ant.

How could we be in any sort of relationship with such a being and how would a transcendent, all-powerful spirit being interact with humans? Even coming before such a God (let alone knowing Him) is fraught. In many cultures in ancient times people were not permitted to come before their king unless summoned. The Old Testament book of Esther tells of the rule in the Babylonian Empire by which coming before the king unbidden would result in death unless the king extended his scepter to the one approaching.[18] How much greater is an omnipotent God than a mere human king? An omnipotent God, such as the God of the Jews and the Christians, or Allah for Muslims, is beyond any human reckoning. The ancient Jews believed that merely being in the presence of God would result in death. At several places in the Jewish scriptures the people exclaim to their religious leader that if they were to come into the presence of the holy God, or even hear His voice, they would die.[19] Moses, the greatest leader in the Jewish tradition, was told by God that he could not see God's face, "for man shall not see me and live."[20] After meeting with God on Mount Sinai, Moses' face was said to glow with the reflected glory of God.[21] So too the God of Islam is a God to be feared and respected, but not a God to be known or befriended. In Islam, the sole means of approach to Allah (the *Wasilah*) involves strict adherence to the pillars of the Muslim religion, the laws of Islam, and what are called the "acts of Ihsan" (excellence in the religion).[22] Approaching the almighty

18. Esth 4:11.

19. See for example Exod 20:18–19: "the people were afraid and trembled; and they stood afar off, and said to Moses, 'You speak to us, and we will hear; but let not God speak to us, lest we die.'"

20. Exod 33:18–23.

21. Exod 34:29–35.

22. For more on differences between Muslim and Christian thought on approaching God, see Qureshi, *No God but One*.

God is not something to be undertaken lightly. So how then is a person to be in a relationship with such a God?

Christianity is again unique in this regard, in that it claims to provide a way to bring us into such a relationship with an omnipotent God. We can already know something about the Christian God by the very fact that He wants to be in a personal relationship with us. Moreover, He has provided the means by which we can achieve it. Jesus Christ claimed to be God incarnate (God in the flesh), saying, "I and the Father are one."[23] Jesus also said if you knew Him, then you would know the Father.[24] Christ calls us into relationship with Him, just as He called His disciples. As He is not in the flesh any longer, you may wonder how this is possible. The answer is that Jesus also promised that for those who believe in Him He will give God's Holy Spirit to dwell with us and in us.[25] This is the same Holy Spirit that God, in the Old Testament, promised to give in the new covenant when He said, "I will put my spirit within you, and cause you to walk in my statutes and be careful to observe my ordinances."[26]

This invitation into relationship has two immediate aspects for believers today (and the promise of a third). We are invited into relationship with God through God's Holy Spirit,[27] and relationship with the other members of the church, Christ's body on earth.[28] Throughout the New Testament we are told that the Holy Spirit dwells within us when we accept Christ as our Savior. Following Christ's death and resurrection, the Holy Spirit came upon His followers at Pentecost, as promised in the Gospels and described in Acts.[29] Pentecost (which is Greek for "the fiftieth day") is a Jewish holiday, celebrating the giving of the Law on Sinai, the Feast of Weeks, which occurs fifty days after Passover. This feast is still celebrated in Judaism as Shavuot. It is no coincidence that in Christianity Pentecost is the day on which the Holy Spirit came to the apostles. This was significant to the early followers of Jesus. Whereas Shavuot, fifty days after the Passover, celebrates the giving of the Jewish Law, the Christian holiday of Pentecost (on the same day of the year, and fifty days after

23. John 10:30.
24. John 8:19.
25. See for example John 14:15–17; Rom 8:11; and 1 Cor 3:16.
26. Ezek 36:27.
27. Acts 2:38. See also Rom5:5; 1 Cor 6:19; and 2 Tim 1:14.
28. See Col 1:18, 24 and Eph 5:23.
29. Acts 2:4.

Christ's death on the cross) celebrates the new covenant and the giving of the Holy Spirit, who the prophet Jeremiah said would write God's law on their hearts. The Holy Spirit sealed those under the new covenant, and the annual celebration of Pentecost was one of the holiest days in the early church, commemorating the new covenant (salvation through the grace of God by faith in Jesus Christ) on the very day that the Jews celebrated the original covenant, the giving of the Mosaic and Levitical laws (recall that all of the disciples and the majority of the first members of the early church were Jews who believed that Jesus was the Jewish Messiah promised in the Jewish scriptures).

> Behold, the days are coming, says the LORD,[30] when I will make a new covenant with the house of Israel and the house of Judah, not like the covenant which I made with their fathers when I took them by the hand to bring them out of the land of Egypt, my covenant which they broke, though I was their husband, says the LORD. But this is the covenant which I will make with the house of Israel after those days, says the LORD: I will put my law within them, and I will write it upon their hearts; and I will be their God, and they shall be my people. And no longer shall each man teach his neighbor and each his brother, saying, "Know the LORD," for they shall all know me, from the least of them to the greatest, says the LORD; for I will forgive their iniquity, and I will remember their sin no more.[31]

The Bible teaches that the Holy Spirit dwells within us when we accept Christ as our Savior.[32] This means that we have the Spirit of the living, omnipotent God at work within us. This is a fulfillment of the promise made hundreds of years before by the prophet Jeremiah, a promise sealed with the Holy Spirit for each of those who accept salvation in Christ.[33]

---

30. Note that by convention, when the Christian Bible uses the word "LORD" in capital letters (as opposed to simply "lord" or "Lord"), this signifies that in the original Hebrew the word translated here is the covenant name of God. Specifically, when God first speaks to Moses (recorded in the third chapter of Exodus) and Moses asks, in effect, "Who shall I say sent me?," God answers, "I am that I am ... say to the people of Israel 'I am sent me to you.'" Translated from the original Hebrew (which contains no vowels), the letters are YHWH (or JHVH, in the medieval Latinized rendering). The four Hebrew letters have, in different Christian traditions, given rise alternatively to the names "Yahweh" and "Jehovah."

31. Jer 31:31–34.

32. 1 Cor 3:16.

33. Eph 1:13.

Text Box 7. In the second chapter of Acts Luke records how the Holy Spirit came to the apostles on the day of Pentecost, after Jesus had ascended. Many see this as the birth of the church, and it is certainly when the apostles went from being afraid and in hiding, to bold preachers of the gospel. As noted in the main text, Pentecost occurred fifty days after Passover. This day was the Jewish Festival of Weeks (also called "Shavuot"), marking the beginning of the harvest, when the first fruits of the harvest were brought to the temple. This is also associated with the giving of the Law at Mount Sinai, as described in Exodus. When Moses first came down from mount Sinai with the stone tablets upon which the Law was written, he found the people engaged in idolatry, worshipping a golden calf. In his anger, Moses called for those loyal to him and to God to punish the idolaters, and Exodus records that "there fell of the people that day about three thousand men."[34] Interestingly, on that first Pentecost recorded in Acts, the newly emboldened disciples preached the gospel (heard by all those present in their own tongue, even languages that the disciples didn't speak) and "there were added that day about three thousand souls" to the nascent church.[35] When Paul wrote, "the sting of death is sin, and the power of sin is the law, but thanks be to God, who gives us the victory through our Lord Jesus Christ,"[36] he may well have had these parallels passages in mind. When the Hebrews in the wilderness broke the Law, "about three thousand" died, but when the Holy Spirit birthed the new church, and they preached the gospel of salvation through faith in Christ, "about three thousand" received eternal life.

In addition to having access to God directly through His Holy Spirit, who dwells within us, Christians may also share in fellowship with the body of Christ. Although this may not sound particularly desirable to some because of the very real failings of the Christian church throughout history (for more on the contributions of the church and Christianity to

34. Exod 32:28.
35. Acts 2:41.
36. 1 Cor 15:56–57.

society, please see chapter 8), the fact remains that the church is referred to in the New Testament as the "body of Christ." That is, the church is called to be the hands and feet of Christ, serving the poor, seeking the lost, preaching the good news. The church also provides avenues for fellowship, accountability, support, and communal worship. The church, at its best, is a light to the world. The early New Testament church described in the book of Acts was such a church, quickly spreading because of the good deeds and changed lives that resulted from its ministries. Within only a few generations of its inception the church had grown and spread across the entire Roman Empire, coming to the notice (and often persecution) of rulers throughout the empire. In a letter to the Roman emperor Trajan, Pliny the Younger wrote of the Christians that they were guilty of no crime, but only of taking oaths "not to commit fraud, theft, or adultery, not falsify their trust, nor to refuse to return a trust when called upon to do so."[37]

The third way in which a follower of Christ can be in relationship with God is actually the promise of a face-to-face relationship in the future. Some ancient Jewish leaders (though not all) believed in some sort of life after death. However, the New Testament clearly teaches that there will be eternal life with God for those who have faith in Christ as their Savior. The idea of heaven (or paradise) is not unique to the Judeo-Christian religion, but as we'll see in chapter 6, the differing views of what this means among the different world religions are profound. To atheists and materialists, the entire idea of a life after death seems foolish. Instead, any allusion to heaven, or to loved ones going to a better place when they die, or to final justice being meted out by a just God, is considered to be merely wishful thinking. Although nearly every culture in history has had some idea of a spiritual life after death, it is worth noting that the Christian concept of heaven is certainly unique from the ideas of the Eastern religions, in that we will be eternally with God, but not dissolved into God. That which we can only now believe through faith and hope for we will one day experience firsthand. The end of Revelation, the final book in the Bible, gives an extensive (if somewhat inscrutable) view of heaven and eternal life.[38] However, one thing is clear from the biblical accounts of the afterlife—we will be conscious, and we will retain our individuality.

37. From a letter (*Epistulae* X.96) from Pliny the Younger (governor of the province of Bithynia et Pontus) to the Roman emperor Trajan, c. 111–13 (quoted in Carrington, *Early Christian Church*, 429).

38. Rev 21:9—22:5.

Finally, we can find comfort in Christ through our relationship with Him. Unlike the God of any other religion, we do not have a God who only judges, nor do we have a Savior who simply pities us. Rather we have a divine Savior who knows what suffering is, one who can sympathize with us. The author of the New Testament Letter to the Hebrews writes, "For we have not a high priest who is unable to sympathize with our weaknesses, but one who in every respect has been tempted as we are, yet without sin."[39] This is discussed in more detail below but suffice it to say that there is no easy answer to all of the suffering on this earth. However, on an emotional level, many have found comfort and peace in the fact that they do not suffer alone. Christians believe that they have a high priest who is indeed able to sympathize with them. To sympathize (from the Greek *sym* for "with" and *pathos* for "suffering") literally means to "suffer with," but in fact Jesus suffered not just with us, but for us, paying the price for the sins of the world through His death on the cross. If you believe that humans have free will, then we must share at least part of the blame for the evil and suffering present in our world. Sin, which may be defined as the exercise of our human will in ways that go against God's will and God's commands, must be seen as at least partly to blame for the evil in the world. Even if you do not believe in God, even if you do not believe that Christ died for your sins, and particularly if you *do* believe that God shares in the blame for all of the evil and suffering that exists on earth, it must be admitted that the Christian claim that God (in Christ) paid the price for sin is entirely unique. Other religions believe that their gods had incarnations (such as the ten incarnations of Vishnu), but no other religion believes in a God who paid the price to make right the evil and brokenness in our lives. No other religion believes in a God who can offer comfort, peace, and sympathy as we struggle for understanding, hope, and meaning amidst our suffering.

The Problem of Evil

It cannot be denied that there is a vast amount of pain and suffering in the world, and that many people throughout history have looked to religion in an attempt to make some sense of it, while many others have turned away from religion. The reality of pain and suffering in the world is a major issue that many people have with accepting a belief in a monotheistic

---

39. Heb 4:15.

God. Much of this pain has been caused by evil, either individual acts of evil or institutional evil (that is corrupt systems, such as apartheid).[40] Evil can be small or large, and it can be found both in what we do, such as lying about a coworker in hopes of getting preferential treatment from the boss, or sending a million Jews to the gas chambers, and in what we do not do, such as when individuals and entire denominations failed to speak out against injustice. Trying to reconcile the existence of evil with the idea of a good, just, and loving God has been referred to by philosophers and theologians as "the problem of evil." Stated simply, the problem of evil can be summarized as follows. An omnipotent God could stop evil. A good God would want to stop evil. There is evil in the world. Among the conclusions that can be drawn from this are that: a) God wants to stop evil but cannot (God is good but not all-powerful), b) God has the ability to stop evil but chooses not to (God is all-powerful but not good), or c) God has neither the power nor the inclination to stop evil from happening (God is neither good nor omnipotent—possibly because God does not exist). People have been struggling with this issue for ages, but it is worth noting at the outset a logical flaw in the problem of evil as summarized above. Dinesh D'Souza rightly points out that the second conclusion (conclusion b above) is not necessarily valid.[41] It is possible that God is both all-powerful and good, but that there is a reason or purpose for the evil in the world that we, being less than God, cannot understand. The distinction is critical. Whatever we conclude about the existence of evil, if God exists, as noted above, His intellect is far superior to ours. Just as a small child may not understand why he has to suffer the pain of an inoculation, we might not expect to understand everything about God's creation or His purposes.

The problem caused by the existence of evil is profound, and addressing it thoroughly is well beyond the scope and purview of this book. Numerous books have been written by scholars, theologians, and Christian apologists that deal with the matter in detail.[42] Although I touch on this issue here and throughout the rest of the book, I encourage

40. A third type of evil is what might be called "natural evil." This could include so-called acts of God (e.g., when an earthquake or hurricane destroys the homes and lives of countless people), or even the evil that occurs in nature when a predator tears into the flesh of living prey (D'Souza, *Godforsaken*, 117, 135).

41. D'Souza, *Godforsaken*, 80.

42. See for example Yancey, *Disappointment with God*; Lennox, "Loud Absence"; Kreeft, "Problem of Evil"; Wright, *Evil and the Justice of God*; and D'Souza, *Godforsaken*.

anyone struggling with this question, which has been a stumbling block for many, to read some of these references. Before addressing the issue, it is worth considering what the problem of evil says, if anything, about the existence of a divine Creator. In short, questioning the goodness or the power of God is not a reason for dismissing His existence. In fact, it has been argued that the obvious existence of evil in the world is actually evidence *for* the existence of God. If one agrees that there is evil in the world, then it also must be agreed that there is also good; if there is both good and evil, there must be some moral law that distinguishes between the two; and if there is a moral law, there must be a moral Lawgiver.[43]

You may choose not to worship God, but the existence of evil is not evidence against the existence of the supernatural. It is also worth noting that discussions of the problem of evil did not start with atheist thinkers of the nineteenth and twentieth century. These very questions that atheists place at Christianity's doorstep, as if they were the first to think of them, have actually been wrestled with within Judaism and Christianity for millennia. This issue of apparently unjust suffering is dealt with matter-of-factly in the Bible, most notably in the book of Job, which is possibly the oldest book in the Bible.

If the problem of evil does not argue against the existence of God, why has it driven so many from the church? Some have suggested that many atheists are actually "wounded theists." Their final decision to reject God is based not on science or reason, but on some terrible thing that happened in their life that has caused them to give up on God. For example, Desmond and Moore, biographers of Charles Darwin (who had considered a career in the clergy at one time), write of the death of one of Darwin's daughters: "Annie's cruel death destroyed Charles's tatters of belief in a moral, just universe. Later he would say that this period chimed the final death-knell for his Christianity."[44] Although it is risky to comment on the motives of others for adopting one belief over another, it is clear that the evil in the world is seen by many as an indictment on God's character.[45] In the face of pain, suffering, and evil, what can religion offer

43. Zacharias, *Shattered Visage*, 176.

44. Desmond and Moore, *Darwin*, 387.

45. It is interesting (as well as poignant and ironic) to note that there is evidence that both Darwin's and his ten children's health issues were genetic in nature. Darwin, who married his first cousin, came from a sickly family. Of his ten children, "three proved infertile as adults, and three died young." When his favorite child, Anne Elizabeth, died at age ten, "it snuffed the last lingering remnant of Darwin's religious

by way of explanation or remedy for the problem of evil? Do any of the forms of religious belief provide answers or comfort, and if so, does this give any real reason to accept such a belief, or is it just wishful thinking to accept a religion only because it provides some illusory hope or meaning?

Not What We Expect

During a discussion amongst friends in graduate school on the biblical stance regarding a contentious theological issue, a colleague of mine said, "I prefer to believe in a more open-minded supreme being." Truly, such a statement is nonsense. If there is a supreme being, His attributes are entirely independent of what we may prefer to believe. I may prefer to believe that a "loving God" (or at least my concept of one) will stamp out all pain and suffering in this life, but that does not make it so. There are no easy answers to the problem of evil and other questions that religion and philosophy seek to address. But there are some bad answers. As noted at the beginning of this chapter, a worldview must deal with four key questions in an internally consistent manner.[46] These are: where do we come from (origins)?, is there any meaning or purpose in life (teleology)?, what is the basis for right and wrong or good and evil (morality)?, and what happens when we die (destiny)? What then can we say about creation based upon the possible kinds of divinity? And what can we conclude about divinity from an investigation of creation?

In short, the other belief systems described do not offer satisfying answers to all four of these questions. Polytheism as practiced throughout history has no logical answer to the origins of the universe. The polytheistic deities of old were themselves physical beings who did not precede matter. Pantheism also stumbles here, for a "life force" made up of the spirit of all living beings cannot have preceded that which gives it existence. With pantheism there is also no way to derive purpose or meaning. We cannot be "called" to anything if there is no "caller."[47] Since individuality is an accident or an aberration, the only thing the pantheist can say with any certainty that he is called to is—nothing. He is called to stop seeking some imaginary call, and instead melt back into the spiritual oblivion of oneness with the universe. Polytheism can provide

---

faith" (Kean, *Violinist's Thumb*, 291).

46. Zacharias, *End of Reason*, 31.

47. Guinness, *Call*, 48.

a purpose—but only to get involved in the petty struggles of the gods in return for some passing earthly reward. Polytheism struggles with a basis for morality as well. If the gods are fickle and flawed and cannot themselves adhere to any moral code, what hope or expectation is there that humans will be different? Pantheism also fails on a basis for morality. One must wonder why an impersonal force would care if we followed a moral code. Caring is something sentient beings do. Rocks, potatoes, and life forces do not care. Finally, the answers related to eternal destiny offered by polytheism and pantheism are unsatisfying. Paradise in the presence of the polytheistic deities is unlikely to be any less volatile than life at their mercy on this side. Giving up everything that we are and all our memories of love and loved ones is all that pantheism has to offer.

Atheism also proposes answers to the four questions, but those answers are singularly unsatisfying. In short: we originated from nothing, there is no meaning in life, there is no absolute basis for morality (as we'll see in the next chapter), and our destiny is death and a return to nothingness. The impersonal material universe offers no comfort, peace, or purpose, only science and determinism. From an evolutionary perspective, there is no adaptive advantage to a sense of meaning, and compassion does nothing to improve the reproductive success of the individual. The cockroach is among the most successful species on earth—there is no evidence that the cockroach experiences individuality, meaning, or compassion.

If, as atheism posits, there is no transcendent reality, then when the biological functions of life cease, we cease. There is no afterlife, and no hope for pleasure or for justice beyond that which we affect in this life. Even if an atheist believes that "good" and "evil" are not meaningless and relative terms, faced with such a hopeless view of the future, is it any wonder that people would ignore what *is* good in favor of what *feels* good? Is it any surprise that as atheism increases people choose to maximize their individual pleasure even if this comes at the expense of others? In seeking to maximize my personal pleasure by answering the Darwinian call to carry my genetic material forward to future generations, why would it be wrong to procreate with every woman I see who seems reproductively fit? Even if the women claim not to want to procreate with me, why would it be evil to force myself upon them? If someone is strong enough to subdue both her and her current mating partner, the species benefits by the passing on of the genetic material of only the strongest individuals.

By contrast, these questions have been an ongoing discussion within Christianity for centuries and are even dealt with frankly in the Bible. As

I hope to show in the next chapter (and the rest of the book), monotheism alone, which conceives of a personal God who is present and active in the created order, provides some comfort and hope in our suffering. Christianity alone deals with questions of origins, meaning, morality, and destiny in an internally consistent manner.

Additional Reading

For additional reading on the nature and character of God, consider the following books: *Mere Christianity* by C. S. Lewis is quite possibly the greatest work of Christian apologetics of the twentieth century.[48] It is a must-read for anyone seriously contemplating God and Christianity. *Knowing God* by J. I. Packer is a classic devotional guide to developing an intimate relationship with God.[49] *Evil and the Justice of God* by N. T. Wright is an excellent treatment on the problem of evil, a primary obstacle that many people cite for accepting belief in the Judeo-Christian God.[50] Another excellent treatment of the problem of evil can be found in *Godforsaken* by Dinesh D'Souza.[51]

48. Lewis, *Mere Christianity*.
49. Packer, *Knowing God*.
50. Wright, *Evil and the Justice of God*.
51. D'Souza, *Godforsaken*.

4

Who Needs God?

Sire, I had no need for that hypothesis

—SIMON LAPLACE[1]

WHEN FRIEDRICH NIETZSCHE WROTE that "God is dead" in 1881,[2] he was simply commenting on the fact that, increasingly, many of the most "enlightened" of his contemporaries in nineteenth-century Europe thought and lived as if there was no God. Though perhaps claiming to be agnostic, they were most often functionally atheistic in that a belief in God no longer directed their actions or informed their decisions. Western culture at large remained outwardly Christian for many decades following and provided popular support and peer pressure to adhere to biblical mores and make a public appearance of Christianity. But privately, individuals were increasingly convinced that there was no need for God. Like Simon LaPlace, they believed that the laws of science made the "god hypothesis" unnecessary. As a result, they increasingly made decisions and held beliefs that were antithetical to the "Christian" way of life. G. K. Chesterton described the absence of belief in the privileged

---

1. Attributed to Simon Laplace (Lennox, *God's Undertaker*, 46).
2. Nietzsche, *Gay Science*, 181.

upper classes: "agnosticism was the established thing . . . There was a uniformity of unbelief among educated people."[3]

The change had been coming for some time. Following the Enlightenment of the 1600s and 1700s, for the first time in human history mankind began en masse to jettison God from everyday life. The Scientific Revolution vastly increased mankind's understanding of natural processes (Aristotle's "efficient cause"), dispelling much myth and superstition. The Industrial Revolution reduced our utter dependence on providence, or "divine intervention," to provide the basic necessities for life. Individualism, a product of the Renaissance and the Reformation, further sapped mankind's reliance on institutions, or at least preached an end to such reliance. In literary circles, Romanticism, characterized by the idealization of innocence and of the past, gave rise to the decadent era, existentialism, then nihilism. People increasingly adopted a worldview that no longer seemed to require a transcendent deity. Humanity, they reasoned (and the likes of Nietzsche and Auguste Comte assured them), had moved from ignorance to increasing states of enlightenment, as their religion moved in lock step from shamanism and nature cults to polytheism, then monotheism, then ending in scientific atheism. Nietzsche wrote:

> God is dead. God remains dead. And we have killed him. Yet his shadow still looms. How shall we comfort ourselves, the murderers of all murderers? What was holiest and mightiest of all that the world has yet owned has bled to death under our knives: who will wipe this blood off us? What water is there for us to clean ourselves? What festivals of atonement, what sacred games shall we have to invent? Is not the greatness of this deed too great for us? Must we ourselves not become gods simply to appear worthy of it?[4]

As Nietzsche asked, what shall we have to invent if there is no God? That is, do we really lose anything of value once we have done away with God? American neuroscientist and author Sam Harris thought not, saying, "Everything of value that people get from religion can be had more honestly, without presuming anything on insufficient evidence."[5] He was mistaken. There is much that materialist science and atheism cannot explain. If science insists upon what has been called "methodological

---

3. Chesterton, *Autobiography*, 143–45.

4. Nietzsche, *Gay Science*, 181.

5. Harris, "God's Dupes."

materialism," it must limit itself to those areas that will submit to empirical methods. Answers concerning purpose, meaning, and morality—why things are the way they are, and how they should be—cannot be arrived at by methodological materialism.

What Science Cannot Prove

As argued in chapter 1, science can neither empirically prove nor disprove the existence of God. But neither can science address many key questions concerning how our universe and how life itself came about. However, one can state that the odds against all of this happening merely by unaided chance are astronomical, and this may be interpreted as evidence for the existence of something that we call "God." Furthermore, although the pursuit of religious and philosophical truth does not lend itself to empirical experimentation, this is not to say that such truths cannot be arrived at in a rational manner; nor does it follow that such truths are relative. Timothy Keller writes of Swinburne's argument (that belief in God can be tested and justified) that a theory or belief can be validated if it explains or predicts reality better than the alternatives. The existence of a God, Swinburne argues, leads us to expect the very things we observe, "that there is a universe at all, that scientific laws operate within it, that it contains human beings with consciousness and with an indelible moral sense. The theory that there is no God, he argues, does not lead us to expect any of these things. Therefore, belief in God offers a better empirical fit, it explains and accounts for what we see better than the alternative account of things."[6]

There is other evidence, independent of empirical scientific proof, for the existence of a divine Creator. Among these are human consciousness, the existence of a clear (and universal) moral sense, what C. S. Lewis and others have called "the argument from desire," and the universal concept of God. Each of these could be treated in much more detail (and have been elsewhere), but the implications of a religious versus an atheistic worldview can be tested and evaluated as they relate to these and other topics. The prominent evolutionary biologist William Provine claimed (I believe wrongly) that if Darwinian evolution (or any mechanism for the origin of life that does not invoke a divine Creator)[7] could be shown to

---

6. Keller, *Reason for God*, 125–26.

7. As noted above (chapter 2), Darwinian evolution does not claim to explain the

explain the origins of life, there would be five "inescapable conclusions."[8] These are:

1. there is no physical evidence for God;[9]

2. there is no life after death;

3. there is no absolute foundation for right and wrong;

4. there is no ultimate meaning for life; and

5. people do not really have free will.

The primary presupposition behind these conclusions is materialism—the theory that there is nothing outside the material world, and that all emergent phenomena (such as consciousness, emotion and free will) are solely the result of material properties and interactions. But nothing that one can prove concerning the material world could possibly speak to the possibility of things outside of the material world. Even if one could prove definitively and empirically that life evolved by chance with no input from a divine external agency, this would prove only that the external agency was not necessary for life, not that the external agency did not exist. Life arose without any input from my Aunt Linda, but this does not prove that my Aunt Linda does not exist. When the modern scientific enterprise demands anti-supernaturalism as a necessary first principle, as Francis Schaeffer noted, "They . . . are doing their materialistic science with no epistemological base. In the crucial area of knowing, they are not operating on facts but on faith."[10] Materialism simply cannot be demonstrated to be true by any empirical method.

Provine is, however, correct in linking materialism to the loss of any foundation for morality and meaning (as discussed below). Materialism also leaves no room for free will, for if true, then our every choice

---

origins of life. Darwin never made this claim for his theory, and no one who knows the theory could possibly make this claim. As Dawkins points out, Darwinian evolution is a theory of the development of "adaptive complexity" (*Blind Watchmaker*, 407).

8. Johnson, *Darwin on Trial*, 126–27.

9. This conclusion is false. Even if a mechanism could be definitively shown to fully explain the origins of life by chance and without the intervention of a supernatural intelligence, such a mechanism is still not even the beginning of proof that God does not exist, only that we do not need to invoke Him to understand the origins of biological life. Even then, divinity is not disproved—perhaps the Creator chose to use the mechanism in question to create life. Empiricism simply can neither prove nor disprove divinity.

10. Schaeffer, *God Who Is There*, 20.

is determined by the laws of nature—physics, chemistry, biology, and genetics. We are a product of our genes and our genes' response to environmental stimuli. If there is nothing but the material world, Camille Paglia argues that "free will is stillborn in the red cells of our body, for there is no free will in nature. Our choices come to us pre-packaged."[11] Just as the rotation of the planets around the sun and transmission of physical traits from parent to offspring follow predictable natural laws, so too the workings of the human brain. Our brains are "wetware"—like a computer that has neither consciousness nor the will to do anything other than that for which it is genetically programmed. Even intelligence does not really exist; there are only differences in the speed and accuracy of the electrochemical synapses in our brains. If everything is predetermined by nature's laws, even our most random-seeming actions and responses are programmed. But in the absence of will, predetermination and randomness seem to be mutually exclusive. In fact, a computer cannot actually generate a random number; it can only do that for which it has been programmed.

> **Text Box 8**. Except in science fiction, computers have no consciousness and no free will. They can do only that for which they are programmed. Among the things that they cannot do is generate a random number. Instead, complex algorithms must be written that rely on a specific (complex) number. For example, a random number generation program may calculate the value of pi to thousands of decimal places. Each time a computer is asked to generate a random number, it may select the next sequential digit and use this digit (or a value derived from it) to generate a "random" number or value. The notion that all emergent phenomena (such as consciousness) are the result of material properties and interactions would have you believe that if I asked you to select a random number between one and one million, and if I intimately and exactly know your genome, your history, and all the laws of the universe, I could predict that you would select, for example, 91,074 on a given day. Conversely, theism, the belief in an eternal God that exists outside of time, predicts that a God who is always in the past, present, and future would know the number you selected

11. Paglia, *Sexual Personae*, 7.

because the future to you (and for that matter the past) is all the present to Him. If intelligence and will cannot produce true randomness, can randomness produce intelligence and will?

If the material world is all that there is, everything must follow physical and natural laws, and everything that happens is determined by those laws. Instinct, inherited behaviors, and programmed adaptation replace free will. Atheism must lead to materialism, and materialism is determinism.

The Myth of Consciousness

That humans possess individuality and consciousness is no surprise to most of us, though to a strict materialist it ought to be. What may be surprising is that, as Johns Hopkins psychiatrist Paul McHugh writes, "We do not have a clue how a material object—even one as complicated as our brain—can produce the light of consciousness in which we experience our thoughts, carry out our enterprises, and in so many different ways conduct our lives."[12] To any unbiased observer, consciousness appears to exceed mere material processes in the brain. To a materialist—who does not believe in anything but matter—what passes for thought, emotion, and consciousness is only neurochemistry. Although humans may seem unique in their ability to think and conceptualize, the materialist would consider this to be an illusion caused (though, as Dr. McHugh and other experts note, we know not how) by the vast neural connectivity in the human brain. There now exist computers that can do as many computations per second as the human brain, but no computer has achieved sentience. Many have tried to demonstrate definitively that consciousness is an "emergent" property and does not transcend the physical world. One such individual, renowned leader in the field of modern neurosurgery Wilder Penfield, has stated that he had sought to "prove that the brain accounts for the mind."[13] Instead, after years of research and the practice of medicine, Penfield came to believe that human beings are both body and spirit. Said Penfield, "to expect the highest brain mechanism or any set of reflexes, however complicated, to . . . perform all the functions of the

12. McHugh, *Mind Has Mountains*, 201.
13. Strobel, *Case for a Creator*, 249.

mind, is quite absurd." Australian physiologist and Nobel laureate John Eccles, after a career studying neuroscience and the physiology of the human brain, concluded that "Naturalism fails to account for our experienced uniqueness . . . I am constrained to attribute the uniqueness of the Self or Soul to a supernatural spiritual creation."[14] Monotheism alone offers a plausible rationale for consciousness and our strong personal sense of selfhood—we were created by a personal God.

The assumption that all thought and emotion can be reduced to neurochemistry is itself not an empirically verifiable hypothesis. It is a belief based upon the materialist presupposition, not a scientific conclusion drawn from empirical evidence. To be sure, electrochemical stimulation of the brain can induce feelings and sensations (tastes and smells). There must be at least some link between neurochemistry and thought, emotion, and perception, or else mood-altering and mind-altering drugs would not work. Some researchers have sought to test brain activity in specific regions of the brains of people undergoing religious experiences. However, the presence of a corresponding electrochemical signal in the brain does not disprove the existence of a supernatural God. If such a God exists, separate from matter and the created world, and if He wished to be in relationship with material beings, He would have had to create some way in which the spiritual and the physical can interact.

To the materialist consciousness is simply a series of electrochemical interactions forming and breaking between and within our neurons. Neurotransmitters are released, bind to their cognate receptors, and the signal is transmitted across synapses, triggering additional electrochemical changes resulting in physiological processes and the appearance of sentience, love, independent thought, and religious experience. A religious experience that one might claim as experiential evidence for the existence of God is discounted as a physiological phenomenon that we simply do not (yet) fully understand, a "religious instinct" caused by electrochemical activity in the brain that passes for sentience and sensation. The fact that this "religious instinct" has been present in virtually every culture and every society ever discovered throughout the history of our earth, regardless of the time, place, or degree of isolation, is no longer seen as evidence for the existence of a divine object of that religious longing. Instead, it is dismissed as a neurological phenomenon that somehow (though we know not how) provided an evolutionary advantage to our

14. Popper and Eccles, *Self and Its Brain*, 93.

ancient ancestors. Altruism and religious experience are evolutionary traits the evolutionary benefits of which have yet to be understood by science. Some researchers have sought to explain the evolutionary advantages of morality and altruism and its development by amoral natural processes. Many have given up the pursuit, while at least one star of the field, working on how our universal sense of morality was designed by nature, was forced to resort to scientific misconduct in an attempt to defend this untenable position.[15] Then again, absent a divine source for ultimate moral truth, why would his academic dishonesty be wrong?

Knowing Right from Wrong

One of Provine's "inescapable conclusions" mentioned above is that there is no absolute foundation for good and bad if there is no God. Provine is not the first to recognize this. In *The Brothers Karamazov* Dostoevsky wrote that if God does not exist, then "all things are lawful . . . for if there's no everlasting God, there's no such thing as virtue, and there's no need of it."[16] Outspoken atheist Madalyn Murray O'Hair wrote in *What on Earth Is an Atheist?*:

> We need a decent, modern, sophisticated, and workable set of standards by which we can get along with ourselves and with others. We atheists . . . try to find some basis of rational thinking on which we can base our actions and our beliefs, and we have it . . . We accept the technical philosophy of materialism. It is valid philosophy which cannot be discredited. Essentially, materialism's philosophy holds that nothing exists but natural phenomena . . . Materialism is a philosophy of life and living according to rational processes with intellectual and other capabilities of the individual to be developed to the highest degree in a social system where this may be possible . . . There are no supernatural forces, no supernatural entities such as gods, or heavens, or hells, or life after death. There are no supernatural forces, nor can there be. We atheists believe that nature simply exists. Matter is. Material is.[17]

It is striking that in Murray O'Hair's admission that atheists need a "workable set of standards by which we can get along with others,"

15. Carpenter, "Government Sanctions," 1283.

16. Dostoevsky, *Brothers Karamazov*, 720.

17. Murray O'Hair, *What on Earth*, 16.

and in Provine's five "inescapable conclusions," they both recognize the absence of any grounds for morality in materialistic atheism. Thank God for honest atheists—too many others delude themselves into believing that a rational basis for morality can be arrived at without a belief in God. As noted earlier, Sam Harris suggested that "Everything of value that people get from religion can be had more honestly, without presuming anything on insufficient evidence."[18] But neither he nor anyone else has developed any valid justification for an absolute moral code. If there is no absolute Lawgiver, there is no standard for determining if something is good or evil, no absolute moral foundation for right and wrong beyond expedience and "survival of the fittest."[19] All of our behaviors, whether we perceive them as good or bad, are reduced to matters of personal or societal preference. Notions of good and evil become constructs based on expedience alone.

I am *not* saying here that only persons who acknowledge a divine authority are moral, or that religious people are more ethical than irreligious people. I suspect everyone has known irreligious people who are good, honest, and upstanding, and some who claim to be religious but for whom lying and cheating seem to be second nature. I am not arguing that only the religious are moral, but that absent a divine absolute, there is no basis for determining something to be right or wrong. Although there is no absolute justification for morality without God, every individual and certainly every culture has a concept of right and wrong, good and evil. C. S. Lewis wrote of the human race that they are "haunted by the idea of a sort of behavior they ought to practice," and that they "did not in fact do [it]."[20] As Lewis argues, supposed cultural differences that many try to point out do not obviate the underlying universal principles such as the virtue of truthfulness, integrity, fidelity, generosity, and courage. The existence of an absolute moral law bespeaks the existence of a moral Lawgiver. The irreligious do indeed have morals, but these definitions of right and wrong are based upon centuries of morality based on and nurtured by religion. As these religious traditions are overturned in increasingly secular societies, it is inevitable that concepts of truth and values will increasingly be perceived to be subjective.

18. Harris, "God's Dupes."

19. The phrase "survival of the fittest" was coined by English philosopher and anthropologist Herbert Spencer (*Principles of Biology*, 444).

20. Lewis, *Mere Christianity*, 26.

If life evolved as the result of impersonal evolution absent a divine, moral intelligence, then we are just another animal species inhabiting the earth. If there is no spirit or soul, no hint of the supernatural within us, we are no different than animals beyond a simple matter of scale. That is, we are simply more intelligent than the next species on a continuum from amoeba and starfish through pigeons, rats, dogs, cats, dolphins, and chimpanzees. There is only animal instinct and Darwinian survival of the fittest. In such a world "good" is simply that which produces the most success for our species (or perhaps for our biosphere if one regards the Gaian earth mother). If I am bigger and stronger than you and I am attracted to your wife, girlfriend, sister, or daughter, I simply take her. If the female objects to my advances, I simply overpower her. Absent a moral standard, this could even be said to be "good," since only the strongest and fittest individuals would thus reproduce. The secular humanist notion of the perfectibility of man—the myth that promises that man, freed from the restraints of oppressive systems (such as religion), will continue to evolve into an increasingly noble race—is an atheist fairy tale. If you doubt that such behavior, driven only by instinct and absent any higher morality, happens in the animal kingdom, simply spend a bit of time observing the behavior of virtually any mammalian species. Rodents will mount literally any female in close proximity, including littermates and even their own dams. Dominant male chimpanzees will similarly force themselves on unwilling females. I worked with rodents and primates for years and observed such behaviors firsthand. Does one chimpanzee chastise his peer for "immoral behavior" when he steals another's mate?

Moreover, if life evolved only through impersonal evolution absent a supernatural Lawgiver, why should we not emulate the behaviors of others in the animal kingdom? If there is overpopulation, is euthanasia not a perfectly acceptable option? Children born with disease or disability would rightly be euthanized as well, since they are also a drain on valuable resources, while producing little of "value" toward advancing the species. If their condition were genetic, they would only harm the gene pool (and thus the success of the species) if they were allowed to survive long enough to reproduce. Just as the females of some species eat their young when they are unfit or when conditions justify (e.g., an absence of sufficient food or other resources), so too we, who are in this deterministic view essentially only smarter primates, ought to euthanize ill and inferior children, the old and infirm, the genetically damaged, and even the uneducated and the exceptionally poor. Science can establish the most "humane" (whatever that means) way to euthanize someone, but science cannot describe why that individual might have some innate worth or value independent of their potential genetic contribution or their abilities. Christianity can. As G. K. Chesterton wrote, in "religion all men are equal, as all pennies are equal, because the only value in any of them is that they bear the image of the King."[21]

A worldview based only on materialism and atheism cannot establish human worth beyond personal preference and expedience (what is "useful" at the time). If you think it unlikely that the practices described in the previous paragraphs could ever be justified by an entire civilization, consider for a moment the fruit of the eugenics movement of the early twentieth century.[22] Consider the Nazi party, which sought to eliminate Jews, gypsies, and other racial minorities, handicapped people, and homosexuals from the human race because they were seen as contributing to genetic and racial impurity. If you think it unlikely that mass infanticide could be justified, consider that nearly every culture in the ancient world engaged in the practice to a greater or lesser extent. In the Roman Empire, for example, the practice of "exposing" unwanted infants to the elements was commonplace. Infants that were not wanted for whatever reason were routinely placed outside to be exposed to the elements. The infant might die of starvation, dehydration, or exposure to the elements. The child might be eaten by wild animals or taken by slave traders and sold into slavery or prostitution. This practice was so ingrained in Roman culture that the very foundation myth of the city of Rome was the story of two infants (Romulus and Remus) born of a vestal virgin (sworn to chastity) and abandoned to spare their family from embarrassment. They were suckled by a wolf and eventually grew up to avenge themselves and establish the city of Rome. It was not until after Christianity took hold that the Christian emperor Valentinian I in 374 AD made "exposure" and infanticide illegal across the empire.[23]

Only through the knowledge of God, and His absolute moral standard, can we know right from wrong with certainty. The belief that rape, incest, child abuse, and infanticide are wrong is neither an evolutionary adaptation nor a man-made construct relative to our culture, but absent an infinite absolute there can be no biological basis for

21. Chesterton, *Charles Dickens*, 10.

22. See for example Black, *War against the Weak*.

23. Radbill, "History of Child Abuse," 175.

such absolute moral standards. The strongest and the most able spread their genes. If they steal mates from the slow or the stupid, or if they euthanize the sick and the mentally retarded, the atheist is left with no rationale by which such actions can be said to be wrong. As Sartre said, "if a finite point does not have an infinite reference point, it is meaningless and absurd."[24] In speaking of the "evils" and ignorance of religious belief following the terrorist attacks of September 11, 2001, Richard Dawkins commented that "Many of us saw religion as harmless nonsense . . . we thought, if people needed a crutch for consolation, where's the harm? September 11th changed all that."[25] Absent an absolute reference point, Dawkins's declaration simply makes no sense. By what standard can he possibly condemn the Al-Qaeda attacks as wrong? What was evil about the attacks? Is it that lives were lost? Lives are lost every day—we are born to die when the biochemical activity in our body ceases. The Al-Qaeda operatives on that day believed that America—which they called the "Great Satan"—was actually the evil one. By what criteria can science alone show them to have been wrong? Just as the fact that there was a beginning to creation suggests that there was a beginner who created, the fact that there is a moral code suggests that there is a moral Creator. Absolute moral laws, just like ordered universes, do not simply pop out of nothing. By contrast, if there is no God, there is no absolute foundation for right and wrong. Without a just and good God there is simply no source for ultimate moral truth. No one has developed a defensible moral code absent a reference to a divinity. Nor can they.

The Argument from Desire

Every culture, every society, and every people group ever discovered or studied throughout history has had religious ideas and a concept of divinity. Atheists might say that this simply reflects some as-yet-unknown selective advantage bestowed upon those that possess the gene for this "religious instinct." Dawkins has stated that "The meme[26] for blind faith secures its own perpetuation by the simple unconscious expedient of

24. Schaefer, *He Is There*, 291.

25. Dawkins, "Has the World Changed?"

26. A *meme* is a concept for an idea, behavior, or style that spreads from person to person within a culture, essentially a cultural analogue to a gene. One wonders, if the material world is all there is, what exactly is an idea? Is it made of atoms like everything else?

discouraging rational inquiry."[27] The notion that religious faith discourages rational inquiry is so entirely false as to call into question the objectivity of anyone making such a claim. As already noted in chapter 1 and elsewhere, the majority of the greatest scientists throughout history have been deeply religious, and a convincing case can be made that the modern scientific enterprise would not have been possible absent a Judeo-Christian foundation.[28] Aside from Dawkins's historically unsupportable bias that faith discourages rational inquiry, what selective advantage does he presume to have been bestowed upon an individual or a species by irrationality? To be sure there are some in any population who seem to be more or less disposed to religious orthodoxy or religious belief at all. But how does one explain (using only genetics) atheist children being born to devoutly religious parents—at rates recently that appear to be quite a bit higher than the usual rates of mutations in the human germ line? How does one explain the children of atheists coming to a belief in religion? Although not empirical evidence for the existence of the divine, the inescapable fact that religion has been a fundamental part of virtually every culture and people group throughout the history of humanity could conceivably be taken as evidence that this belief is based on something real.

The drive to search for God reflects a longing that is also ubiquitous amongst humans regardless of their time and place or their degree of isolation from other people. Perhaps you have at one time or another experienced this longing, a desire for something transcendent. In German this "blessed longing" is called "selige sehnsucht."[29] C. S. Lewis referred to this longing as the primary reason that led to his conversion to the Christian faith. Lewis wrote:

> Creatures are not born with desires unless satisfaction for these desires exists. A baby feels hunger; well, there is such a thing as food. A duckling wants to swim; well, there is such a thing as water. Men feel sexual desire; well, there is such a thing as sex. If I find in myself a desire which no experience in this world can satisfy, the most probable explanation is that I was made for another world.[30]

27. Dawkins, *Selfish Gene*, 219.

28. See for example Schaefer, *Escape from Reason*; Mangalwadi, *Book That Made Your World*; and Metaxas, *Is Atheism Dead?*

29. Kreeft, *Heaven*, 204.

30. Lewis, *Mere Christianity*, 120.

This longing for something more, something transcendent, is most certainly not simply a phenomenon found amongst Christians, or only the religious; it is a universal condition of humanity that spans millennia. The church father Augustine wrote, "thou hast made us for thyself and restless is our heart until it comes to rest in thee,"[31] while mathematician Blaise Pascal wrote of a God-shaped vacuum in the heart of every man, and that "this infinite abyss can be filled only with an infinite and immutable object; in other words by God himself."[32] More recently, professor Bart Ehrman, a self-described agnostic, has written of "a void inside me, a void of wanting someone to thank, and I don't see any plausible way of filling it."[33] Atheist Bertrand Russell said "The centre of me is always and eternally a terrible pain, a searching for something beyond what the world contains, something transfigured and infinite—the beautiful vision—God. I do not find it. I do not think it is to be found, but the love of it is my life."[34] What could possibly be the evolutionary advantage of such painful emptiness, of desiring the supernatural, if there is no object of that desire? As is often the case, the Bible has anticipated this emotion—Ecclesiastes states that God has placed "eternity in the hearts of men."[35]

Abandon All Hope, Ye Who Enter Here[36]

Just as science alone can provide no answers regarding absolute moral truth and no answer to the longing within us to know and be known, neither can science provide any basis for purpose or meaning. In the world of deterministic materialism left to us by the atheists, we are no different than animals, or even plants (for even plants sense and respond to their environment, and to the materialist consciousness is a myth of neurochemistry). We are simply more complex biological machines. Some atheists today will have us believe that purpose, meaning, and value can be derived without relying upon the divine, but they are mistaken. They cannot produce any logical construct that delivers on this promise. They

31. Augustine, *Confessions*, 11.
32. Pascal, *Pensees* (425), 113.
33. Ehrman, *God's Problem*, 128.
34. Quoted in Bryan, *Chapter and Verse*, 65.
35. Eccl 3:11.
36. This is the inscription over the gates of hell in Dante, *Inferno*, 18.

have not, and they cannot. We may derive a sense of purpose in our work or our progeny, but this is meaningless to others, and, ultimately, meaningless to even ourselves once we're dead. The early existentialists and the nihilists acknowledged this fact, and Albert Camus, a leading thinker amongst the nihilists, stated, "There is but one truly serious philosophical problem and that is suicide. Judging whether life is or is not worth living amounts to answering the fundamental question of philosophy."[37] This is the only logical end for a belief that there is no God. There is no escape from the meaninglessness and absurdity of our existence. Poet Ernest Dowson wrote:

> They are not long, the weeping and the laughter,
> Love and desire and hate:
> I think they have no portion in us after
> We pass the gate.
> They are not long, the days of wine and roses:
> Out of a misty dream
> Our path emerges for a while, then closes
> Within a dream.[38]

When you're dead, there is nothing, and while you're still alive, there is nothing with any meaning—this is the final truth of atheism. Psychologist Carl Jung reported that a third of his cases suffered from no definable neurosis other than "the senselessness and emptiness of their lives."[39] Stephen Jay Gould is quoted as saying, "We are here because one odd group of fishes had a peculiar fin anatomy that could transform into legs for terrestrial creatures; because comets struck the earth and wiped out the dinosaurs thereby giving mammals a chance not otherwise available . . . We may yearn for a 'higher' answer—but none exists."[40] We live, we die, and we are forgotten forever. Nothing we do has any lasting meaning or value. If you think that I am simply a judgmental Christian, remember that these are not my pronouncements, but they are the pronouncements of men who have rejected God. Consider a few more words from atheist thought leaders—more fruit from their poison tree. Meursault, the protagonist in Camus's book *The Stranger*, says, "It makes little difference whether one dies at the age of thirty or threescore and ten, since in either

37. Camus, *Myth of Sisyphus*, 3.

38. Dowson, "Vitae Summa Brevis," ii.

39. Yancey, *Bible Jesus Read*, 144.

40. Keller, *Reason for God*, 36–37.

case, other men and women will continue living, the world will go on as before."[41] Sartre said that man finds it disquieting that "God does not exist, for there disappears with him all possibility of finding values in an intelligible heaven . . . and man is in consequence forlorn, for he cannot find anything to depend on within or without himself."[42]

Much of Western literature since nihilism has tried to derive some sort of meaning ex nihilo, but it has failed. From Hemmingway's "grace under pressure," in which his protagonists stoically face meaninglessness and oblivion with vast quantities of alcohol, through Tom Robbins's irreverent and adolescent romps, poking fun at all things Christian while conveniently avoiding the burden of developing any actual lasting meaning or any working worldview beyond the pleasures of impiety, to the inane dictums of our present commercial culture, which insist that we "keep it real" and "coexist," there is little that honestly admits of the overwhelming emptiness of life without God. Peter Kreeft has written, "Our divine discontent is our humanity. Even the atheist Sartre saw this and rose to the dignity of despair. Pop psychology, infinitely inferior to honest existential anxiety, offers a prescription fit for cabbages and pigs, not men and women."[43] If you identify yourself as an atheist and have come to any other conclusion regarding whether life is really worth living, then perhaps you are not really living according to your beliefs. Perhaps the charge of "hypocrite" should not be limited to the religious.

By contrast, to the Christian life has meaning precisely because the divine and eternal God created us in His image and gave us a purpose, from which we derive meaning and fulfillment. What we do today can have implications for eternity. When the book *The Purpose Driven Life*[44] by Rick Warren came out in 2002, it was an immediate success, appearing on various bestseller lists for as many as ninety weeks. Nominal Christians, agnostics, and atheists alike are hungry for some semblance of meaning in the harsh, materialistic world left to us by empty philosophies in which truth and morality are seen as relative, mindless adolescent skepticism is confused for great intellectualism, and depravity and meaninglessness are considered to be wisdom. The Bible paints a very different picture. In the Eighth Psalm the psalmist marvels, "What is man that thou art

41. Camus, *Stranger*, 21.

42. Lucado, *No Wonder*, 34.

43. Kreeft, *Heaven*, 46.

44. Warren, *Purpose Driven Life*.

mindful of him, and the son of man that thou dost care for him?[45] In the book of Job, Eliphaz taunts, "Can a man be of benefit to God . . . what would he gain if your ways were blameless,"[46] but God later roundly chastises Eliphaz and the others for their false wisdom, and commands them to make reparations to Job. And of course, after His acts of creation, including the creation of humans, God Himself declared it "very good."[47]

Why So Much Suffering?

Richard Dawkins has written:

> The total amount of suffering per year in the natural world is beyond all decent contemplation. During the minute that it takes me to compose this sentence, thousands of animals are being eaten alive, many others are running for their lives, whimpering with fear, others are slowly being devoured from within by rasping parasites, thousands of all kinds are dying of starvation, thirst, and disease. It must be so . . . In a universe of electrons and selfish genes, blind physical forces and genetic replication, some people are going to get hurt, other people are going to get lucky, and you won't find any rhyme or reason in it, nor any justice. The universe that we observe has precisely the properties we should expect if there is, at bottom, no design, no purpose, no evil, no good, nothing but pitiless indifference.[48]

How can Christians continue to say that God is good in light of the evil in the world? In dealing with the problem of evil, it is worth distinguishing between pain and suffering. Pain is a physiological response to the stimulation of pain receptors, while suffering is the result of a conscious awareness of the presence or even the mere possibility of pain. D'Souza suggests that the majority of the "pain" that people experience is actually suffering.[49] We humans suffer even when someone other than ourselves—a loved one for instance—is suffering or in pain. Loneliness, rejection, job loss, the death of a loved one, and a broken heart all cause suffering, though in most cases not the physiological response of pain.

45. Ps 8:4–6.
46. Job 22:1–3.
47. Gen 1.
48. Dawkins, *River Out of Eden*, 131–32.
49. D'Souza, *Godforsaken*, 153–55.

Is all pain bad? Perhaps counterintuitively, Paul Brand and Philip Yancey in their book *Fearfully and Wonderfully Made* make a compelling case for the benefits of pain.[50] Yancey and Brand (an MD who studied the disease leprosy for much of his professional life) point out that without the ability to feel pain, people with leprosy lose digits and limbs due to otherwise minor injuries. Without a functional physiological pain response, a leper cannot tell if his hand is on a hot stove, or if he has a minor injury that without attention could become life threatening. Brand notes that the single greatest gift that he could have given his patients with leprosy would have been the ability to feel pain. Too much pain can be a very bad thing, but so too can too much food, yet no one bemoans God the creation of food or the need to eat. Not all pain is evil: if it warns of danger (e.g., placing your hand on a hot stove) or signals underlying issues (e.g., a head ache that alerts an individual to a brain tumor), the pain felt is serving the very purpose for which pain exists. Similarly, not all suffering is bad. If one suffers remorse for some wrongdoing and this motivates the person to seek forgiveness and restoration of a broken relationship, such suffering is actually a good thing. Someone who is incapable of suffering remorse is not usually considered to be emotionally healthy.

Other religions have offered some answers, but it is worth noting that, as D'Souza has written, "The problem of suffering is first raised in the book of Job, and the vigorous debate about this topic is unique to Christianity. You won't find it in Hinduism or Buddhism or even Islam."[51] It is worth a brief investigation to see if it is possible to glean some hope or meaning in all the suffering in the world from these other religions. Unfortunately, such an investigation is likely to result in disappointment. To begin with, the pantheistic religions cannot give any explanation for consciousness—if the deity/life force does not have personality, will, sentience, and intellect, how can this have emerged in the created (and therefore derivative) world? If consciousness is an illusion, then much of suffering (as distinguished above from actual pain) is also an illusion, and even pain is just a matter of a series of neurons firing in our nervous system. The primary answer to be found in the pantheistic Eastern religions is a denial that suffering really exists. Buddhism, in its strictest form, says that all of our perceptions of this reality are illusions based upon our own cravings and desires, and "Hinduism explains . . . [the] perception

50. Brand and Yancey, *Fearfully and Wonderfully Made*.

51. D'Souza, *Godforsaken*, 13.

of evil as induced by ignorance . . . There is no way for classical Hindu-ism to deal with the problem of evil. To deny that evil is real does not diminish wickedness . . ."[52] Another "answer" can be found in the fact that some Eastern pantheistic religions tend to place blame for evil squarely on the individual, through the concept of Karma. When evil things hap-pen to you, you deserve it because of the evil things you did in previous lives. The "atheistic religions, such as Buddhism, and monistic ones, such as Hinduism, invoke the Karmic law to work out evil and prosper the good."[53] Thus the pantheistic religions either deny the existence of suf-fering or place the blame squarely on humanity, wherein any suffering is earned by the "bad" Karma accumulated in previous lives.

Neither does polytheism offer any answers. One possible differenti-ator (though it can hardly be called an "answer" in any meaningful sense) of polytheism is that the so-called problem of evil is no longer even a question. With polytheism, the gods themselves are capable of significant acts of evil. The gods of polytheism are little more than created beings with superhuman power but very human failings and foibles. They are fallible, capricious, spiteful, and petty. That humans can also perform evil should come as no surprise in a polytheistic universe. However, this does nothing to provide any hope or meaning in our suffering.

The atheist view in some ways has arisen specifically in response to the problem of evil. That is, as D'Souza and Bryan have pointed out, many people seem to turn to atheism (or agnosticism) because they cannot make sense of the evil and suffering present in the world. For this reason, atheism does in some ways address the problem of pain. Sadly, the answers it gives are hopeless, contradictory, and demeaning. To begin with, at least some of the suffering in the world is again illusion to the atheist, essentially unconstructive electrochemical reactions in our brain. Since, as D'Souza described, much human suffering is not due to actual pain that we experience firsthand, but rather to our fear or anticipation of pain for ourselves or others, this sort of suffering is simply neurochemistry run amok. Chemistry is neither good nor evil; overactive neurons are morally neutral. Just as higher consciousness in humans is an illusion to a materialist, an outgrowth of the size and complexity of our brains relative to that of our next nearest cousins in the animal kingdom, anticipating pain is simply a more complicated electrochemical response that we have

---

52. Zacharias, *Jesus among Other Gods*, 119–20.
53. Zacharias, *Jesus among Other Gods*, 100–101.

evolved in order for us to adapt better to our environment and to plan ahead for dire contingencies. One could propose that suffering is an adaption that is partly behind our success as a species and can therefore hardly be called "evil" at all. As already noted, even the real pain that we feel when our pain receptors are activated (if for example we were bitten by a shark) must be seen as an evolutionary advantage, as evidenced by the horrible reality of the absence of pain in those with leprosy. To the Darwinist, pain is a signal that has evolved to protect—it tells us to remove our hand from the flames and warns us that a particular joint or muscle may be weak or about to fail. Although the pain response, like any biological response designed to be triggered by external stimuli, can go out of control and be activated inappropriately, it can hardly be said to be evil. As described above, even evil is a meaningless term to the materialist. Those individuals who commit what we call "evil" or "selfish" acts are simply "dancing to their DNA"—answering the genetic call to improve their own reproductive success at the expense of weaker members of the species. Dawkins writes that "DNA neither cares nor knows. DNA just is. And we dance to its music."[54] The materialist must accept that an individual has "value" only insofar as he or she can contribute to the success of the species. Culling the herd to favor the strong and the intelligent (as Hitler claimed to be doing) is no evil; it is simply speeding the evolutionary process along.

Atheism can make sense of the problem of evil only by removing belief in evil, or rather removing the belief in any absolutes other than matter and the material world. By their own admission, the logical conclusion of atheism is that there is no absolute truth, there is no absolute basis for morality, and there is no meaning or purpose. In believing thus, we are left with all of the evil with which we began, but none of the comfort that people have for generations derived from religion, and no hope for the future, either in this life or the next one. Alexander Solzhenitsyn, in his commencement address at Harvard University in 1978, said, "The humanistic way of thinking that has proclaimed itself as our guide did not admit the existence of intrinsic evil in man, nor did it seek any task higher than the attainment of happiness on earth. It started modern Western civilization on the dangerous trend of worshipping man and his material needs as if human life did not have any higher meaning."[55]

---

54. Dawkins, *River Out of Eden*, 133.

55. Quoted in Bryan, *Chapter and Verse*, 59.

With the exception of the intellectual surrender of deism, monotheism alone can begin to address the problem of evil in an honest fashion without denying that evil exists. With monotheism, the problem of evil as classically stated comes acutely into view, because theism confirms moral absolutes (that evil and good exist), transcendence (consciousness is real and human beings have inherent value), and absolute truths (that God is both good and all-powerful). For more than three thousand years, beginning with the book of Job, Jewish and Christian religious leaders have been engaged in *theodicy*, that is, the effort to reconcile the presence of evil, pain, and suffering in our world with the existence of a loving and omnipotent God. Pascal wrote that "Solomon and Job have known and spoken best about man's wretchedness, one the most fortunate, the other the most unfortunate of men; one knowing by experiencing the vanity of pleasure, the other the reality of affliction."[56] What do we learn from God's Word? We learn first of all that pain and suffering are the result of sin. John Piper writes, "Suffering . . . portrays sin's horror for the world to see. It punishes sin's guilt for those who do not believe in Christ. It breaks sin's power for those who take up their crosses and follow Jesus."[57] If we are in Christ, at least some of what we suffer is meant to sanctify us. James wrote that we should "count it all joy, my brethren, when you meet various trials, for you know that the testing of your faith produces steadfastness."[58] God will also discipline His children. As the author of Hebrews wrote, "God is treating you as sons; for what son is there whom his father does not discipline?"[59] Whereas some of our suffering is the result of our own sin, some is the result of the sin of others. But all of it is the result of the fall. What's more, the Bible claims that none of our suffering is without meaning or purpose. The apostle Paul wrote that "in everything God works for good with those who love him, who are called according to his purpose."[60] Expanding upon this concept, Augustine wrote that "God would not allow any evil to exist in His works unless His omnipotence and goodness were such as to bring good even out of evil."[61] Indeed, an honest reading of human history suggests that we learn and grow from

---

56. Pascal, *Penses* (50), 174.

57. Piper, *Don't Waste Your Life*, 58.

58. Jas 1:2–3.

59. Heb 12:7

60. Rom 8:28.

61. Augustine, *Enchiridion*, 11.

the bad things much more than the good. Malcolm Muggeridge wrote that "if it ever were to be possible to eliminate affliction from our earthly existence . . . the result would not be to make life delectable, but to make it too banal or trivial to be endurable."[62]

Comfort in Suffering?

None of this makes the pain and suffering any easier. Although the problem of evil does not disprove the existence of a divine Creator, the existence of evil is a profound and troubling matter, not to be taken lightly. As noted above, addressing the issue thoroughly is beyond the scope of this book, though many of the more simplistic answers that have been proffered by other religions have been found wanting, and none is entirely satisfying intellectually. Theologian N. T. Wright has said that "solving" the problem of evil would in some ways cheapen the very real suffering that people experience as a result of evil, and that, as the book of Job reveals, "the theological insistence that to 'solve' the problem of evil in the present age is to belittle it."[63] Any attempt to address evil, pain, and suffering that does not treat the sufferer with sympathy may make sense intellectually, but would almost certainly be unable to provide healing. By providing the hope of justice, the eventual victory of good over evil, and comfort for sufferers, Christianity alone offers an answer for the problem of evil. Biblical Christianity alone tries to make sense of the pain and suffering without acting as if they do not exist. The longing that we all share for justice, the unmistakable sense that life should be better, is also evidence for the existence of God, and that all is not as it should be.

In our everyday lived experience, people share an innate sense of self, a basic moral sense, a longing to know and be known, and a desire for meaning and purpose. People suffer when they perceive life as meaningless, when they feel unloved, and when they feel disconnected from others. A belief in an impersonal deity, or in no deity at all, cannot explain these universal facts of human existence. We suffer even when someone we love is suffering or in pain. Compassion is a part of that which is most noble about humanity, but pantheism, polytheism, deism, and (especially) atheism posit no reasonable answer for this. The Eastern religions see suffering (as well as individualism) as an illusion to

62. Muggeridge, *Homemade*, July 1990 (referenced in Piper, *Desiring God*, 266).

63. Wright, *Evil and the Justice of God*, 71.

be overcome, or as the just reward for past sin (the concept of Karma). Islam also sees suffering as the justice of Allah. The gods of these religions may be questioned regarding the origins of evil in creation, but they will not be available for response. Neither will atheism's "god" be available for questioning—as Stephen Crane wrote:

> A man said to the Universe,
> Sir, I exist!
> Nevertheless, replied the Universe,
> That fact has not created in me
> The slightest feeling of obligation.[64]

Atheism has sought to make sense of the problem of evil by denying the existence of God. In so doing, we are left with all of the pain and all of the evil (but no absolute basis upon which to call it evil), but none of the comfort, and no way to derive any purpose for either our existence or our suffering. In the purely Darwinian view of life, suffering is just as much of a fiction as consciousness, and even pain itself is an evolutionary advantage of higher organisms that have evolved the obligate pain receptors. As Dawkins stated in the quote at the beginning of the previous section, not only is there "no evil," there is also "no good," and "no purpose." If it is true that there is no God, has atheism honestly considered the inevitable conclusions that arise from this belief—the very conclusions that Dawkins himself hints at? The nihilists alone have done so. Albert Camus concluded that "there is but one truly serious philosophical problem and that is suicide. Judging whether life is or is not worth living amounts to answering the fundamental question of philosophy."[65] Atheism's only answer for all the suffering and evil in the world is to lay it at the feet of the God in whom they claim not to believe—the God who redeems our suffering and who alone can bring good from it. But if, as the atheists charge, Christians have the problem of evil to explain, atheists have the problem of good. A worldview based on random chance and Darwinian survival of the fittest may reward those who find pleasure in beneficial things such as eating, mating, and nurturing young. But there is no easy explanation for joy, or for taking pleasure in small and seemingly meaningless things, the undeniable enchantment of simple human pleasures. Why should it be that art and music moves the soul? Why should it be that throughout history peoples around the world have believed that we have a soul at all?

---

64. Crane, "Man Said to the Universe."
65. Camus, *Myth of Sisyphus*, 3.

Where does all the good in our universe come from, and if the evil sends atheists running to deny and condemn God, why does the good not lead them to acknowledge and thank Him?

Science has not disproved the existence of God. If one can put aside unsupported preconceptions (i.e., materialism and a slavish adherence to empiricism), the conclusion that "God is" is much more rational than the opposite conclusion. Without God, there is, as stated in the *Atheist Manifesto*, no place for "charity, temperance, compassion, mercy, and humility, but also love of one's neighbor and the forgiveness of offenses."[66] Since even consciousness and sentience are a myth without God, the logical conclusion of atheism is that "there isn't actually a 'you' at the heart of all of [your] experiences . . . You are the sum of your parts . . . if everything else in the universe is like this, why are we different? Why do we think of ourselves as somehow not just being a collection of all out parts, but somehow being a separate, permanent entity which has all those parts?"[67] G. K. Chesterton foresaw this conclusion when he wrote that "Evolution . . . does not especially deny the existence of God; what it does deny is the existence of man."[68] Atheism leaves us meaningless and cold, arguing ultimately that human history is "a trash bag of random coincidences blown open by the wind."[69] By contrast, as author Philip Yancey writes, "the Old Testament's overwhelming lesson about God is that He is personal and intimate, its overwhelming lesson about human beings is that we matter."[70]

Whatever He is, God is likely to be as much unlike as like anything we've seen or experienced in this world. One thing seems clear: the presence of such a being, if He were to materialize in all His power and glory, while dispelling all doubts in His existence, would not allow for a relationship of loving obedience, which appears to be what the Judeo-Christian God desires. The Israelites were firsthand witnesses to the glory and power of God in the exodus, as they traveled through the wilderness to the promised land, but this certainly did not excite in them faithfulness or obedience. If the all-powerful God wished for whatever purpose to have a people who could relate to Him in any way other than shock and

66. Onfray, *Atheist Manifesto*, 57.

67. Baggini, "Is There a Real You?"

68. Chesterton, *Collected Works*, 196.

69. Heller, *Good as Gold*, 72.

70. Yancey, *Bible Jesus Read*, 35.

awe, it would seem that He would have to manifest Himself in something other than His complete, unfathomable glory. If He wished for us to have and exercise free will, His own influence would have to be somehow self-limited or we would simply be awed into obedience out of fear (but not willing submission out of love). For example, driving from the airport to the hotel while traveling on business, we might choose to visit a "gentleman's club" for a little diversion, or we might choose to hurry to the hotel to call our wife and report on our safe arrival. If an omnipotent God sat hovering over the entry to the club waiting to smite us with His holy wrath, it would require neither faith nor a relationship with God to choose the right option, nor would this excite any sort of love for God on our part. If God truly wished to honor our free will, He would have to tread lightly lest His unimaginable presence and power usurp any inclination we might have to exercise that will.

There is no easy answer to the problem of evil but being alive must entail at least as much good as evil, at least as much pleasure as suffering. In the final analysis, being "in the flesh" is good (else there would be more suicides), just as God concluded in summation of His creation of man. With N. T. Wright, it seems to me that "solving" the problem of evil would in some ways belittle the very real suffering that is present in the lives of so many. As many others have noted, if our Creator wished to create beings capable of love, it seems as though He would have had to give us a degree of free will. Love requires choice; we cannot compel others to love us; we must have the freedom to choose to love, or to reject love. This freedom makes it possible to insist on our will, our way, to the exclusion of the will of our maker. That is in fact one definition of "sin," and pain and suffering are the result of the fall—the result of sin. Lewis wrote, "There are only two kinds of people in the end: those who say to God, 'Thy will be done,' and those to whom God says, in the end, 'Thy will be done.' . . . Without that self-choice there could be no Hell."[71]

Additional Reading

For additional reading on how Christianity uniquely makes sense of our lived experience, consider the following books. *Is Atheism Dead?* by Eric Metaxas argues convincingly against the intellectual bankruptcy of the

---

71. Lewis, *Great Divorce*, 75.

"New Atheists."[72] *The Case for a Creator* by Lee Strobel provides insightful answers to some of the questions and challenges raised against the Judeo-Christian God.[73] In *The Weight of Glory* C. S. Lewis develops the concept of the argument from desire, and the universal longing for the divine.[74]

72. Metaxas, *Is Atheism Dead?*
73. Strobel, *Case for a Creator.*
74. Lewis, *Weight of Glory.*

5

The Bible Is Just a Book

Hammer away, ye unregenerate hands. Your
hammer breaks, God's anvil stands.

—INSCRIPTION ON A MONUMENT TO THE FRENCH
PROTESTANT GROUP THE HUGUENOTS[1]

IF YOU PRESS MANY Christians for what they believe and why, you often
don't get a very convincing or satisfactory answer, just vague references
to what "the Bible says." Many Christians simply cannot verbalize why
they believe the things that they claim to believe, and fewer still seem
to know what is in the book that they claim to be "the Word of God."
Of course, this is true of many adherents to other beliefs as well. There
are any number of people who, if pressed, could give only a very simple,
halting explanation for why they believe what they claim to believe. I
once heard a young woman describe why she was a Democrat rather than
a Republican by exclaiming, "I just hate the whole idea of the welfare
system!" Ignorance is not the singular domain of the religious.

Even if you press a devout Christian for what they believe and why,
you often get a pointed and assured reference to what the Bible says. You

---

1. Lutzer, *Seven Reasons*, 31. The French Protestant group called the "Huguenots,"
many of whom died as martyrs, faced religious persecution in the seventeenth and
eighteenth centuries.

may have noticed that your author has referenced the Bible numerous times already. Many Christians memorize passages in the Bible so that they have answers at hand for questions about faith, morality, and salvation. Some evangelicals speak of "the Roman Road," a series of three verses from the book of Romans (an epistle, or letter, written by the apostle Paul) that takes one through a sort of basic overview of the fundamentals of the Christian salvation story.[2] The Bible is the most complete source of information about the life of Jesus Christ. It is also the most detailed source of information about the early Christian church, as well as the earliest religious beliefs of the ancient Jewish people. The Jewish Bible (that is, the "Old Testament" in the Christian Bible) is the Bible that Jesus read, and from which He quoted extensively.[3]

So what? What exactly is this book that so many Christians claim to believe, yet remarkably few seem to know very well? Why would anyone not affiliated with Christianity want to read a book that many self-proclaimed Christians can barely seem to open?

What Is the Bible?

Many people who do not actively participate in any organized religion assume that the religious texts of all religions are comprised mainly of rules that must not be broken. "Thou shalt not" do this and "thou shalt not" do that. Everyone has heard of the Ten Commandments. Most have seen media coverage of some religious group or other trying to impose their rules and beliefs on someone else, whether it is Christian groups picketing porn shops or abortion clinics, or Muslim groups trying to impose Sharia law on entire populations. A cynic might conclude that all religions are simply groups of egomaniacs trying to impose their views on others. Many outspoken critics of religion have suggested this publicly.

Although the Bible is so much more than just a book of rules, the scriptures of every religion do indeed contain rules for right living. The Jewish scriptures are comprised of three main sections: the Law (the Torah—literally "teaching"), the Writings (Ketuvim), and the Prophets (Nevi'im). The Law, which includes the Ten Commandments, the basic Jewish kosher laws, laws concerning the Levitical priesthood and

---

2. Although the details from different sources vary, the most illustrative verses are Rom 3:23; 6:23; 10:13.

3. See for example Yancey, *Bible Jesus Read*.

acceptable sacrifices, instructions regarding the tabernacle that was in the midst of the Israelites in the wilderness, and details regarding prescribed religious ceremonies and holy days, is a set of five books called the "Torah." These five books—Genesis, Exodus, Leviticus, Numbers, and Deuteronomy (known in Christianity as the "Pentateuch")—are shared between Judaism and Christianity. The Book of Mormon also contains a great number of rules, providing structure and guidance for how a practicing Mormon ought to live, and what practices and activities are not allowed. In the Muslim tradition, a significant portion of the Koran is comprised of rules and laws for how to live and how to worship, as well as instructions concerning other practices (for example, the halal dietary laws, which are broadly similar to the Jewish kosher laws). Many Westerners, ignorant of the full tradition of the Eastern religions, assume them to be less prescriptive and doctrinaire; but the scriptures of these religions also contain a great deal of rules for right living. It has been pointed out that "much of Hindu worship is steeped in purification rites. That is why the entire corpus of popular Hinduism is filled with the forms of worship, fear of punishment [and] means of obtaining God's favor."[4] In this regard, the moral dictums of the major world religions are not very different from one another in their basic essentials. Books have been written highlighting the parallels and similarities between the Bible and, for example, the Buddhist religious writings. Recall that the moral law, an argument for the existence of God, is based upon the apparent existence of a universal set of principles for morality and right living.

The Bible does include rules and wisdom for living well, both in the Pentateuch (the law), and in the Writings (e.g., Proverbs), respectively. A legalistic (and, ironically, not very aligned with the teachings of Jesus) view of the Bible would focus only on orthopraxy (right practice) to the exclusion of what is actually the primary message of the Bible. This is a view that the Bible itself speaks against, in words attributed to Jesus as well as the apostle Paul and other biblical authors. Paul writes in the letter to the church at Ephesus, "For by grace you have been saved through faith; and this is not your own doing, it is the gift of God—*not because of works*, lest any man should boast."[5] The Old Testament prophet Amos, speaking for God, said of the Jewish people, who were going through the motions of following the Law but without any meaningful relationship

---

4. Zacharias, *Jesus among Other Gods*, 120.
5. Eph 2:8–9, emphasis added.

with God, "I hate, I despise your feasts, and I take no delight in your solemn assemblies. Even though you offer me your burnt offerings and cereal offerings, I will not accept them, and the peace offerings of your fatted beasts I will not look upon."[6] Jesus condemned the religious leaders of His time, who made a great show of obeying the letter of the Jewish Law but were found wanting in regards to compassion and the spirit of the law: "Woe to you, scribes and Pharisees, hypocrites! for you tithe mint and dill and cummin, and have neglected the weightier matters of the law, justice and mercy and faith; these you ought to have done, without neglecting the others."[7] Jesus saved His most scathing rebukes for the religious elites of His day, those who followed the letter rather than the spirit of the Law (though He never approved of ignoring the letter of the Law, saying, "Think not that I have come to abolish the law and the prophets; I have come not to abolish them but to fulfil them.")[8]

The Bible can be thought of in many ways. To be sure, it is a book of rules and guidelines for right living. Independent of its divine inspiration, there is value in reading such a book. It contains tried and true wisdom that, even though some think it wildly outdated, still has relevance for our time. In fact, many well-known truisms of our day (e.g., "do unto others as you would have done to you" and "pride goes before a fall," to name but two) derive from the Jewish and Christian scriptures. But the Bible is more than simply a list of rules. The Bible can also be read as a historical text, as literature, as prophecy, and as the story of God and His people. Above all, the Bible is a revelation of an otherwise unfathomable God. As a source of history, *Judaism Online*, notes, "An enormous amount of information in the Bible has been borne out by archeology."[9] As literature, the Bible is unparalleled. Not only has it had a profound influence on many of the greatest artistic and literary works throughout the history of Western civilization, but it is itself art and literature. Camille Paglia, no friend to evangelical Christianity, has said that the "Bible is a masterpiece . . . one of the greatest works produced in the world,"[10] that it is "the basis for so much great art," and that it "moves deeper than

---

6. Amos 5:21–22.

7. Matt 23:23.

8. Matt 5:17.

9. Spiro, "Bible as History."

10. Birnbaum, "Camille Paglia."

anything coming out of the culture today"[11] She has expressed dismay at "how distant young people have become from the Bible. The unintended consequence of this is that most liberal young people are losing the ability to understand Western art."[12] Rosario Champagne Butterfield notes that the Bible contains "an engaging literary display of every genre and trope and type."[13] The Bible also contains prophecy, some that has already been fulfilled, and some that speaks of the future of humanity. Finally, the Bible is a revelation—the story of God and His chosen people. It is how an unfathomable God has chosen to reveal something of Himself—His character and His plan—in the story of how He has related to a specific people (the Jews) and how they have related to Him.

The Bible as a Book of Laws

The Bible most definitely contains rules. Although it is among the first written codes of law in history, there is often nothing particularly unique in many of the rules and laws that it prescribes. While the rites and rituals of any religion differ in detail, essentially all religions include rules for right living as well as purification rites prior to coming before their deity. What Christians refer to as the "old covenant" is an agreement made by God with (or more accurately for) the Israelites, as described in the Old Testament. God says, in effect, if you pay attention to and follow these rules, you will be blessed, and it will go well with you. But if you break these commandments, it will go poorly.[14]

While it is easy to see that the Bible is a book of law, it is also easy to stop there and think that the Bible is *only* a rulebook, or to misapprehend the nature of Old Testament law. There were several purposes for the Old Testament laws. The first deals with right behavior or right practice (*orthopraxy*, as opposed to *orthodoxy*, or right belief) toward God. The second deals with right behavior toward our fellow man. In fact, when Jesus was asked by one of the scribes, "what is the greatest commandment?," He answered, "you shall love the Lord your God with all your heart, and with all your soul, and with all your mind, and with all your strength. The second is this; you shall love your neighbor as yourself. There is no

11. Paglia, in "For Camille Paglia, the Spiritual Quest Defines All Great Art."
12. Kelly, "Gospel According to Paglia."
13. Butterfield, *Openness Unhindered*, 15.
14. Deut 30:16–18.

other commandment greater than these."[15] The first of these is from what is called the "Shema," and it appears in the book of Deuteronomy.[16] The second appears in the book of Leviticus.[17] A third purpose for the Law is to show us our sinfulness, and our need for a Redeemer.[18]

It is important to note that the Jews believed that they were set apart by God as God's "chosen people," not because of their having obeyed the Old Testament laws—God chose them long before He gave them the Law—but because of the covenant that God made with Abraham (Abraham, the father of Judaism, is also acknowledged in the Koran and Arab tradition as the father of modern Arabs). It is also important to note that, as God's chosen people, the Jews were immune neither from obeying the Law nor from punishment when they broke those laws. The Israelites were told clearly, "Behold, I set before you this day a blessing and a curse: the blessing, if you obey the commandments of the LORD your God, which I command you this day, and the curse, if you do not obey the commandments of the LORD your God, but turn aside from the way which I command you this day."[19] The Jews were set aside for a purpose not because they were particularly powerful, or educated, or righteous; rather, they were blessed to be a blessing. God states clearly in His earliest promise to Abraham, ". . . I will make of you a great nation, and I will bless you, and make your name great, so that you will be a blessing."[20] Christians believe that this is an allusion to the fact that Jesus Christ, the Savior of all humanity, would come from the Jews, and all the world would be blessed by His coming. This is believed to be true both for those who accept Him as Lord and Savior, as well as for the entire world, which will benefit from Christian morality (e.g., other-regarding as opposed to self-regarding ethics) and from the charity and good deeds performed by God's people and in God's name (see chapter 8). Although the Jews do not consider their scriptures to be only a book of rules, it is clear that the laws detailed in the Pentateuch were adhered to (with varying degrees of sincerity and success) in ancient times, in Christ's time, and up through today.

15. Mark 12:30–31.

16. Deut 6:4–9.

17. Lev 19:18.

18. Gal 3:19, Rom 4:15.

19. Deut 11: 26–28.

20. Gen 12:2.

The view that "religion is just a bunch of laws," or that "the Bible is just a list of somebody else's rules" implies that laws and rules are a bad thing. In our age of extreme individualism, rules are immediately assumed to be bad. Anything that would limit our absolute freedom to do whatever we want to do is considered to be bad. This is an adolescent, knee-jerk response, endemic in advertising slogans and pop music. Though some may claim to be anarchists, no one would really welcome a society without laws. Think of the morning commute without the benefit of traffic laws, to say nothing of the grave moral crimes that could be committed and go unpunished. Your bank account, your home, your spouse, and your daughters—all fair game for whoever wished to prey on them, and you would have no recourse to any laws or courts. Laws bring order, and rules bring an understanding of expectations. Every religion has rules, every society has laws, and every culture has codes to which it expects people to adhere. Even professional societies have rules to which members must submit in order to remain members in good standing. Considering for even a moment what the world would be like without laws should quickly disabuse us of any notions that rules and laws are things to be scorned. You may disagree with a particular law, and you may even question my right to impose "my laws" on you, but dismissing a religion or a religious text as "just a bunch of laws" is not only specious; it also ignores the critical role that laws play in making life with other people livable.

The Bible as History

Although the Bible is not primarily a history book, it is also not separate from history. It is the revelation of the very real and present God in history. The Bible claims to report actual historical occurrences, and the Bible's historicity has consistently been verified. A number of academic pursuits, including history, archeology, linguistics, and comparative literature, rely on the Bible and compare it to other recorded accounts. It is used frequently to provide insight into ancient cultures, practices, and beliefs. Just as the historical content in the Bible is studied and verified (or debated), so too the history of the times in which a particular biblical book was written can be examined to try to understand the historical context of a particular biblical passage. In this way both the dating of particular books and the overall historicity of the Bible can be examined.

Although there has been much scholarly debate over the centuries as to whether and to what degree the Bible is historically accurate, the Bible has been used from time immemorial as a source against which other sources of history are compared. Not everyone accepts the Bible as the inerrant Word of God, but all scholars agree that the Bible is overwhelmingly and without doubt the most well-documented and carefully conserved ancient text.[21]

The Jews widely regard their scriptures as a source of the early history of their people. Although some more liberal historical scholars question the historicity of some sections (for example, many see the early portions of Genesis more as a creation "myth" than actual literal or historical fact), the fact remains that the Old Testament of the Bible contains a history of the Jewish people and of their religious system. In his book *Seven Reasons Why You Can Trust the Bible*,[22] Erwin Lutzer includes a chapter summarizing inquiry into the historical accuracy of the Bible. Engineer Dr. Henry Morris concluded that "there exists today not one unquestionable find of archeology that proves the Bible to be in error."[23] This is not to say that independent archeological evidence has been found to support every historical detail in the Bible. Rather, in every case where the archeological evidence is unequivocal, it supports the historicity and accuracy of the biblical accounts. An exhaustive analysis of the final chapters of the book of Acts[24] reveals eighty-four confirmed facts, including place names and geographical details.[25] New Testament scholar William Mitchell Ramsey began as a skeptic and set out to disprove the book of Acts. After visiting every site mentioned in Acts and studying the details, Ramsey concluded that Luke was possibly the greatest historian of all time, writing that "Further study . . . showed that the book could bear the most minute scrutiny as an authority for the facts of the Aegean world, and that it was written with such judgment, skill, art and perception of truth as to be a model of historical statement."[26]

21. Wallace, *Revisiting the Corruption of the New Testament*, 30.

22. Lutzer, *Seven Reasons*, 63–87.

23. Lutzer, *Seven Reasons*, 70.

24. Luke was an eyewitness of the events he reports in the final chapters of the biblical book known as the "Acts of the Apostles." Starting in chapter 16, verse 10, Luke begins to use "we" rather than "they" in describing the events upon which he is reporting.

25. Geisler and Turek, *Faith to Be an Atheist*, 256–58.

26. Ramsay, *Bearing of Recent Discovery*, 85.

In short, historians and archeologists have found significant evidence supporting the historical accuracy of much of the Bible.

The Bible as Literature

The Bible may also be thought of as great literature, containing literary devices such as allegory, aphorism, metaphor, simile, and foreshadowing. Throughout the Bible there is poetry as well as poetic and strikingly powerful prose. The Song of Solomon and the Psalms represent poetical writing and a collection of prayers, songs, and responsive readings. The Magnificat in the New Testament and the Song of Hannah in the Old Testament are two of the more striking poetic passages. That they happen to have been spoken by actual people as acts of worship and praise makes them no less beautiful, even if you do not happen to believe in the God that they believed in. For the literary value alone, the Bible is worth reading simply as the literature of a certain culture and a certain time. The literature in the Old Testament shows how the Israelites, through whom God chose to bless the world, worshiped, spoke to, and even complained to their God. There are poems and songs praising God's might and glory, some thanking Him for His providence, and even some questioning God's silence, His timing, and His justice. These were a people in passionate relationship with their divine creator God, and their literature shows it.

Songs in the Bible

The Psalms are a series of poems, hymns, prayers, and meditations that comprise a significant portion of the Old Testament. Some, such as Psalm 136, are meant to be read or sung responsively in congregational worship. Others, such as Psalms 133 and 134, are songs sung in worship. A contemporary version of Psalm 137 was recorded in the early 1970s by folk/rock musician Don McLean. Songs in the Bible are not limited to the Psalms—the first eighteen verses of the fifteenth chapter of the book of Exodus records a song of celebration and praise sung by the Israelites upon their deliverance from the armies of the Egyptian Pharaoh.

Poetry in the Bible

As Pastor Ray Ortlund has preached, "It takes a poet to describe what God has done, because there is nothing prosaic about it." The Bible contains poetry that speaks to readers even today. The Bible is uncompromising in its honesty in dealing with the full range of human emotion, showing peace, faith, joy, anger, despair, and longing. For example, Psalm 42 records King David's longing (Israel's king from ~1010 to 970 BC, and an ancestor of Jesus) to know God better, the longing to know and be known.

> As a hart longs for flowing streams, so longs my soul for thee,
> O God.
> My soul thirsts for God, for the living God.
> When shall I come and behold the face of God?
> My tears have been my food day and night,
> While men say to me continually, 'Where is your God?'
> Why are you cast down, O my soul, and why are you disquieted
> within me?
> Hope in God; for I shall again praise him, my help and my God.[27]

Poetry is not limited to the books called the "Writings" (Ketuvim). In the book of First Samuel in the Old Testament, the early chapters tell of a woman named Hannah. Hannah desperately wanted a child but was unable to conceive. When at last she does conceive and bears a son, she dedicates him to the Lord. That son, Samuel (which means "God has heard"), becomes the last of Israel's judges and a prophet. He goes on to anoint Saul and David, the first two kings of Israel. When Hannah dedicates Samuel to the service of God, she utters the words known as "Hannah's Song."[28]

Poetry is not only found in the Old Testament; in the Gospel of Luke, Mary (the mother of Jesus) is credited with an expression of praise, known as the "Magnificat," which she spoke upon meeting her kinswoman Elizabeth. Mary was pregnant with a child though she claimed not to have been with a man. Mary was promised (betrothed) to a man named Joseph. It was common practice in that time for betrothed people to be considered to be married in all ways, except they did not live together, nor did they have sex for a period (typically about one year), while the groom prepared a house or rooms in his father's house for them to live. Jewish law said that a woman could be stoned to death for the sin of adultery.

27. Ps 42: 1–3, 5.
28. 1 Sam 2:1–10.

Mary would have known this and been frightened and full of doubts. She claimed that an angel had appeared to her and foretold the event, and also told her that her kinswoman Elizabeth, who had been barren into her old age, would conceive and bear a son. When Mary, pregnant and frightened, went to see Elizabeth, Elizabeth exclaimed, "Blessed are you among women, and blessed is the fruit of your womb! And why is this granted me, that the mother of my Lord should come to me?"[29] Upon hearing this blessing, confirmation of what she had been told by the angel, Mary responded with her Magnificat, which begins, "My soul magnifies the Lord, and my spirit rejoices in God my Savior, For He has regarded the low estate of His handmaiden. For behold, henceforth all generations will call me blessed."[30]

Other Literature in the Bible

Other stories and passages from Scripture have found their way into contemporary idiom and literary traditions. For example, a passage from the Old Testament book of Ruth, "for where you go I will go, and where you lodge I will lodge; your people shall be my people, and your God my God,"[31] is commonly read in weddings. Although the words were actually spoken by a Moabite woman named Ruth to her Jewish mother-in-law, they are a fitting expression and tribute to the power of love. Similarly, a number of common phrases originate in the Bible. For example common homespun wisdom such as "take the plank out of your own eye before you try to remove the splinter from another's eye"[32] is from the Bible, as is the concept of a "scapegoat"[33] and the "good Samaritan."[34] Perhaps everyone is familiar with the biblical account of creation, the parting of the Red Sea during the Israelites' exodus from Egypt, and wise King Solomon directing that a baby be cut in half to determine which of the two women claiming the child was the mother. All of these and other passages, and in fact the entire Bible, has been studied in the field of comparative literature. Even critics of Christianity

29. Luke 1: 42–45.
30. Luke 1: 46–55.
31. Ruth 1:16.
32. Matt 7:3–6.
33. Lev 16: 20–22.
34. Luke 10: 25–37.

acknowledge this, stating that the Bible should be taught "because it underlies so much of our literature and our culture."[35]

The Bible as Prophecy

In the days and weeks after the terrorist attacks on the World Trade Center of September 11, 2001, it came to light that the sixteenth-century mystic Nostradamus had predicted the cataclysmic events. A hauntingly specific passage written in his characteristic quatrains predicted:

> In the year of the new century and nine months,
> From the sky will come a great King of Terror . . .
> The sky will burn at forty-five degrees.
> Fire approaches the great new city . . .
> In the city of York there will be a great collapse,
> Two twin brothers torn apart by chaos
> While the fortress falls the great leader will succumb
> Third big war will begin when the big city is burning.

This was of course an Internet hoax—no such lines appear in Nostradamus's writings. The farce was apparently based on his actual writings, including predictions of a future war in which he wrote, "At forty-five degrees the sky will burn, fire to approach the great new city: In an instant a great scattered flame will leap up, when one will want to demand proof of the Normans."[36] Although it is not the purpose of this book to refute predictions made by Nostradamus, suffice it to say that a great number of prophecies have been made by various mystics, soothsayers, and mediums over the centuries. The vast majority have not come true.

The Bible is most certainly a prophetic book. It is important to note that "prophecy" in the biblical sense does not always mean a shadowy prediction, often in riddle form, of some future cataclysm. Often "prophecy" refers simply to speaking the word of God into a situation. Although most people today focus on the often vague and confusing prophetic writings in the Revelation of John, the Bible includes prophecy throughout. Both the Old and the New Testaments speak generally of the ill effects of sin and a broken relationship with our creator God. Much of the prophecy in the Old Testament is simply a warning to a people or

---

35. Beckford, "Richard Dawkins."
36. Nostradamus, *Les Propheties*, quatrain 6–97.

nation to repent or face the wrath of God. Some prophecies (e.g., Jonah's prophecies to Nineveh) specifically did not come to pass, because those to whom the prophecy was directed heeded the prophetic warnings and repented of their wrongdoings. Still, there are numerous very specific prophesies in the Bible that have demonstrably come true. Among these are countless predictions regarding the Jewish Messiah, and it is upon these that I will give the most attention. Jesus uniquely fulfilled hundreds of predictions made of the Messiah in the Jewish scriptures.[37] Although all of the oldest manuscripts in existence today are not original documents, many are thousands of years old. Among the oldest existent copies of the Old Testament, the Dead Sea Scrolls were found near Qumran in caves about a mile inland from the northwest shore of the Dead Sea. They have been dated to about (or before) the time of Christ, with the dates ranging from the third century BC to ~70 AD.[38] These documents, which contain many of the most well-known messianic prophecies, demonstrate that these passages were already well known to the Jewish scholars at the time of Christ. Throughout their history Jewish religious leaders referred to the passages in their scriptures, including those that spoke of a Messiah—an "anointed one" who would free the Israelites. When the wise men came from the East (sometime after Christ's birth), the religious leaders referred to the books of the Old Testament that spoke of the Messiah. They interpreted them correctly to say that the Messiah would be born in the town of Bethlehem, referring to the passage in the book of Micah, "But you, O Bethlehem Eph'rathah, who are little to be among the clans of Judah, from you shall come forth for me one who is to be ruler in Israel, whose origin is from of old, from ancient days."[39] Unlike the fictional predictions of September 11 by Nostradamus, the predictions in the Bible contain genuine prophecies that predate the events that they predict. Although there is a great deal more in-depth analysis of this topic in other books,[40] a summary of some key messianic prophecies follows.

37. McDowell, *Evidence That Demands a Verdict*, 141–75.

38. Vermes, *Complete Dead Sea Scrolls*, 13.

39. Mic 5:2.

40. See for example Jeremiah, *Prophecy Answer Book*; Efird, *Daniel and Revelation*; and Walvoord, *Daniel*.

Foreshadowing in the Bible

Prophecies concerning the future, particularly concerning the Messiah, God's "anointed one" that will serve as Savior for His people, occur
throughout the Old Testament of the Bible. Many are mere foreshadowing, while others are quite pointed, but they span the entire Jewish
scriptures. Foreshadowing is a common literary technique. Even if you
do not believe that the Bible is the inspired Word of God, as a work of
literature alone the Bible is quite masterfully written. However, unlike a
novel written by a single author, the Bible is a collection of sixty-six books
written by about forty authors over hundreds of years. In spite of this,
there is remarkable consistency in the foreshadowing, almost as if it were
written by a single, particularly adept Author. Allusions to a Savior or
Messiah occur from the very beginning of the Bible up to and including
the last book of the Old Testament. For example, in the account of the fall
of man in the garden of Eden, God declares, "I will put enmity between
you [the serpent, who tempted Adam and Eve to sin] and the woman,
and between your seed and her seed; he shall bruise your head, and you
shall bruise his heel."[41] This is called the "protoevangelium," the first good
news. Many see this as foreshadowing the manner in which Christ would
achieve His ultimate victory over death and sin—specifically, that Satan
would wound the Messiah, but that in His victory over death on the cross
Christ would deal a mortal blow to evil and the evil one. In fact, even the
reference to Eve's seed in verse 15 may be an allusion to the virgin birth.
In ancient texts, including the Bible, the term "seed" is uniquely used
for the male gamete (sperm), never the female gamete (except in this
instance); and children are referred to as the seed of their father.

The story of Abraham's almost-sacrifice of his son Isaac is a
foreshadowing of the Messiah, the "Son of God," and the manner
in which He would die. In Genesis 22 the Bible tells of God testing
Abraham's faith by telling him to go to a certain place (called "Moriah" in
the Genesis account, which many believe to be the eventual site of King
Solomon's temple in Jerusalem) to sacrifice his only son—a son who was
born under miraculous circumstances. Although the thought of child
sacrifice seems barbaric to us today (thanks in large part to the influence
of Christianity on our culture), Abraham lived in a time when the gods
worshipped by other peoples, including those who were living in the land
that God had promised to Abraham and his offspring, practiced child

41. Gen 3:15.

sacrifice. Abraham dutifully took his son Isaac to the place to which he was directed. Just as Christ carried the wooden cross upon which He was crucified on his back for part of the way to the crucifixion site,[42] so Isaac carried the wood for his sacrifice on his back.[43] In the end God stayed Abraham's hand—God does not require the blood sacrifice of children, as the priests of many false gods do. Instead, God provided a sacrifice for Abraham,[44] and He has provided a sacrifice for all humanity in the form of Jesus. God did not withhold His own Son from being a willing sacrifice to redeem the fallen creation.

It may be that foreshadowing is dismissed as less than an actual specific prophecy. Foreshadowing in literature is simply a literary device an author uses. The author knows ahead of time what the end of the book will be, so it is no great accomplishment to hint at that ending earlier in the book. But remember that the Bible was written by multiple authors over hundreds of years. These earthly authors did not know the manner in which the Messiah would come, yet the foreshadowing that occurs throughout the Bible is remarkable in its frequency and uniformity. This is just one piece of evidence that the Bible is no mere human book.

Prophesies Concerning the Messiah

Although some allusions to the Messiah could be dismissed as lucky guesses and/or non-specific foreshadowing, there are also many very specific prophecies regarding the Messiah. These are not simply revisionist interpretations invented by Christians to provide the appearance of credibility to their stories of Jesus. Hebrew scholars of today, those of Christ's time, and scholars from both before and between these two eras broadly agree concerning the portions of the Old Testament that deal with the Messiah. As noted above, when King Herod (called "Herod the Great"), the ruler of the Jews at the time of Jesus' birth, asked the chief priests and scribes where the Christ was to be born, they told him, "In Bethlehem of Judea; for so it is written by the prophet: 'And you, O Bethlehem, in the land of Judah, are by no means least among the rulers of Judah; for from you shall come a ruler who will govern my people Israel.'"[45] The Jewish

42. John 19:17.
43. Gen 22:6.
44. Gen 22:13.
45. Matt 2:4–6.

religious leaders at the time of Christ's birth already acknowledged these passages in their scriptures, and they considered them to be prophetic concerning their long-awaited Messiah (see Text Box 9).

> **Text Box 9.** The name Bethlehem, the town in which the Jewish Messiah, according to the prophecies, was to have been born, is derived from the Jewish words *beit* ("house") and *lechem* ("bread"). The town is quite literally the "House of Bread." When Jesus referred to himself as the "bread of life,"[46] He may have been alluding to His birthplace and its significance in the Jewish scriptures. Significantly, the shepherds of Bethlehem, among the first witnesses to Jesus' birth,[47] were in charge of raising lambs for the temple sacrifices.[48] This would have included the *paschal lamb*, the spotless lamb sacrificed on Passover.[49] At the beginning of Jesus' ministry, John the Baptist proclaimed Him as "the Lamb of God, who takes away the sin of the world."[50] Jesus would eventually be crucified on Passover, the Jewish holiday that commemorates the Jews' liberation from slavery in Egypt. The parallels between the Jewish religious calendar, derived from events in the Old Testament (well before Jesus' birth), and events in the life of Christ are remarkable.[51]

Perhaps the most well-known verses that speak of the coming of the Messiah are found in the book of Isaiah, specifically the passages dealing with the "suffering servant," in the fifty-third chapter. Isaiah writes, "But he was wounded for our transgressions, he was bruised for our iniquities; upon him was the chastisement that made us whole, and with his stripes we are healed"; "He was oppressed, and he was afflicted, yet he opened not his mouth; like a lamb that is led to the slaughter, and like

---

46. John 6:35.

47. Luke 2:8–20.

48. Bailey, "Christmas Means More."

49. The paschal lamb is the lamb offered during the Jewish Passover meal (see Exod 12:21–27).

50. John 1:29.

51. See for example: https://jewsforjesus.org/jewish-resources/community/jewish-holidays/.

a sheep that before its shearers is dumb, so he opened not his mouth"; "They made his grave with the wicked and with a rich man in his death, although he had done no violence, and there was no deceit in his mouth"; and "by his knowledge shall the righteous one, my servant, make many to be accounted righteous; and he shall bear their iniquities."[52] In this passage we see a summation of the entire Christian theology of salvation through substitutionary atonement for our sin and our taking on the righteousness of Christ. We also see reference to key events regarding the manner in which Christ died. Specifically, Christ did not make any attempt to defend Himself, either to the Jewish chief priests or to the Roman political leaders (Pontius Pilate, the governor of Judea, and Herod Antipas, tetrarch of Galilee and son of Herod the Great);[53] instead He "opened not His mouth." And just as Christ would be killed along with insurrectionists and His body taken away and buried in the newly carved tomb of the wealthy Jewish leader Joseph of Arimathea,[54] so the passage in Isaiah predicts that He would make "His grave with the wicked and with a rich man." All this in spite of His innocence. Even Pontius Pilate found no crime in him.[55]

Upon His death on the cross, Jesus cried out, *"Eli, Eli, la'ma sabach-tha'ni?,"* which means, "My God, my God, why hast thou forsaken me?"[56] These words, among the last words Christ uttered before His death on the cross, are actually a quotation from the Twenty-Second Psalm, attributed to King David (the ancient Israeli king and ancestor of Christ, to whom God promised that his "line shall endure forever, his throne as long as the sun before Me"[57]). This psalm was written by David hundreds of years before crucifixion was invented, yet the verses after those quoted by Christ on the cross read, "a company of evildoers encircle me; they have pierced my hands and feet—I can count all my bones—they stare and gloat over me; they divide my garments among them, and for my raiment they cast lots."[58] What did David mean when he said "they have pierced my hands and feet"? There is no recorded history that David

---

52. Isa 53:5, 7, 9, 11.

53. See for example Matt 26:55–56 and 27:11–14; Mark 14:60–61 and 15:2–5; and Luke 23:2–9.

54. See for example Matt 27:39, 57; Mark 15:43–46; and Luke 23:32, 50.

55. Luke 23:4, 14–15.

56. Matt 27:46 and Mark 15:34.

57. Ps 89:36.

58. Ps 22:16–18.

himself ever had his own hands and feet pierced. Nor is there any reason to believe that David would have known of crucifixion, a method of torture and capital punishment that was not invented or used until shortly before the time of Christ. Furthermore, the staggering specificity of these verses, which predict that the Roman soldiers would divide some of His garments amongst themselves and cast lots for one item of His apparel, is astonishing. Note too that the psalmist writes, "I can count all my bones," and in Psalm 34 David writes, "He keeps all his bones; not one of them is broken,"[59] (in God's instructions concerning the paschal lamb He tells the Israelites, "You shall not break any of its bones."[60]). In many crucifixions, if the person being executed stayed alive too long, the Roman soldiers would break their legs to speed death. Hanging by nails through the wrist, the crucified person would have difficulty drawing breath. The individual would have to put weight on their legs (which would have hurt a great deal, due to the nails through their feet or ankles) to lift themselves up a bit and reduce the pressure on their lungs and allow them to inhale. By breaking the victim's legs, the Roman soldier would cause them to die by suffocation.[61] In fact the apostle John (a witness to the crucifixion) tells us, "The soldiers came and broke the legs of the first one, and the legs of the other who was crucified with him. But when they came to Jesus and saw that he was already dead, they did not break his legs."[62] As the psalmist wrote, Jesus could count all His bones; not one of them was broken.[63]

Were these (and numerous other) prophesies simply lucky guesses? By some reckonings there are hundreds of specific details about the Messiah in the Old Testament,[64] all of which came true in Jesus of Nazareth. Some of these—that the Messiah would be born of a woman,[65] and a virgin, and that they would call Him "Immanuel" (which means "God with us")[66]—demonstrate that He would be human, God in the flesh, something that was unheard of at the time. The various polytheistic religions in history had half-gods born of a tryst between a god and a

59. Ps 34:20.

60. Exod 12:46.

61. Edwards et al., "On the Physical Death of Jesus Christ," 1461.

62. John 19:32–33.

63. Ps 22:17.

64. McDowell, *Evidence That Demands a Verdict*, 141.

65. Gen 3:15.

66. Isa 7:14.

human, and incarnations, but no other religion believed that God-made-flesh would come as our Savior. Other prophecies tell of the lineage of this God-man, that He would descend from Abraham,[67] from the tribe of Judah,[68] and in the lineage of David.[69] These prophecies limit the number of humans that could make the claim of being the promised Messiah even before they were born. Still other prophecies tell of the particulars of His birth and His life, such as that He would be born in Bethlehem[70] and that He would be from Galilee[71] (note that the land of Galilee was far removed from Bethlehem, north of the land of the despised Samaritans and not even in the Jewish kingdom of Judea during Jesus' lifetime). Finally, there are passages, including those detailed in the paragraph above, that tell of the manner in which the Christ would be killed. Killed? The very thought that the promised divine Deliverer of a people who considered themselves chosen by God would be killed strained the imagination, so much so that many Jewish scholars believed that the "suffering servant" foretold in Isaiah 53 and the victorious Messiah predicted in other passages were two different individuals. But Christ fulfills all of these prophecies in one person. The Old Testament prophecies even foretold of Christ's being raised from the dead, and of His second coming in the distant future. It has been reckoned that the odds against even a subset of the more specific prophecies being fulfilled in a single man are well over a trillion to one,[72] more than the number of people who have ever lived on earth. Given that the prophecies of Christ's birth, life, death, and resurrection have all come to pass, one must give pause to easily dismissing the Bible and its many prophecies concerning His return.

Other Specific Prophecies

Finally, numerous other specific prophecies in the Bible have come to pass as prophesied. For example, the prophet Jeremiah, who wrote before and during the time of the fall of the southern kingdom of Judah (the northern kingdom of Israel fell to the Assyrians between 740 and 722

---

67. Gen 12:3 and 22:18.
68. Gen 49:10.
69. 2 Sam 7:12–13 and Isa 9:7.
70. Mic 5:2.
71. Isa 9:1–2.
72. Strobel, *Case for Christ*. 183.

BC), predicted that the kingdom of Judah (the land inhabited by the tribe of Judah, from which the Messiah would arise) would be subject to the Babylonians for seventy years.[73] The fall of Jerusalem occurred in 606 BC, with the elite being deported to Babylon the following year. The Babylonian Empire fell to the Persian Empire in 539 BC, and in 536 BC an edict from the Persian king Cyrus II allowed the Jews to return to their home.[74]

The prophet Daniel, who wrote during the Babylonian captivity, predicted that "seventy weeks of years" (490 years) were decreed before God would "put an end to sin, and . . . atone for iniquity."[75] Although a complete description of the fulfillment of this prophecy is beyond the scope of this book, the time between the decree to rebuild Jerusalem (issued in 457 BC[76]) and the crucifixion, resurrection, and ascension of Christ, who died in atonement for our sins and to free us from slavery to sin and death,[77] was in fulfillment of that prophecy. Daniel also foretold of a leader and his earthly kingdom that fits well with the life and reign of Alexander the Great from 356 to 323 BC.[78] In fact some have questioned the early dating of Daniel simply because the prophecy contained in the book is so very accurate. Since there is, in their view, no omnipotent God; prophecy so strikingly accurate cannot be for real, and must have been written after the facts that they claim to predict occurred. That is, their questioning of the early dating of the book is not based on any independent scholarship, but rather on their own incredulity that any prophetic book could be so accurate. There are many more specific prophecies in the Bible that have come to pass. For a more thorough account, please consider some of the texts referenced throughout and at the end of this chapter.

The Bible as a Story

The Bible is also a story of how God created the world, how it fell in rebellion, how He redeemed it through Christ, and how He is restoring it through the work of His Holy Spirit. In referring to the Bible as a story,

73. Jer 29:10.
74. Stökl and Waerzegger, *Exile and Return*, 7–11.
75. Dan 9:24.
76. Lanzer, "Did Ezra Come to Jerusalem?"
77. See for example Rom 6:20–23; 1 Cor 15:3; and 1 John 2:2.
78. "Alexander Reads about Himself."

I am emphatically not saying that the Bible is akin to a myth or fairy tale. Rather, it is a story that contains other stories because humans love and learn through stories. Especially in ancient times, when literacy in the general population was low, people learned through stories. Anyone with children knows that this is still true today; children love and remember stories. They want to hear the same stories again and again, until they remember them well enough that they can recite them as they page through their books long before they can read. Adults love stories too. Long before the development of the written word, cultures shared what was most important to them through stories. Culture, cultural identity, and shared morality are relayed through stories. We share stories when we fellowship with friends and family; we remember our past in stories that we tell and retell. This is part of the image of God in which we were created. Our Father God loves a good story too, and He invites us into His story. In fact, the four Gospels, the complementary stories in the New Testament of Christ's life and ministry, can be read as a story, without the interruptions of chapters and verses, in a series available from Crossway.[79]

> **Text Box** 10. The Bible as we have it today, split into chapters and verses, is a relatively recent format. Although the Scriptures were routinely divided into sections to facilitate liturgical reading on Sabbath days, the chapter divisions found in most contemporary Bibles were developed by Stephen Langton, Archbishop of Canterbury from 1207 to 1228.[80] The Bible was further divided into verses by Robert Estienne (among others) in 1551.[81] The Geneva Bible, published in 1560, was the first Bible to use the common contemporary chapter and verse divisions. Although ideal for referencing passages of the Bible, anyone who has read the Bible will have noticed how irrational some of the verse and chapter breaks seem. Some have argued that these artificial divisions make routine reading of the Bible more difficult. Glenn Pauuw writes, "We have tended to follow the modern estimation that only by dissection can a thing be known. What if, rather than always 'studying' the

---

79. https://www.crossway.org/bibles/esv-readers-gospels-cob/.
80. Paauw, *Saving the Bible from Ourselves*, 28.
81. Paauw, *Saving the Bible from Ourselves*, 30.

smaller pieces of the Bible . . . we were simply to spend more time reading or listening to the Bible at length?"[82]

The biblical story can be seen as a story in four parts: creation, fall, redemption, and restoration. God created the world (the physical universe) and "saw that it was good."[83] At some point, humanity fell from grace, and sin and death entered into creation.[84] Humanity, now separated from God, needed to be redeemed or bought back, and Jesus Christ, God incarnate, accomplished this by paying the price for our sins through His death on the cross.[85] Following His victory over death (His resurrection), He then called His church to join Him in restoring all things.[86] The concept of the Bible as story is captured well in *The Children's Storybook Bible* by Sally Lloyd-Jones. She writes that the Bible is "a love story about a brave Prince who leaves his palace, his throne—everything—to rescue the one he loves. It's like the most wonderful of fairy tales that has come true in real life! You see, the best thing about this Story is—it's true."[87]

The Bible as Revelation

Above all, the Bible is revelation. By "revelation" I am not referring specifically to the New Testament book that includes that word in its name. Rather, I am referring literally to the fact that God reveals Himself in this, His Word. As mentioned earlier, thinkers in several cultures developed some concept of a divine Creator. For many of the reasons discussed in the earlier chapters, belief in God is at least as rational as the idea of the eternality of the material universe, or that nothing could have blown up into everything. The apostle Paul wrote in his letter to the Roman churches, "Ever since the creation of the world his [God's] invisible nature, namely, his eternal power and deity, has been clearly perceived in the things that have been made."[88] But such knowledge

---

82. Paauw, *Saving the Bible from Ourselves*, 179–80.

83. Gen 1:1—2:25.

84. Gen 3:1–24.

85. See for example Rom 3:24; Eph 1:7; Col 1:14; and Heb 9:12.

86. See for example 1 Pet 5:10 and Rev 21:3–5.

87. Lloyd-Jones, *Jesus Storybook Bible*, 17.

88. Rom 1:20.

represents only knowledge *about*, not knowledge *of* the Creator. There is a profound difference in knowing about someone verses actually knowing them. When I was dating my wife, I knew something about her. But in order to really know her, I needed to form a relationship with her, and she needed to reveal something of herself to me. Some of the earliest ancient Greek thinkers had a concept of God (consider Anaximander's concept of *apeiron*, "that which is boundless or without limit"). But God did not reveal himself to them, and so they did not attribute personal attributes to their ideas concerning the uncaused cause.

Imagine that there is a God, a transcendent being who is spirit, and is immeasurably more intelligent and powerful than the creatures He created and with whom He wishes to communicate. We could come to know something about Him by studying His creation. But if He wanted us to know Him, He would need to reveal Himself to us. As noted in chapter 4, if you wished to communicate with ants, you might place barriers in front of them to steer them in the direction that you wished them to go. Such is the Law. But if you wished to have an actual relationship with these creatures, what would you do? In the example of communicating with the ants, you could synthesize a pheromone that the ants could sense and that would elicit a response ("Sehnsucht" is in some ways like a receptor that God designed into us, a receptor for which the cognate ligand is God's Holy Spirit). But in this scenario the ants would be simply responding to a chemical pheromone for which they have receptors. There would be little choice for the ant to sense and respond to such a chemical stimulus, and indeed ants have no real will of their own. In contrast, having been created in the image of God, human beings have the ability to understand and communicate, to love and feel, to obey and disobey.

If an immeasurably powerful God wished to communicate with His creation, with humans created in His image, He could act through personal revelation, as He did in the biblical accounts of Abraham, Moses, and others. But as we've seen, the Jewish people claimed that if they were to come into the presence of their God, or even hear His voice, they would die,[89] and Moses was told by God that he could not see God's face, "for man shall not see me and live."[90] Furthermore, for reasons of His own choosing, there have been periods when God has seemed silent. Another way to communicate, one that could potentially

89. Exod 20:18–19.
90. Exod 33:20.

last for a long time, provide a record of those communications, and be spared the vagaries of human memory, would be the use of the written word. Such an account would not only capture those times when God worked through personal revelation to one individual or a small group of individuals; it would also capture details about the circumstances under which that communication took place. In this way, individuals throughout time could learn about the nature and the character of God.

Furthermore, in His Word we can see how God has revealed Himself to the human race over time. Some have claimed that the God of the Old Testament does not seem to be the same as the God of the New Testament, that the "Jewish God" and the "Christian God" seem to be two different Gods. This is not true; everything that Christ teaches in the New Testament is prophesied and hinted at in the Old Testament. Furthermore, the Bible claims that God is unchanging, "the same yesterday and today and forever."[91] Yet much of the Old Testament seems to deal with law, and with God's justice and mercy, while Jesus emphasizes grace and God's love in the New Testament. Indeed, the word "grace" appears 118 times in the New Testament, but only six times in the Old, and in two of those places it is referring to a person, and not to God.

Assuming for a moment that the Bible is the true Word of God, and that God is unchanging, why the apparent difference in two Testaments? The answer seems to be that God has chosen to reveal Himself over time. Although God does not change, humans do. The primary message of Christ and the New Testament, hinted at in the Old, is one of grace and love. Mercy (not getting a punishment that we deserve) and grace (getting a reward that we have not deserved) are opposite sides of the same coin, and both bespeak God's love for us. But as Paul and others warn in the New Testament, God's grace cannot be taken for granted. It is free, but it is not cheap. Among the primary heresies of the early Christian church was a belief that since Christ paid the price for all of our sins, and those sins would not be counted against us, Christians were in effect free to sin all the more. The apostle Paul roundly criticizes this view in the book of Romans.[92] If the early church (and Christians today) struggle with "cheap grace," how much more would the Old Testament peoples have struggled. These primitive cultures were self-regarding, honor-based societies that could barely have recognized the concept of grace (many still do not).

91. Heb 13:8.

92. Rom 6:1–15.

As a parent, one does not treat very small children the same as teenagers, or teenaged children the same as adult children. Toddlers have a will, but they have little ability to reason, little experience with which to judge right from wrong, and little predisposition to question sources of authority. The rationale of "because I said so" works in most cases. Not so with teenagers. A teenage child seems entirely predisposed to question everything, including the source of authority. Simple rules are best when dealing with a small child. The child does not need to know that a flame is hot, they only need to know to "not touch." As the child grows the parent may still expect and insist upon obedience, but a good parent will begin to explain the rationale behind the rules, as much to educate the child as to justify the rules. I have a friend who tells his teenage son, "I have a reason for what I have told you to do. I'll tell you what those reasons are, but I expect your immediate obedience first, and I will explain myself afterwards." God's dealings with the humans He created can be seen broadly as dealing with children as they grow up. The Old Testament people did not question God's authority. They were often willful and disobedient, like a headstrong two-year-old, but they were less likely to ask of God, "Who are you to set these rules over me?" They acknowledged the authority of God's Law, even if they did not always follow it. Imagine telling your two-year-old child that if he put his fingers into a flame, you will take his punishment for him—would he ever learn not to touch a flame? Imagine if you never punished your child, no matter how bad or disobedient he was, and if you somehow suffered the consequences of all of his bad decisions. What would such a child grow up to be? The Jews in the Old Testament recognized God's authority (while not always obeying His commands) and were thankful for His mercy when they broke the Law but did not receive the full punishment that was promised.

As the human race "grew up," we got to a point where God saw that we were ready for a fuller version of truth. The Law was still very much in place, but God had always known that laws do not evoke the response of love and relationship that He has always desired. Teenagers the world over seem to share an astonishing sense of privilege—as if their parents owe them something, even though parents routinely give the teenaged child everything he has and ask for almost nothing in return. A parent could insist on a thoroughly authoritarian approach, and the teenager might continue to be obedient until the day he moves out, but his relationship with such a parent might well be strained for years to come, possibly for life. Instead, most parents try to reason with and teach their teenagers about the implications and repercussions of good and bad choices. In effect, parents are trying to prepare their children for increasing responsibility and independence. So too, the grace of the New Testament, if received by the spiritually immature, may be seen as license to do wrong in a consequence-free world. Without an understanding and appreciation of rules and their natural consequences, one cannot appreciate freedom from those consequences. Without understanding God's mercy (we do not always pay the full price for our bad deeds), it would be difficult to truly understand God's grace (we often do not deserve the good gifts that God gives us).

The focus in the Old Testament on God's mercy does not disappear in the New Testament. Just as Jesus said, "Think not that I have come to abolish the law and the prophets; I have come not to abolish them but to fulfill them,"[93] God's mercy is not replaced in the New Testament by grace. The New Testament mentions God's mercy sixty-one times (verses seventy-seven times in the much longer Old Testament). Just as a parent wishes to eventually produce a mature adult who contributes to society, so too God wishes for His people to grow into mature Christians who will be a blessing to those with whom they interact. Jesus did not die only so that you or I could be saved; He died so that you and I could be saved (blessed) *and* so that we would in turn be a blessing to those around us. God desires for us to be in fellowship with Him. He does not force us to love Him—love cannot be forced; it can only be freely offered. The law was a good start, and it prepared the way for the grace that Jesus proclaimed. Just as you can legislate obedience but not morality, so you can command respect but not love. If God's intention for us were to be obedient and respectful, the Law would suffice. But God's will is for us to be in loving relationship with Him, and for us to share that love by serving our fellow man. Such love can only be evoked in gratitude for what has been given; it is not legislated by divine fiat.

Can We Really Know What the Original Manuscripts Said?

We do not have the original manuscripts (called "autographs") of any book of the Bible. As Bart Ehrman, professor of New Testament studies at the University of North Carolina, is fond of pointing out at debates and public speaking events, we don't even have copies of the autographs,

---

93. Matt 5:17.

or even copies of the copies—we have copies of copies of copies.[94] A cursory look at the basic facts upon which everyone agrees may initially seem discouraging. Ehrman is correct that we do not have the original documents for any of the books of the New Testament, and we don't even have copies. It is also true that most of the copies we have are from a few hundred years (or longer) after the events, and the oldest universally accepted manuscript fragments we have are from the second century. There are ~5,600 ancient Greek New Testament manuscript fragments, and virtually no two are identical. There are more textual variations (~2.5 times more, that is, between 300,000 and 400,000) than there are words (~140,000) in the New Testament. In light of this evidence, with which even evangelical biblical scholars agree, it seems fair to ask, with Ehrman, "What does it mean to say that God inspired the words of the text if we don't have the words?" and "Why should one think that God performed the miracle of inspiring the words of the Bible if He didn't perform the miracle of preserving the words of the Bible?"[95]

While it is true that there are more textual variants than there are words in the New Testament, this is due to the enormous number of copies and fragments that we have of the New Testament. As Daniel B. Wallace, professor of New Testament Studies at Dallas Theological Seminary, notes, there are 2.6 million pages (from ~5,600 manuscripts and fragments) of the Greek New Testament.[96] Although the majority are from the second century or later, several fragments are earlier. Among these, P52 (which contains John 18:31–33 on front and John 18: 37–38 on back) has been dated to ~100–150 AD.[97] Fragment 7Q5 is possibly a portion of Mark from ~50 AD.[98] There are also more than 10,000 ancient manuscripts in Latin and about five thousand to ten thousand ancient manuscripts in other languages (e.g., Coptic, Syriac, Armenian, etc.). Finally, there are countless references to and quotations of passages from the New Testament from the church fathers. Just three of the early church fathers (Clement, Ignatius, and Polycarp, who were themselves disciples of the original Apostles and were active from ~95 to 110 AD) recorded

---

94. Ehrman, *Misquoting Jesus*, 10.
95. Wallace and Ehrman, "Can We Trust the Text?"
96. McDowell, *Evidence That Demands a Verdict*, 39.
97. Wallace, *Revisiting the Corruption of the New Testament*, 28.
98. Union of Catholic Christian Rationalists, "Early Date of Mark's Gospel."

citations of vast portions of the New Testament,[99] including portions of twenty-five of the twenty-seven books.[100] By comparison, there are only about eighty copies of Herodotus (from five hundred years after the originals), twenty-seven copies of Livy (from three hundred or more years later), and three copies of Tacitus (from eight hundred years later). Furthermore, as Wallace points out (and Ehrman agrees), of the ~400,000 variants, the vast majority are minor errors in grammar or spelling. Many of the variants cannot be translated from the Greek because they're differences in word order, while another large portion of the variants are related to vagaries of Greek grammar.[101] A few of the variants are bigger. For example, some of the earliest manuscripts do not contain Mark 16:9–20 and John 7:53—8:11, while the number of the beast in Revelation 13:18 is 616 rather than 666 in some early manuscripts. But Wallace and other New Testament scholars emphasize that no major theological concept is affected by textual variants.

The issue remains, though, that speaking of God's Word as "inerrant" may seem preposterous if we cannot get to those actual words. For this, it is illustrative to consider an example using DNA alignment technology. As discussed above in chapter 2, DNA, comprised of nucleotides containing one of four nucleic acids, encodes proteins, comprised of twenty amino acids. Three DNA nucleotides (called a "codon") encode a single amino acid. I spent time as a postdoctoral fellow doing DNA sequence alignments. In an "experiment" with friends and family, the letters of a short passage of Scripture were encoded into a hypothetical DNA sequence. Three copies of the encoded message were made, including several intentional errors. Four errors were introduced into copy 1, and three different errors each into copies 2 and 3 (Figure 7). Each of these three copies were given to three different friends or family members and they were asked to make hand-written copies of the copies, which they then passed to friends and family members to make further copies. In the end, there were seven copies and copies of copies from sequence 1 (the most error prone), and three copies each from sequences 2 and 3. Given

99. Geisler and Turek, *Faith to Be an Atheist*, 236.

100. The books for which early citations from the three church fathers mentioned exist are Matthew, Mark, Luke, John, Acts, Romans, 1 and 2 Corinthians, Galatians, Ephesians, Philippians, Colossians, 1 and 2 Thessalonians, 1 and 2 Timothy, Titus, Philemon, Hebrews, James, 1 and 2 Peter, 1 and 3 John, and the Revelation to John. Only 2 John and Jude are missing from the citations of these three church fathers.

101. Wallace, *Revisiting the Corruption of the New Testament*, 27–28.

that these were (at least to my "scribes") meaningless DNA sequences, the nature of some of the transcription errors are likely different than those made by actual New Testament scribes, but there is no reason to expect that untrained individuals copying unintelligible DNA sequences would make fewer errors than trained New Testament scribes, who saw their work as their Godly vocation. In the end, all of the sequences were aligned using the MAFFT DNA sequence alignment method.[102, 103] Since the errors in the original three sequences were different, most of the errors were corrected in the final alignment. Predictably, since there were more copies from the more error-prone sequence 1, by sheer dint of the number of sequences in the multiple alignment, the errors in sequence 1 "overruled" the correct code from sequences 2 and 3. Thus, although the final consensus sequence was close, it was not perfect. But if we wish to debate finer points of theology, "close" is not good enough.

However, that was not the end of the "experiment." Historically there have been four regions of the Roman Empire from which families of manuscripts were generated through the copying of New Testament manuscripts (though I used only three groups of sequences in my experiment). If a molecular biologist has multiple copies of a gene, and the majority are from one taxonomic order (for example, twelve sequences from primates and only three from rodents and two from carnivores), a simple multiple alignment will generate a consensus sequence that would favor variations unique to primates. To address this one could first align sequences from each order separately, to get an order-specific consensus sequence. The three consensus sequences could then be aligned to try to identify a progenitor sequence. A similar approach was taken with this "experiment," generating a consensus from each of the three main groups, then aligning the three consensus sequences. This resulted in the removal of the errors in group one that previously remained simply because there were more copies from that group of sequences. The alignment of the three consensus sequences and translation back into the twenty corresponding amino acids resulted in the complete and correct message with which I began

102. Katoh et al., "MAFFT."

103. The errors made in copying "meaningless" DNA sequences are likely to be different that those made by trained scribes copying (or translating) passages in languages known to them. I reasoned that the gaps introduced by manually copying short sequences would be shorter and more frequent than those introduced by sequencing errors or genetic variations, so I reduced the gap penalty to the smallest allowable value.

(Figure 7).[104] Similar approaches have been utilized to identify ancestral progenitor sequences of genes and viruses, including a recent analysis of SARS-CoV-2, the coronavirus that causes COVID-19.[105]

```
Cons1 ATG TAC GAG CAA GAT ATG TAT GGA GAC GAC TGG
Cons2 ATG TGC GGG CAA GAT ATG TAT GGA CAG GAC TGG
Cons3 ATG TAC GGG CAA GAT ATG TAT GGA CAG GAC TGG

Err        *   *                         * *

Final ATG TAC GGG CAA GAT ATG TAT GGA CAG GAC TGG

AA     M   Y   G   O   D   M   Y   G   O   D   W


Cons1 CAC TAT CAT GCC TCA ACG ACT CAC CAA GTT TTT
Cons2 CAC TAT CAT GCC TCA ACG ACT CAC CAA GTT TTT
Cons3 CAC TAT CAT GCC TAA ACG TAC CA- --A GTT TTT

Err                    *       *** * **

Final CAC TAT CAT GCC TCA ACG ACT CAC CAA GTT TTT

AA     H   Y   H   A   S   T   T   H   O   U   F


Cons1 CAG AGA GGC GCA AAA AAA -AT ATG GAA TAG   95
Cons2 CAA AGA AGC GCA AAA GAA AAT ATG GAG TGA   96
Cons3 CAG AGA AGC GCA AAA GAA AAT ATG GAG TAG   93

Err    *       *           *   *       *   **

Final CAT AGA AGC GCA AAA GAA AAT ATG GAG TGA   96

AA     O   R   S   A   K   E   N   M   E   stop
```

Figure 7. Alignment of Consensus Sequences and Translation. The three consensus sequences (representing related manuscripts from three "sites" or repositories) were realigned, and the final consensus sequence was translated into the correct amino acid sequence of the original code.

104. Note that the codons for the amino acid Glutamine (abbreviated Q) were used to encode an O, since there is no O in the protein alphabet (there are no DNA codons that encode the amino acid ornithine), and the Bible passage quoted did not need any Qs.

105. Kumar et al., "Evolutionary Portrait of the Progenitor SARS-CoV-2."

The biblical quotation used in this "experiment," "My God, my God, why have you forsaken me," appears in both Matthew[106] and Mark.[107] One of the errors that I introduced in sequence 3 was to change "thou" to "you." This sort of minor change a scribe might make in the original language would have no effect on the meaning of the passage. Along with minor changes in spelling and obvious slips of the pen, such are the vast majority of textual variants. Interestingly, in the original Greek, Matthew spells "God" as "*Eli*," the Hebrew spelling, while Mark uses the Aramaic spelling, "*Eloi*." This could give rise to multiple textual variants, as some well-meaning Jewish Christian scribes might "correct" one or both "*Eloi*" in Mark to "*Eli*," while a well-meaning scribe in Rome might switch the "*Eli*" in Matthew to "*Eloi*." Every manuscript or fragment with such a switch would be counted as a textual variant. Clearly the large number of textual variants in the New Testament is a direct result of the huge number of manuscripts. In the original multiple alignment of thirteen sequences in my own "experiment," there were fifty errors (textual variants) in a sequence of only ninety-six nucleotides. This high number of variants was due to the large number of copies, and it did not impede the ability to get to the original sequence.

> **Text Box 11.** The quote above from the Gospels of Matthew and Mark are among Jesus' final words from the cross, and are, as noted in the text, actually a quotation from the Twenty-Second Psalm. Another of the last utterances of Christ from the cross is a quotation from the Thirty-First Psalm.[108] The Gospel of Luke records Jesus' last words: "Then Jesus, calling out with a loud voice, said, 'Father, into your hands I commit my spirit!' And having said this he breathed his last."[109] According to writer Shawn Brix, in Jesus' day Jewish children across the Holy Land were taught to pray these words from Psalm 31:5 as a bedtime prayer.[110] Just as my brother and I said the prayers "Now I lay me down to sleep" and "Ich bin klein, mine herz ist rein," Jewish children spoke these words of comfort and trust

106. Matt 27:46.
107. Mark 15:34.
108. Ps 31:5.
109. Luke 23:46.
110. Brix, "Childhood Prayer."

in God from the Psalms, the hymn book of the Jewish people. As Brix notes, it is quite likely that Jesus was taught that prayer as a child, a prayer He returned to when He was forsaken by His heavenly Father to pay for our sins.

With more than twenty to twenty-five thousand ancient manuscripts and fragments of the New Testament in existence, to say nothing of very early extrabiblical documents that contain direct quotations of significant portions of the New Testament, Sir Frederick Kenyon was safe in pointing out that "no unbiased scholar would deny that the text that has come down to us is substantially sound."[111] As for the Old Testament, the Dead Sea Scrolls, discovered in caves near the Dead Sea, contain portions (and in some cases complete books) of every Old Testament book except Esther. When discovered, these scrolls, which date to around the time of Christ, were approximately eight hundred to one thousand years older than the oldest Old Testament manuscripts then in existence. Yet the text revealed in these scrolls had been remarkably well preserved when compared to those from 800 AD, and those available today. It has been estimated that the scrolls containing the book of Isaiah were "word for word identical in 95 percent of the text," with the variations consisting mostly of obvious slips of the pen and variations in spelling.[112] With respect to the fifty-third chapter of Isaiah, which contains the pointed prophecies of the crucifixion of Christ, of the 166 words of this chapter, there are only seventeen letters that are different between the Dead Sea Scrolls and the newer sources that have been held to be authoritative. Of these, ten are simply spelling differences, four were minor stylistic differences, three were the addition of the word "light" (added in verse 11), and none changed the meaning or interpretation of the passage.[113]

Is the Bible True?

Although I have written much on what the Bible is, I have not dealt with the truth of the Bible. All of the copies of the New and Old Testament

---

111. McDowell, *Evidence That Demands a Verdict*, 47.

112. Geisler and Nix, *General Introduction to the Bible*, 263.

113. Geisler and Nix, *General Introduction to the Bible*, 367.

documents, separated by hundreds and even thousands of years, tell us that the scribes who copied the texts down through the ages paid remarkable attention to their work. They would have—these were held to be the inspired Word of God. Even so, there are discrepancies in the various texts as noted in the previous section. Remarkably, these differences are not hidden in some great conspiracy to hide the truth. Rather, they are footnoted plainly in any good version of the Bible. Biblical scholars pour through these minor textual variants to get to the original text and meaning of the original inspired words. What other religion is so open with such information?

All of this demonstrates that we have something exceptionally close to the original words written by the biblical authors, but this still does not prove that the Bible is the inerrant and inspired Word of God, as evangelical Christians believe. What other evidence is there that the Bible is true? First, perhaps a restatement is in order for what is meant here by "true." Many Christians would agree that everything in the Bible is true, but that not everything that is true is in the Bible. That is, the statement 2 + 2 = 4 is true, though it is not spelled out in the Bible. Most Christians would agree that "all truth is God's truth"; that as the Creator of everything, God created mathematics, physics, chemistry, biology, etc., so we need not fear that there is some truth out there that God does not already know or that did not come from God. There is therefore no reason why a Christian should not read books other than the Bible and study subjects like science and mathematics. Richard Dawkins's statement that "religion . . . teaches us that it is a virtue to be satisfied with not understanding"[114] misrepresents Christian teaching. To be sure, there have been individual Christians who have chosen to put their heads in the sand and not learn, discuss, or deal with scientific pursuits, but this is not a teaching of the Bible. Christianity is and has always been a reasonable faith, not simple fideism.

Secondly, although perhaps opening the door to a potentially theologically questionable view of biblical inerrancy, there is also the matter of what types of truth the Bible contains. For example, to be sure the Bible contains a great deal of *factual truth*. Factual or empirical truth (such as 2 + 2 = 4) is relatively common. Factual truth can be found everywhere and is often easily proved empirically. The Bible may also be said to contain *moral truth*, that is, rules and guidelines for living

---

114. Dawkins, *God Delusion*, 152.

well. This type of truth (or wisdom for living well) is less common than factual truth, but again the Bible does not (nor does it claim to) hold the corner on the market of this sort of truth. All truth is God's truth, and so the Book of Mormon, the Vedic scriptures from Hinduism, and the writings of the Gautama Buddha may all contain moral truth, some of it overlapping with that found in the Bible. Although it is difficult to establish empirically if a particular bit of moral truth is indeed true, the overall fruits of those proclaiming and those practicing a given moral truth can provide insight into its value. Finally, the Bible contains what may be called "*salvation truth*," that is, guidelines for how to be saved. Christians believe that the Bible is *the* source of truth about the God who is there; His nature and what He expects of us. As such, the Bible is also a unique source of truth regarding the nature of creation—where we come from, how we got here, how we are to live and derive meaning, and where we are going. It is the transcendent God's revelation of Himself.

The overall message of the entire Bible, a message of God's love for fallen creation and His efforts to reconcile that creation to Himself, is conserved throughout book. The Bible is not an exhaustive source of all factual truth, nor was it intended to be. The Bible is also not (nor does it claim to be) an exhaustive source of all moral truth. It is an infallible source of such truth, truth that is timeless and just as applicable today as it was when it was written. But rather than being an exhaustive source of moral truth, it is instead the standard against which moral truth from other sources must be evaluated. However, the Bible is the sole inspired written source of what I have here called "salvation truth," and it is re-markably consistent in its dealing with salvation truth. As discussed in chapter 6, Christianity is unique in that it teaches salvation by faith (not works), and this truth is hinted at (though missed by many) in the Old Testament. In fact, the entire "new covenant" that God makes through Jesus Christ is hinted at throughout the Old Testament; evidence that this was God's plan all along.

Is the Bible true? Is it inerrant? The Judeo-Christian belief in a "personal-infinite God"[115] of love and relationship is unique. So too is the Judeo-Christian belief in man created in God's image; a personal-finite being capable of knowing (truly, though not completely) the personal-infinite Creator. As Francis Schaeffer has written, if the uncreated, personal-infinite God "really cared for the created personal [man], it

---

115. A term used by Schaeffer, *He Is There.*

would not be unthinkable for Him to speak things of a propositional nature to the created personal; otherwise, as a finite being, the created personal would have numerous things he could not know if he just began with himself as a limited, finite reference point."[116] Such is the case with humanism—beginning with finite man, there is no infinite reference point, and we are left with meaninglessness and no absolute truth. But as Schaeffer argues, "why would it be unthinkable that the non-created [*sic*] Personal should communicate with the created personal?" and "if the non-created Personal placed the communication . . . in a book of history, why would it then be unlikely that [He] would communicate truly concerning the space-time history in that book? How strange if the non-created Personal is not a liar or capricious, that He should give 'religious truth' in a book in which the whole structural framework . . . be false or confused."[117] In other words, a loving God would have wanted to provide the fundamentals of His truth to all of his followers. In the Holy Bible God has done just that. Although, as finite beings, we cannot know God fully, we can know Him (and His universal truth) truly.

Additional Reading

For additional reading regarding the truth, accuracy, and inerrancy of the Holy Bible, please see the following resources. *Seven Reasons You Can Trust the Bible* by Erwin Lutzer is a thorough defense of the Bible, demonstrating that the Bible is exactly what it says it is—the inerrant Word of God.[118] *The Bible Jesus Read* by Philip Yancey is an excellent book describing the Bible that Jesus and His disciples read, quoted, and relied upon—that is, the Old Testament.[119] An excellent reference describing archaeological evidence in support of the New Testament is *Archaeology and the New Testament* by John McRay.[120] *Saving the Bible from Ourselves* by Glenn Pauuw is an excellent book in which the author (a veteran of the Bible publishing industry) argues for more holistic reading and studying of the Bible.[121] Finally, *Revisiting the Corruption of the New Testament:*

---

116. Schaeffer, *He Is There*, 344.
117. Schaeffer, *He Is There*, 345.
118. Lutzer, *Seven Reasons*.
119. Yancey, *Bible Jesus Read*.
120. McRay, *Archaeology and the New Testament*.
121. Pauuw, *Saving the Bible from Ourselves*.

Manuscript, Patristic, and Apocryphal Evidence. Text and Canon of the New Testament, edited by Daniel B. Wallace, is a scholarly and thoroughly researched work addressing questions raised concerning our ability to know or derive the original text of the biblical autographs.[122]

---

122. Wallace, *Revisiting the Corruption of the New Testament*.

6

All Religions Are the Same

All religions are connected to the same Ultimate Reality
and lead people toward a common goal.

—ANDREW WILSON[1]

MANY PEOPLE EXPRESS DISTASTE and contempt for the hatred, fighting,
and wars that are spawned by differences in religious beliefs. Atheists,
agnostics, and nominal adherents to the world's major religions routinely
express the feeling that all major religions are basically the same. "What,"
they ask, "is all the fighting for?" Many religious scholars have said
essentially the same thing. Marcus Borg has noted that Buddha and
Jesus, though hailing from vastly different cultures, eras, experiences,
and socioeconomic backgrounds, preached a parallel morality—in some
places nearly identical. Borg cites this as the basis for his belief that "I do
not think that Christianity is the only adequate religion, even though it
is my 'home.'"[2] There is a great deal of moral truth shared between the
Christian and Buddhist religions (as well as with the Jewish, Mormon,
and Muslim religions). This fact lies behind the universal moral law as
an argument for the existence of God. However, there is a difference

1. Wilson, *World Scripture*, prologue.
2. Borg, *Jesus and Buddha*, 8.

between right living (orthopraxy) and right belief (orthodoxy), and all religions are not the same. There are particulars of each that make them unique, but do these make any fundamental difference? If all religions do not teach the same thing, is one of them unique in that it alone holds ultimate truth for salvation? Hinduism proclaims multiple pathways to God. But if an Eastern religion that allows for multiple paths to eternal life (or paradise, or oneness with the universe) is correct, then all of the major monotheistic religions that claim an exclusive path to paradise are wrong, because each claim to be the sole source of salvation truth, to the exclusion of all other religions. If the more "permissive" Eastern religions are wrong and there really is only one way to salvation, then at least two of the big three monotheistic religions must still be wrong; again, because each is unique and claims to exclusively hold the one true way. Perhaps you have therefore concluded, like so many seem to have done, that all religions are essentially wrong. Even if there is a God, there must be multiple ways to get to Him, and the exclusionary belief systems of the major world religions are simply a will to power.

If you accept that there is a God, that this God is alive and active in His creation, and that being in relationship with Him is a desirable thing, then how we come to that relationship matters. Furthermore, if you believe that humans somehow need to be in relationship with our Creator in order to have some sort of life after death, then it is imperative that you be right with God, whoever He is. On the assumption that you're open to the idea that being in right relationship with God matters, and that life after death in some sort of heaven or paradise is a possibility, then it would be well to consider the claims of each religion to see if one of them makes more sense than the others, to see if one of them is true.

What you believe matters, but religious belief is more than just intellectual assent. Imagine that a group of people on an island in the middle of a large far-northern lake is facing death from starvation and exposure, and you have been charged with the job of delivering food, fuel, shelter, and supplies to them. A person who lives near Madeline Island in Wisconsin will know that bodies of water can freeze over to the point where cars and trucks can drive over them safely (Madeline Island, on Lake Superior, is connected to Bayfield, Wisconsin, in the winter by an ice road). Armed with such knowledge, you may choose to drive out onto a frozen lake, believing that the ice will support your weight, and you will be able to drive to the island to rescue the people in need. But if it is too early or too late in the season, or if it simply hasn't been cold enough for the ice to be very thick, you may well break through the ice and drown. What you have faith in matters—if you have faith that the ice is thick enough, but it is not, your faith is misplaced. But suppose you are a cautious person by nature, and you believe that, although it is possible to cross over the ice, it is uncertain if the ice is thick enough and you are unwilling to risk it. Even in the dead of winter in Wisconsin, where the ice is thick enough, your lack of faith means that you are unwilling to risk going onto the ice, and the starving people on the island die. How strongly you believe what you believe also matters. In this case you had faith in the right thing (the thickness of ice in the Wisconsin winter), but you did not have a sufficient faith to act on what you claimed to believe. The key to being in right relationship with God is much the same; it matters both what you believe and whether or not you are willing to act on that belief. Knowing that it is possible to drive across a frozen lake is not the same as moving out onto the ice and seeing for yourself that you can do it. Conversely, taking a step of faith, if your faith is in the wrong thing, could have potentially disastrous results. The claim that what you believe doesn't matter and only leads to misunderstanding is only true if all beliefs are the same or if all truth is relative. Both of those two possibilities are demonstrably untrue.

All Religions Point to the Same God

There are many who proclaim that there is one God, and that there are multiple, equally legitimate paths to achieve oneness with Him. They claim that He has revealed Himself by different names to different cultures, creating different religious traditions. Such people, and the religious beliefs they proclaim, may be called "universalists." Many universalists would ask of a Christian (or a Jew, or a Muslim, or a Mormon), "Why would a loving God reveal Himself to just a select few?" But a different question could be asked of the universalist—"Why would an all-powerful creator God reveal Himself to different people and proclaim conflicting paths to reach him?" Even a cursory investigation shows that even the universalist Eastern religions have marked differences in their teachings not just of how to get to God, but of what that means as well. Did God Himself change His mind with each successive revelation to each new culture? It seems a bit absurd to believe that all paths lead to God when the definitions of God and of the afterlife are different between each religion. Any serious investigation into the different world religions will reveal both similarities as well as stark differences. The similarities tend to be in the moral truth, the rules and guidelines for living well. But when it comes to the nature of God, the nature of creation, and salvation truth, the differences are many, even among those universalist religions that claim that there are many ways to salvation. Although this is not meant to be a book on comparative world religions, a brief overview of some of the key points of the various major world religions is pertinent.

East vs. West

Although perhaps a gross oversimplification, it may be said that many of the Eastern religions, which are a mix of pantheism and polytheism, tend to be universalist, at least in theory. Hinduism, Buddhism, and Taoism generally understand their various deities to be expressions of a single absolute reality, and the various paths prescribed by each religion lead to one supreme goal, even if, as we'll see, that supreme goal is not universally agreed upon. The Buddha teaches. "But of whatsoever teachings you can assure yourself . . . of such teachings you may with certainty affirm, 'this is the Norm. This is the Discipline. This is the Master's Message.'"[3] Hinduism, in the Bhagavad Gita, teaches that "Whatever path men travel is my path: No matter where they walk it leads to me."[4] Taoism teaches, "Let some worship the Truthful One [a Taoist deity], and revere the Northern Constellation, while others bow before the Buddha and recite sutras."[5] Confucius claimed, "In the world there are many different roads but the destination is the same. There are a hundred deliberations but the result is one,"[6] while the Sikh religion proclaims, "The Hindus and the Muslims have but one and the same God."[7] The Baha'i religion teaches, "There can be no doubt that whatever the peoples of the world, of whatever race or religion, derive their inspiration from one heavenly Source, and are the subjects of one God. The difference between the ordinances under which they abide should be attributed to the varying requirements and exigencies of the age in which they were revealed. All of them, except for a few

---

3. Vinaya Pitaka ii.10. Referenced in Wilson, *World Scripture*, 38.

4. Bhagavad Gita 4.11, 51.

5. Tract of the Quiet Way. Referenced in Wilson, *World Scripture*, 38.

6. I Ching, Appended Remarks 2.5. Referenced in Wilson, *World Scripture*, 34.

7. Adi Granth, Bhairo, p. 1158. Referenced in Wilson, *World Scripture*, 35.

which are the outcome of human perversity, were ordained of God, and are a reflection of His Will and Purpose."[8]

All of these religions claim that there is one true and universal "godhead," and that there is more than one way to reach that truth. But this claim is suspect in light of the fact that they do not agree on the nature and attributes of that deity, nor on what happens after we die. If there is but one all-powerful creator God, but He had to reveal Himself to different cultures at different times and He apparently promised different rewards to those different people, can we really say that there is just one truth? For example, Buddhism's concept of heaven is Nirvana. Nirvana is not exactly a place; it is more of an awakening to truth, resulting in freedom from suffering and from worldly attachments and delusions. After death an individual is reborn in successive incarnations until he/she "awakens" (as the Buddha did) and becomes liberated from the cycle of life and death. Similarly, in Hinduism the ultimate goal is Moksha, self-realization and release from the cycle of death and rebirth. When Moksha is achieved, the soul becomes one with god, a sort of melting of one's identity into a universal (e.g. pantheistic) divinity. In Taoism, death (*shijie* or "release from the corpse") is followed by ascension to heaven, and it is said that the Yellow Emperor ascended directly to heaven in plain sight (suggesting that heaven is an actual place, not simply a state of mind or a melding with the universal godhead). In Baha'i, "heaven" represents the joy experienced by a soul that is spiritually close to god (while "hell" symbolizes the suffering a soul endures when it is far from its creator), suggesting that our soul retains some aspect of individuality. Can all roads lead to one true God if that God is different? Or perhaps God really is like a cosmic soda machine—all roads end in Him, or one version of Him, and when you get there, you can opt for regular or diet, eternal joy or dissolution into eternal peace.

The "Big Three" Monotheistic Religions Are All Exclusive

In contrast to the Eastern religions, which tend to be universalist in that everyone will eventually reach some final level of paradise or enlightenment, the major monotheistic religions of Western culture are not universalist. Although there are some who claim to be advocates of one of these traditions but try to wrench their beliefs into a universalist view,

8. Writings of Baha'u'llah, 111. Referenced in Wilson, *World Scripture*, 35.

such individuals must effectively gut the religion to which they claim to adhere in order to spin such a view. For example, it is noteworthy that many who try to claim that religions are the same seem to willfully leave out key differences between the religions. For example, Borg cites similarities between a passage of teaching from Buddhism and the sixteenth and seventeenth verse of the third chapter of the Gospel of John[9] ("For God so loved the world that he gave his only Son, that whoever believes in him should not perish but have eternal life. For God sent the Son into the world, not to condemn the world, but that the world might be saved through him"), while conveniently leaving out the eighteenth verse ("He who believes in him is not condemned; he who does not believe is condemned already, because he has not believed in the name of the only Son of God.").[10] Similarly, multiple passages are cited in which Jesus claims to speak on behalf of God (as though He were a prophet or teacher), but the passages in which He claims divinity for Himself are suspiciously absent from this "comparison." To the best of this author's knowledge, Buddha never claimed to be divine on this side of the grave—a grave that no one has ever claimed to be empty. You may choose to ignore or disbelieve one or all religions, but even the most cursory inspection will review that they are not identical.

Contrary to the claims of some critics of religion, believing that one religion is the only true or correct religion is no more closed-minded than believing that any one thing is truer or more correct than all others. Any statement of truth is in effect saying that something else is untrue. A statement of truth may make the one making the statement incorrect, but it says nothing of how open- or closed-minded they are.

Although Muslims accept that, like them, Jews and Christians are descended from Abraham, the differences between these three religions are significant. Some more moderate Muslims claim that Jews and Christians, as "people of the book," may be able to get into paradise when they die (albeit a lower plane, for paradise in Islam is believed to have seven levels); however in practice, and in the scriptures of Islam, Jews and Christians are at best second-class citizens, and at worst infidels. Islam teaches that the God of the Jews and Christians is the same God (Allah) that they worship, but that the scriptures of these religions have been compromised and polluted over time, and therefore these religions do

9. Borg, *Jesus and Buddha*, 85.

10. John 3:16–18.

not have the truth (it is not clear how Muslims deal with over two thousand years of textual fidelity of the Bible, as noted in chapter 5). To get to paradise, one must observe the Five Pillars of Islam: belief in only one God and His Messenger, Muhammad; a pilgrimage to Mecca (the Hajj); regular fasting; prayer (the Salat, consisting of five daily prayers); and prescribed acts of charity. Jesus is recognized as a prophet and (at least in theory) a great man, but Jesus is not considered in Islam to be God incarnate, and indeed is not even the greatest of God's prophets.[11]

The Jewish religion most certainly agrees with Islam that Jesus was not God, and in fact it is likely that most Jews, if they think of Jesus at all, would not even consider Him to be a prophet of God. Rather, Jesus is seen as a teacher (rabi) and even a would-be reformer, but is ultimately dismissed as a blasphemer.[12] The Jewish religion of the Old Testament included a complex system of Levitical laws and rituals for right worship and sacrificial offerings. Following destruction of Solomon's temple in Jerusalem and the Babylonian captivity, new Jewish traditions arose around the synagogue (house of worship) and the rabi (teacher or religious leader). The study and teaching of the Torah (the Jewish scriptures) became the focal point of worship in the synagogue. However, throughout the history of Judaism salvation has been based on righteousness, achieved by adherence to the Law and sacrifice. Although different traditions within the history of Judaism had different views of the afterlife (for example, in Jesus' day the Sadducees did not believe that there was any life after death, while the Pharisees did), in general for those within Judaism who believe in an afterlife, it is the righteous who goes there. Personal righteousness is ultimately related to the Mosaic laws, as well as the Talmud (the central text of Rabbinic Judaism), which arose around the time of the revolt against Roman rule and the destruction of Herod's temple in 70 AD.

One of the ways that Christianity is different from other religions is that Christians believe that God seeks to be in personal relationship with His people. No other religion has such an emphasis on this aspect of relationship. Many Christians would say that we were uniquely created to be in relationship, and so we long for relationship, both with our Creator and with each other. Perhaps the primary difference with all other

11. For a comparison between key aspects of Islam and Christianity, *No God but One* by the late Nabeel Qureshi (a former Muslim turned Christian) is an outstanding source.

12. Schäfer, *Jesus in the Talmud*, 106.

religions, conservative Christianity makes the claim that Jesus Christ was more than just a man, that He was in fact the incarnate Creator God of the universe. Among the names by which the Bible refers to Jesus, Immanuel, meaning "God with us," arises from the messianic prophecies in the Old Testament, in the seventh chapter of Isaiah. Jews today, and indeed the Jewish authorities of Jesus' time,[13] would say such a belief (that Jesus is God) is blasphemy. The Jews believe that Yahweh is one God. As has already been noted, their "greatest" commandment, called the Shema and found in the sixth chapter of Deuteronomy, begins, "Hear, O Israel: The LORD our God is one LORD . . ."[14] The Christian idea of the Trinity (the triune Godhead, comprised of God the Father, Jesus Christ the Son of God, and the Holy Spirit), and the idea that Jesus was God made flesh, are blasphemy to the Jew and Muslim alike. Yet Christianity claims that Jesus Christ is the only path to salvation.

Heaven and How to Get There

In spite of what many believe, the universalist Eastern religions do have concepts of sin and the need for purification and right action as a way to get to heaven (or paradise, or Nirvana, or ultimate enlightenment). In the Hindu religion there are four paths to *moksha* (freedom from the mortal world): the path of meditation, the path of knowledge, the path of devotion, and the path of good works. To all who achieve *moksha* there is release from this cycle of death and rebirth. As noted earlier, "much of Hindu worship is steeped in purification rites. That is why the entire corpus of popular Hinduism is filled with the forms of worship, fear of punishment, means of obtaining God's favor, etc."[15] The Hindu scriptures state:

> Accordingly, those who are of pleasant conduct here—the prospect is, indeed, that they will enter a pleasant womb, either the womb of a Brahman, or the womb of a Kshatriya, or the womb of a Vaisya. But those who are of stinking conduct here—the prospect is, indeed, that they will enter the stinking womb of a dog, or the womb of a swine, or the womb of an outcast.[16]

13. Matt 26:65; Mark 14:64; John 10:33, 36.

14. Deut 6:4–5.

15. Zacharias, *Jesus among Other Gods*, 120.

16. Brihadaranyaka IV:4:5–6, in Hume, *Thirteen Principal Upanishads*, 91. Note

In Buddhism, the emphasis for reaching enlightenment is on spiritual practice rather than adherence to a particular belief system or the development of a relationship with God. Individuals can improve their karma and advance toward enlightenment through moral conduct and other guidelines prescribed by the Buddha. The Buddha wrote, "I am the owner of my kamma, the heir of my kamma; I have kamma as my origin, kamma as my relative, kamma as my resort; I will be the heir of whatever kamma, good or bad, that I do."[17] Thus, one's actions determine the advancement (or regression) of one's soul toward or away from Nirvana.

The idea of morality as a means to achieving salvation is present in the monotheistic religions of Islam and Judaism, as well as the Jehovah's Witnesses and the Church of the Latter-Day Saints (Mormons). Essentially every religion that believes in a concept of a personal God, and many that believe in an impersonal pantheistic god-force believe that mere mortals are in some way unworthy to come before this god. Just as Esther, in the Old Testament book that bears her name, knew that coming before the Babylonian king unbidden could result in death,[18] religions throughout the history of the world have believed that coming before their deity is a serious matter, and not to be undertaken lightly. The major monotheistic religions of the West add the wrinkle that their way to God and to heaven is the *only* way. Islam teaches that good deeds (works) and morality are the key to pleasing Allah and earning one's way into paradise on death. But unlike the Hindu religion, Islam insists that this includes acknowledging that Allah is the one true God, along with adherence to the other Five Pillars of Islam. Judaism has laws and practices set by Yahweh that must be adhered to, and the Mormon religion also prescribes specific laws that must be obeyed to reach paradise.

As stated earlier, if the various universalist Eastern religions are right, then essentially all of the exclusionary monotheistic religions are wrong. According to the universalist view, adherents to Islam, Judaism, and Christianity (and the Mormon Church and the Jehovah's Witnesses) can all still achieve enlightenment (or get to Nirvana), but the religions

---

that Brahman is the priestly class, Kshatriya is the warrior or royal class, and Vaisya is the working or professional class. The "outcast" mentioned in this passage refers to the very lowest class, the so-called untouchables, to whom Mother Teresa ministered.

17. Bodhi, *Discourses of Buddha*, 686. Note that *kamma* here in the Pali language is the word *karma* in Sanskrit.

18. Esth 4:11.

themselves are wrong, and are presumed to include errors in both the moral truth and the salvation truth that they teach. Note that the Eastern religions, in claiming that right practice and right belief alone are sufficient to achieve enlightenment, really do not require much of a belief in any god at all. In such a mechanistic belief system, god is almost incidental. One could as easily believe that god is a faceless impersonal force, a mighty king with a long flowing white beard, a vengeful, wrathful supreme being, a wise and kindly old grandfather, or a cosmic soda machine—so long as you put in the requisite number of good deeds, right thoughts, or spiritual awakenings, eternity comes out. Furthermore, if any god (or no god at all) will do, then the three main monotheistic world religions (along with any others) that insist on a specific named god are at best misguided, insisting on belief in a god when simple morality and enlightened thinking is all that is needed.

While it certainly seems that these "open-minded" religions are more lenient, that they make it easier to satisfy the moral strictures required to achieve the reward at the end of life, what is that reward? Mostly the Eastern religions teach in essence that paradise is realized by the loss of self in some higher universal consciousness. Individual cares and worries are gone, but so too are individual will, consciousness, and selfhood annihilated as the person's spirit falls back into the universal (un) consciousness. That is, you cease being you. In what way is this paradise or eternity? This is starkly different from the monotheistic religions, in which you retain some portion of your individuality and are actually able to enjoy eternity as you. The vast differences in the concept of heaven, paradise, Nirvana, Sheol, and eternity among the major world religions points out more than anything the vast differences of these belief systems. So, if we can state definitively that the world religions are indeed different, can we say that one is better?

Faith vs. Works

As we have seen, all world religions do preach a need to overcome sin and/or human failing and frailty in order to achieve a good outcome after death. All of this may seem to point to the superiority of the more "open-minded" religions—those that do not insist on belief in and worship of a specific, individual God. But is ease really a criterion that ought to be included in one's decisions about religion? What if one of the harder

monotheistic religions is really true? What if we simply are not—or cannot be—good enough to meet whatever eternal measuring stick is used
to determine if one earns his or her salvation? What is good enough,
and where does one find out what good enough is? How can you have
any peace—on this side of the grave anyway—that you have achieved a
sufficient level of morality to be confident of the disposition of your soul
after death? To this question Christianity has a unique concept worth
consideration.

It is often pointed out by Christians that all of the other world religions are "works-based," while Christianity is "faith-based." Please do not
misunderstand; by saying "faith-based," this is not saying that the truth
of Christianity must be accepted by faith in the absence of reason. As we
have seen, any religious belief (including atheism) requires both faith and
reason to believe some of the claims for which empirical evidence is not
available. The Christian concept of faith is not faith *that*, but faith *in*. That
is, in every other religion salvation must be earned by good deeds and
personal morality in this life; whereas with Christianity, salvation from
sin and eternal life are not earned, but are based on faith alone—faith in
the person of Jesus Christ. Christianity is unique in this regard. Indeed,
this is a founding belief of the Reformation, to which Western civilization owes so much. So what? Faith vs. works—these Christians still insist
on adherence to a set of beliefs that includes belief that God became a
man named Jesus who lived about two thousand years ago, performed
miracles, died on a cross, then rose from the dead. Even provided that all
of this is true, is anything so remarkable about salvation by faith instead
of morality? That is, does salvation by faith make any more sense than
salvation by works?

In fact, salvation by faith has been a stumbling block within and
outside of Christianity since the time of Christ. It seems foolish to say that
salvation can be independent of how good you are. Someone can be truly
wicked for their entire life, the argument goes, then on their death bed
they say a little prayer of faith, and all is forgiven—they go to heaven. This
sounds not just foolish; it sounds downright unjust. Good people who
have lived good, moral lives but deny or renounce Christ go to hell, while
the most despicable person in the world who happens to feel remorse
on his death bed gets into heaven after a simple expression of faith.[19] It

19. If this seems unfair, as has often be charged, consider the contrary (often
unspoken) belief that many seem to hold, that God will honor our intentions. If we
simply try to be good, to be true to ourselves, God will understand. This puts the

is not quite so simple of course—the prayer of faith mentioned above must include genuine repentance—but Jesus essentially offered this sort of "no-strings-attached" salvation to one of the two insurrectionists that was crucified at His side.[20] One of the two confessed that Jesus was indeed the Christ, saying, "Jesus, remember me when you come into your kingdom," and Jesus promised him, "Truly, I say to you, today you will be with me in Paradise." This man would have had no opportunity to change his life or to do enough additional good deeds to somehow make up for all of the bad things he had done, yet Jesus assured him that he would be in heaven simply because he professed faith in Jesus as Savior. Such a system of salvation based on faith may seem foolish or unfair, but this is because we like to believe that we earn our place in heaven with our good works. To the contrary, Christianity teaches that salvation is a gift, earned by Christ and given freely to those who accept it in faith. During His ministry Jesus told a parable about a householder who went out in the morning to hire laborers to work in his vineyard. Every few hours throughout the day until the eleventh hour, the householder hired additional laborers. At the end of the day, the householder paid all of the laborers the same wage, whether they had worked all day or only for the last hour of the day. The householder's response, when challenged by those who had worked all day, was, "Friend, I am doing you no wrong; did you not agree with me for a day's wage? Take what belongs to you and go; I choose to give to this last as I give to you. Am I not allowed to do what I choose with what belongs to me? Or do you begrudge my generosity?"[21]

If this salvation by faith to any who accept it seems unfair, consider the full implications of the alternative: salvation based on works. Consider for a moment the nature of the people who get into heaven, and the nature of the God who judges those who do or do not get in. If one earns their way to heaven by being good, who does not get to heaven? Presumably, there is some sort of metric. That is, one must be, on the whole, more good than bad; otherwise the most despicable person to ever live could just do as many good deeds as bad and get into heaven. In

---

means above the ends. In this view, even if the outcome of much of what we have done is truly despicable, if we were simply trying to be good, we're home free. By this logic, even though communism has been the cause of much evil in the world, Karl Marx, who was simply trying to make a better world and replace the false doctrines of the Judeo-Christian religious tradition, is not ultimately culpable.

20. Luke 23:39–43.
21. Matt 20:1–16.

such a works-based system there must be a sort of goodness ratio of good deeds verses bad deeds that is the primary article of evidence presented to the divine court at judgment. For the most part, we can suppose that most people are pretty average, neither great saints nor great sinners. If the goodness ratio for all of humanity could be expressed on a single graph, it seems likely that there would be what is called a "normal distribution," similar to that seen with any continuous measurable phenomenon for a very large population. For example, one could graph the percentage of correct answers for every student that took a particular standardized test in a given year, and there would be a normal distribution. For any measurement within a large population, most individuals fall within one or two standard deviations from the mean. In such a graph, the possible test scores are along the (horizontal) x-axis. On the (vertical) y-axis would be the number of people who got any particular score. Connecting all of the dots for the number of people who got any particular score would reveal a curve reminiscent of a steep-sided hill, symmetrical on both sides. This is a normal distribution, and it suggests that the majority of the people fall within a range of scores near the middle. A small portion of the population who did very well will be on the right side of the graph, while a small portion of the population who did particularly poorly will be on the left. The vast majority of the people taking the test got something very near to the average score, right in the middle of the graph. A well-designed test will aim to have a normal distribution of scores. The test can distinguish the average from the very good, and from the very bad as well. But within the middle part of the curve, it may be difficult to differentiate one test taker from the next.

Imagine a similar graph for the "goodness ratio" of everyone who ever lived. This goodness ratio would be calculated based upon every good deed relative to every bad deed over the course of each person's life (Fig. 8). If you did ten thousand good deeds and only two thousand bad deeds, your goodness ratio would be five (10,000 ÷ 2,000 = 5). If you are like most people, not a bad person but also not particularly saintly either, you would fall near the average, say 6,100 good deeds and 5,900 bad deeds, giving you a ratio of 1.03 (6,100 ÷ 5,900 = 1.03). A particularly evil individual might have done ten thousand bad deeds and only a few hundred good ones and would get a goodness ratio significantly less than one (300 ÷ 10,000 = 0.03). If reaching heaven is based on works, where does God draw the line? Perhaps you see God as being a "fair" or "just," and so the line is drawn right at the absolute average (Fig. 9). In this case, a person who did 5,001 good works and only 5,000 bad deeds would have a goodness ratio only fractionally greater than one (1.0002) and would be admitted to heaven. But a person who did 5,001 bad deeds but only 5,000 good ones (with a ratio of 0.9998) would be lost, despite their ratio being only fractionally less than one, and not significantly different than the first person. That person might exclaim, "Oh nuts—if only I had helped two more little old ladies across the street," but too late—judgment has been rendered. How arbitrary would such a God be? Can such a God be said to be either loving or just? A significant portion of the human race would not get to heaven, and most of them would not be markedly worse than the majority of those who did get in. If God makes an exception for one such person, must He not also make the exception for the millions of others with the same ratio? If He then moves the line just a bit, what about the fellow who did 5,000 good deeds and 5,002 bad deeds (and the millions like him)? Is this person really significantly worse than the one who did 5,001 good deeds and 5,000 bad deeds?

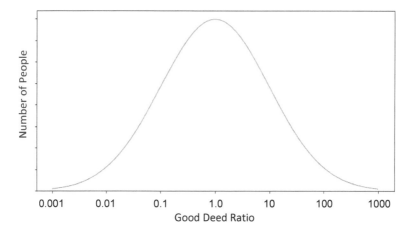

Figure 8. The Goodness Ratio. A hypothetical goodness ratio could be calculated based upon every good deed relative to every bad deed done over the course of each person's life. Such a ratio might be the primary article of evidence presented to the divine court at judgment.

While such data can distinguish an average person from a particularly good or bad one, it cannot distinguish two relatively average people from one-another.

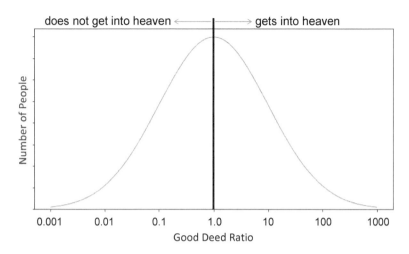

Figure 9. A "Just" God. As with any normal distribution, outstanding individuals (either very good or very bad) can be distinguished, but most people fall within the middle, and are not statistically significantly different from someone with a slightly better or worse ratio. Salvation based on works, shown here by the hypothetical goodness ratio, reveals the arbitrary nature of such a God.

Perhaps you think God is actually very kind and loving. He wants a lot of people to get to heaven, so He draws the line at a ratio of 0.2 instead of 1.0 (Fig. 10). In this case, a person who did only two thousand good deeds but ten thousand bad deeds (with a goodness ratio of 0.2) gets in. Now there is another problem—some not very good people are getting into heaven. I could have beaten my spouse, cheated on her a dozen times, and embezzled money from the charity that I ran, but so long as I helped enough people to get that ratio over 0.2, I'm in. And there is still the problem that a person with 2,000 good deeds but 10,001 bad deeds does not get in, even though they are really not significantly more evil than I was. God still seems arbitrary, and now He is also quite unjust—letting some pretty bad people into heaven.

Perhaps you see God as being very harsh and demanding, requiring a goodness ratio of five (for example, ten thousand good deeds and only two thousand bad deeds) for admittance to heaven (Fig. 11). In this case Mother Teresa and Gandhi may get in, but do you seriously believe that you are of their caliber? And even if you are, the vast majority of the human race is not, so the vast majority will be denied admittance into heaven. Furthermore, God is still arbitrary, since someone with only

9,999 good deeds but 2,000 bad ones, while clearly a good person, misses the mark.

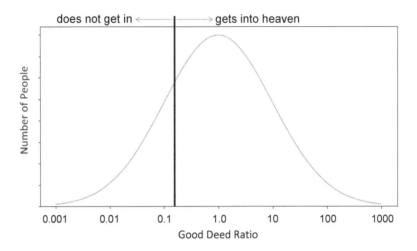

Figure 10. A "Kind" God. An allegedly kind and loving God, one who wants a lot of people to get into heaven, might draw the cutoff at a generous good deed ratio of 0.2 instead of 1.0, essentially grading on a curve so that more people will make it into heaven. Such a God is still arbitrary and also somewhat unjust—letting some pretty bad people into heaven.

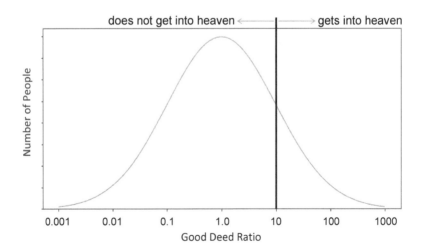

Figure 11. A "Harsh" God. A particularly harsh and demanding God might require a large goodness ratio for admittance to heaven. In this case Mother Teresa and Gandhi get in, but most of the rest of us would likely fall short.

What if God is so good, so holy, and so righteous that He simply cannot abide any sin at all (Fig. 12)? This is the kind of God that the Old Testament Jews and the New Testament church believed in, as evidenced by numerous passages in the Bible.

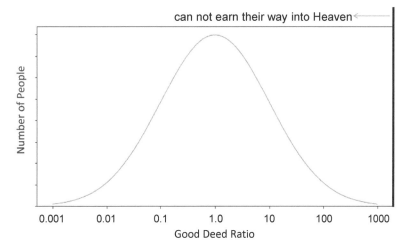

Figure 12. A Holy God. Only a God who is perfectly holy, just, and pure is truly loving and fair. Since none of us are holy or sinless, none of us can earn our way into the presence of such a God. But God is a God of mercy, grace, and love as well as a God of holiness and justice. He has provided the Way for us to get to heaven, which does not depend on our works or merits.

When they said that even if they were to hear His voice they would die,[22] the Jews did not mean that God would strike them with lightning simply because He was hateful and mean. What they meant was that He is so holy and pure that sin simply cannot exist in His presence. Imagine that you're at a party and there is a very large bowl filled with punch. As you go to ladle yourself a glass of punch from the bowl, the host asks you, "How much raw human sewage would be acceptable for me to have placed into this punch? If I placed one gallon of raw sewage into one hundred gallons of punch, would that be pure enough for you to drink?" Can we agree that the answer would be an emphatic "No!"? What if there were only one pint of sewage? Or one milliliter? What about even just a single ten-microliter drop (which would equate to only about 0.000025 percent)? Aside from the "ick" factor, keep in mind that a ten-microliter drop could still contain millions of live bacteria or virus particles, and it

22. Exod 20:18–19; Deut 5:24–25.

really only takes one for you to become infected with something pretty terrible. Obviously, the right answer is "None." You would hope that your host had placed no raw human sewage in the punch. How much purer is a holy God? To God, who is holy beyond our experience or our imagining, even what we call "righteousness" is like "filthy rags."[23] They are in effect raw human sewage. God simply cannot abide sin. To allow sin would be to become less than He is—less than God. Sin is rebellion against God. Just as the prince in fairy tales must abdicate his throne in order to marry a commoner, a perfect, just, and holy God would have to cease being God to be in communion with one who has sin, injustice, and impurity in their life. The king cannot be married to someone who rebels against the kingdom and denies that he is the king. This is not a case of God being intolerant or cruel; it is simply a fact of His being—an immutable law of His holiness that He cannot be who He is if He allows sin and rebellion. God is not just a God of love; He is also a God of justice and holiness.

Fortunately, God *IS* a God of love, and He found a way to satisfy His justice and holiness while also achieving His desire to be in loving relationship with His fallen and sinful children. That way—*THE* Way— is that God became flesh and paid the price for our sins. He clears our guilt. Just as our universe is fallen and imperfect, with the second law of thermodynamics predicting that chaos and disorder (entropy) will always increase until the universe winds down, so is man fallen and imperfect, slouching ever toward sin and death. N. T. Wright has written that "Death is not an arbitrary punishment for sin; it is its necessary consequence, since the turning away from the living God which constitutes idolatry is the spiritual equivalent of a diver cutting off his own breathing tube."[24] We are bound by time, so once we have sinned—once we have rebelled against and rejected the God of love, light, and life—we cannot undue it. It is as though we have fallen into debt, and we must go into debtors' prison until we can pay back the debt. We might try to do all manner of good deeds to overcome the debt, but we cannot undo it. Neither will good intentions repay the debt. But whereas you might conceivably be able to somehow come up with even an unimaginably large sum of money with which to pay a very large financial debt in this analogy, you simply don't have any of what it takes to pay for your sins. You do not have purity; you do not have sinlessness. You cannot go back in time to undo a sin, and you

23. Isa 64:6.

24. Wright, *Evil and the Justice of God*, 109.

lack God's holiness with which to make a suitable sacrifice. Something is either pure or it is not. If you are not pure and holy, you cannot scrape together some purity to try to become pure. You essentially have zero in your bank account, and no ability to get above zero. Fortunately, Jesus Christ, the second person of the Godhead, emptied Himself into human form and lived a perfect life, so that He could offer Himself up in payment of this cosmic debt. Only Christ, who was without sin, can pay that price of purity and holiness. And all you need to do to receive this gift is to accept it and to live in it. The debt has already been paid in full. Nothing you could have done yourself could have paid the price, but it is available to you for free. Since there is no quota, no goodness ratio, God does not need to resort to arbitrary decisions based on some formula. Since sins are thus paid for, your debt is paid; God does not need to compromise His holiness or His justice. And all it takes from you is stepping out in faith, and you will be justified in Christ.[25] Another way to think about it is this: If you go before a judge and are guilty of a crime, he must by law sentence you to whatever punishment the law dictates. But if you are an ambassador of a foreign country, you may well have diplomatic immunity. By your faith in Christ, you have in effect become a member of a foreign country—a kingdom "not of this world."[26] As a citizen of His heavenly kingdom, your new job is to serve as an ambassador for Christ, and for that you are exempt from the punishment for breaking the laws of this world. This does not mean we can live however we want; Jesus said that He came not to overturn the Law, but to fulfill it.[27]

Forgiveness

There is another way in which Christianity is unique among all of the other religions of the world, and this is seen in its emphasis on forgiveness. Every religion includes rites and rituals in order to seek purification from sins, a way to make the penitent believer right with the deity. This is just as true of the inclusive Eastern religions as of the Western monotheistic religions. But Christianity is unique in its emphasis on forgiveness of one another. This is another example of the common grace that has accrued to the world because of Christ's life and words. One example of

25. Rom 3:28.

26. In John 18:36 Jesus says, "My kingdom is not of this world" (NIV).

27. Matt 5:17.

this can be found in the Marshall Plan and the Government and Relief in Occupied Areas (GARIOA) program that came before it.[28] Although there was certainly a degree of self-interest in such programs, seeking to avoid chaos and anarchy in the recently vanquished foes at the end of World War II, these programs were unprecedented. Never before had a victorious nation rushed in so quickly to provide humanitarian aid to recently defeated enemies (enemies that had committed grave human rights abuses). Although the Marshall Plan was largely the creation of the Truman State Department and the Brookings Institute, the role of George C. Marshall, who advocated for the plan, served as Secretary of State during its implementation, and received the Nobel Peace Prize in 1953 for the plan, should not be dismissed. Marshall was baptized and confirmed in the Episcopalian Church, and though intensely private, at several times in his career he expressed his own faith as well as a concern for the religious welfare of those in the services. Of Marshall's religious beliefs David Hein has written, "We live in an era in which American young people . . . see religious belief expressed in public action as a baleful thing; [but] within this cultural atmosphere, an exemplar such as George Marshall offers a thought-provoking alternative, indeed a salutary challenge. Not a saint, Marshall was nonetheless a Christian gentleman whose core convictions were threaded all through his ethical leadership."[29] In spite of all of its faults, it is doubtful that any nation other than the United States, founded overtly in Christianity and at that time resoundingly "Christian" in culture, could have produced a plan that at once required forgiveness of a recent foe and sacrifice for that foe's well-being.

Another example of the power of forgiveness can be found in the South African Truth and Reconciliation Commission. Following the dismantling of apartheid in South Africa, there was the specter of emotional scars from decades of violence, injustice, and abuse. The way that Nelson Mandela's government chose to try to address this was with the Truth and Reconciliation Commission. The commission, chaired by Anglican Archbishop Desmond Tutu, was tasked with discovering and revealing past wrongdoing by government and non-state actors in the hope of resolving past conflicts. Rather than prosecuting individuals for past crimes, its emphasis was on gathering evidence from both victims

28. See for example Hogan, *Marshall Plan*.
29. Hein, *In War for Peace*.

and perpetrators, allowing both to testify and often allowing victims to confront perpetrators and perpetrators to publicly apologize and ask forgiveness in an open and transparent forum. The fact that both Mandela and Tutu come from Christian backgrounds is no mere coincidence. Mandela, who received the Nobel Peace Prize in 1993, was educated in Methodist schools and was baptized in the Methodist Church. Mandela attended church services every Sunday and Christianity was a significant part of his formative years.[30] Desmond Tutu, a recipient of the Nobel Peace Prize in 1984, has been a tireless opponent of apartheid and an advocate for human rights. Following in the footsteps of his mentor and fellow activist Trevor Huddleston, Tutu was ordained as an Anglican priest in 1960. Tutu has written passionately and convincingly of the virtues and necessity of forgiveness in peacemaking and reconciliation.[31] N. T. Wright has said of Tutu's achievements through the Truth and Reconciliation Commission, "I have no hesitation in saying that the fact of such a body even existing, let alone doing the work it has done, is the most extraordinary sign of the power of the Christian gospel."[32]

In a way that is difficult to understand, our own forgiveness depends on our ability to forgive others, as evidenced by the prayer that Jesus gave to His disciples when they asked Him to teach them to pray. In this prayer, called the "Lord's Prayer," Jesus prays, "forgive us our sins, as we have forgiven those who have sinned against us."[33] He later explains to His disciples that "if you forgive men their trespasses [sins], your heavenly Father also will forgive you; but if you do not forgive men their trespasses, neither will your Father forgive your trespasses."[34] According to N. T. Wright, forgiveness is part of God's answer to the problem of evil brought up in chapter 3.[35] This is not simply a cheap or easy "forgive and forget" mentality. Wright says that the evil must be named, and there must be no silly attempts after the fact to dismiss it or pretend that it was not really so bad. Rather, once the evil and the evildoer have been identified, only then can true forgiveness and true repentance occur. Jesus taught this

30. Mandela, *Long Walk to Freedom*, 19–20.

31. See for example Tutu, *No Future without Forgiveness*; and Tutu, *Book of Forgiving*.

32. Wright, *Evil and the Justice of God*, 134.

33. Matt 6:12 (ISV).

34. Matt 6:14–15.

35. Wright, *Evil and the Justice of God*, 133.

very concept, as found in a passage in Matthew that is often narrowly interpreted to deal only with church discipline. Jesus said:

> If your brother sins against you, go and tell him his fault, between you and him alone. If he listens to you, you have gained your brother. But if he does not listen, take one or two others along with you, that every word may be confirmed by the evidence of two or three witnesses. If he refuses to listen to them, tell it to the church; and if he refuses to listen even to the church, let him be to you as a Gentile and a tax collector.[36]

These verses have sometimes been cited as evidence of how judgmental and closed-minded the church is, challenging any who disagree with the established orthodoxy. Certainly, there have been instances where the church abused these passages, instances that church critics are quick to point out at every opportunity. Read more broadly, however, these verses represent a means by which one who has been wronged can seek redress. This is not the same as seeking revenge; rather, the victim confronts the guilty party, first in private, then with dispassionate witnesses, to adress the wrongdoing. If the guilty party responds favorably, confessing the wrongdoing and seeking forgiveness, the guilty party has "gained a brother." If the guilty party never does repent of the wrongdoing, the victim is still free to forgive, thus freeing the victim from the psychological repercussions of continually mulling over the crime and a means for gaining vengeance. Forgiveness, even forgiveness that is not accepted by the guilty party, is freeing. No other religion has such an emphasis on forgiveness.

The Trinity: God in Three Persons

In the previous section and throughout this book there is mention of God's Holy Spirit. Throughout the book, particularly in the next chapter, there is mention of the Christian doctrine of Jesus Christ as God. Belief in a triune God, God in three persons, is yet another way in which Christianity is unique. Christianity differs from all other religions, the Abrahamic monotheistic, the polytheistic, and pantheistic alike, in the concept of a triune God. In fact, this concept is a stumbling block and even an affront to devout Muslims and Jews. It must be noted at the outset that this is not, as many Muslims charge, a veiled form of polytheism.

36. Matt 18:15–17.

Christians believe in one God, one divine being, but this God has three distinct persons, referred to in the Scriptures (including by God Himself) as the "Father," the "Son," and the "Holy Spirit."[37] Among Jesus' last recorded words to His disciples is what has come to be called the "Great Commission," in which He directs His followers, "Go therefore and make disciples of all nations, baptizing them in the name of the Father and of the Son and of the Holy Spirit."[38]

The concept of a triune God is difficult to understand, and difficult to explain. However, as Nabeel Qureshi pointed out, there is a difference between defining who we are and defining what we are.[39] That is, there is a difference between my being and my person. I am a human being—that is *what* I am—and I am also Jeff Kramer—that is *who* I am. God is God, the great I Am,[40] the divine creator God, sovereign over all. But that God exists in three distinct persons, the Father, the Son, and the Holy Spirit.[41] Figure 13 shows the Scutum Fidei, a traditional Christian symbol that expresses the basic aspects of the doctrine of the Trinity. God is one divine being. All three persons of the Godhead are fully God, but each is a distinct person. To be sure, this is difficult to fathom, but why ought we to expect that an eternal omnipotent God would be easy to understand? Nor is the concept unprecedented. As every physicist knows, the electron has a virtue that is referred to as "duality," as does electromagnetic radiation (e.g., light). Louis De Broglie proposed that electrons, which are subatomic particles with mass, have a wave nature.[42] Conversely, under some conditions light, which is a massless transverse energy wave, behaves like a particle. If you were to ask a quantum physicist, "Is light a wave or a particle?," they would answer "Yes." Nobel Prize–winning physicist Werner Heisenberg noted that an "important consequence of the principle of relativity is the inertia of energy, or the equivalence of mass and energy."[43] These "dualities" of mass and energy, and of particle and wave, are difficult to comprehend, but are widely accepted and indeed taught in every chemistry and physics textbook.

37. John 1:18, Matt 3:17, John 14:26.

38. Matt 28:19.

39. Qureshi, *No God but One*, 56.

40. Exod 3:14.

41. John 14:16–18. Jesus here clearly speaks of the Father and the Holy Spirit as distinct persons.

42. De Broglie, "Recherches."

43. Heisenberg, *Physics and Philosophy*, 91.

It should come as no surprise that a complex universe sprung from the hand of a complex God. Nor should we, as finite beings, expect to easily (or fully) comprehend an infinite Creator.

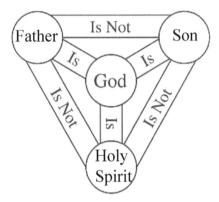

Figure 13. The Scutum Fidei. The Scutum Fidei is a traditional Christian symbol that expresses the basic aspects of the doctrine of the Trinity: God the Father, God the Son, and God the Holy Spirit—God in three persons. God is one divine being, and all three persons of the Godhead are fully God, but each is a distinct person.

What of the apparent contradictions to the Trinity within the Bible, said to be God's revelation of Himself to humanity? For example, Jews reject the concept of the trinity. In fact, The Shema, a Jewish prayer, and a mantra of Judaism, begins, "Hear, O Israel: The Lord our God, the Lord is one."[44] The Shema is a clear statement in support of monotheism, and is perhaps the greatest stumbling block to Jewish acceptance of Jesus as the divine Son of God. As noted above, however, Christianity agrees that God is a single being. However, there are places, even in the Jewish scriptures (that is, the Old Testament), that support the concept of the Trinity, starting with the very first chapter and verse. In Genesis 1, beginning in verse 1 we read, "In the beginning God created the heavens and the earth."[45] The word used in the Hebrew for God is *Elohim*, which is a plural form of *eloah*. A devout Jew would claim this is an "honorific plural," in which the plural is used as a sign of God's great power and majesty. However, in the very next verse we read that "the Spirit of God

44. Deut 6:4.
45. Gen 1:1.

was moving over the face of the waters."[46] The Spirit of God seems to be a separate entity from God Himself. Later in Genesis, God says "Let us make man in our image, after our likeness,"[47] again suggesting a plurality in the Godhead. Even the Hebrew word translated in the Shema as one (*echad*) can be used to denote a compound unity. The same word is used to refer to a bunch of grapes,[48] and when a man and woman joined in marriage become one.

Relationship

Yet another way in which Christianity is unique amongst all other religions is its emphasis on God as a loving Heavenly Father. The Bible reveals that humanity was created to be in fellowship with God. Philip Yancey writes that "the Old Testament's overwhelming lesson about God is that He is personal and intimate, [and] its overwhelming lesson about human beings is that we matter."[49] The Westminster Shorter Catechism states that "Man's chief end is to glorify God, and to enjoy Him forever."[50] This catechism provided much of the material for the *New England Primer*, which was used as the beginning textbook for students in American schools from 1690 until the early twentieth century.[51] Pastor and author John Piper has argued that the statement makes even more sense when modified slightly to "Man's chief end is to glorify God *by* enjoying him forever."[52] Piper's point is that God is a God of relationship. As Francis Schaeffer argued, God is both infinite and personal,[53] and human beings are created in His image. Although humans are finite, part of the image of God, the *imago Dei*, is that we too have personality and will. Starting from an impersonal God, such as that of the Eastern pantheistic religions, one cannot make a convincing case for the development of personality

---

46. Gen 1:2.

47. Gen 1:26.

48. Numbers 13:23.

49. Yancey, *Bible Jesus Read*, 35.

50. Westminster Shorter Catechism. This is the answer to Question #1, "What is the chief end of man?"

51. See for example *New England Primer*.

52. Piper, *Desiring God*, 18.

53. Schaeffer, *Escape from Reason*, 221–22.

except as an aberration from the ideal.[54] As Chesterton noted, "This is the intellectual abyss between Buddhism and Christianity; that for the Buddhist . . . personality is the fall of man, for the Christian it is the purpose of God, the whole point of his cosmic idea."[55] This is why "salvation" in the Eastern religions always involves the giving up of personality. By contrast, the Judeo-Christian God is a personal God. Moreover, the Christian God was a God of relationships even before He created humanity. The Holy Trinity was in perfect relationship before anything was created, and man was created to join in that relationship. As Piper writes (quoting the eighteenth-century American preacher Jonathan Edwards), "The impulse to create the world was not from weakness, as though God were lacking in some perfection that creation could supply. 'It is no argument of the emptiness or deficiency of a fountain, that it is inclined to overflow.'"[56] French mathematician Blaise Pascal spoke of a God-shaped vacuum in the heart of man. Pascal wrote of this vacuum that man ". . . tries in vain to fill with everything around him, seeking in things that are not there the help he cannot find in those that are, though none can help, since this infinite abyss can be filled only with an infinite and immutable object; in other words, by God himself."[57]

More than just a God who values relationship, the Christian God is a God of love. You will often hear it said in cultures that are heavily influenced by Christianity that "God is Love." This is in fact a direct quote from John's first epistle.[58] But as the great twentieth-century Christian apologist C. S. Lewis (himself a convert to Christianity) noted:

> All sorts of people are fond of repeating the Christian statement that 'God is love.' But they seem not to notice that the words "God is love" have no real meaning unless God contains at least two Persons. Love is something that one person has for another person. If God was a single person, then before the world was made, He was not love.[59]

---

54. Schaeffer, *He Is There*, 280–85.

55. Chesterton, *Orthodoxy*, 138.

56. Piper, *Desiring God*, 44 (including a quote from Jonathan Edwards's "Dissertation Concerning the End for Which God Created the World").

57. Pascal, *Pensees* (425), 113.

58. 1 John 4:8b.

59. Lewis, *Mere Christianity*, 151.

Lewis's point here is profound. A unitary God, existing alone before all things, could not have known (much less "been") love before creating a second being to be the object of that love. Love and relationship are shared between two or more individuals. So, love and relationship could not have been an eternal attribute of a monotheistic God as understood by the Jews and the Muslims. The Tawhid, Islam's single most important concept, insists on the absolute unity of Allah. Eastern religions have no personal God at all. But Timothy Keller notes that in John's Gospel we read that the Son is described "as living from all eternity in the 'bosom of the Father,' an ancient metaphor for love and intimacy."[60] Keller writes that in all of his studies of other religions, he "found no other religious text outside of the Bible that said God created the world out of love and delight."[61] Keller writes, "If God is unipersonal, then until God created other beings there was no love, since love is something that one person has for another. This means that a unipersonal God was power, sovereignty, and greatness from all eternity, but not love. Love then is not of the essence of God, nor is it at the heart of the universe. Power is primary."[62] This is where critical theory leaves us today—without the Judeo-Christian God of love, everything is power and the struggle for power. Without the Judeo-Christian God of love, love is an afterthought, a biochemical coping mechanism thrown up in response to the terrible weight of a cruel and totalitarian god.

Additional Reading

For additional reading regarding the pronounced differences between Christianity and other religions, consider the following works. *Orthodoxy* by G. K. Chesterton is a classic work by one of the greatest Christian apologists of the twentieth century, in which the author argues convincingly for the orthodox theology espoused all along by the church.[63] *No God but One* by Nabeel Qureshi is an outstanding and thorough evaluation of the truth claims of Christianity and Islam, written by a convert to Christianity from Islam.[64] Finally, *The Myth of Religious Neutrality* by Roy

---

60. Keller, *Reason for God*, 223.
61. Keller, *Reason for God*, 84.
62. Keller, *Reason for God*, 225.
63. Chesterton, *Orthodoxy*.
64. Qureshi, *No God but One*.

Clouser, though philosophically heavy, is a scholarly and carefully argued work that makes a compelling case that the presuppositions underlying allegedly neutral and non-sectarian social and political positions are, at their core, religious beliefs.[65]

65. Clouser, *Myth of Religious Neutrality*.

7

Jesus Was Just a Man

Christ Jesus, who, though he was in the form of God, did not
count equality with God a thing to be grasped, but emptied
himself, taking the form of a servant, being born in the likeness
of men. And being found in human form he humbled himself
and became obedient unto death, even death on a cross.

—THE APOSTLE PAUL'S LETTER TO THE CHURCH AT PHILIPPI[1]

THERE IS NO DOUBT of the historical Jesus. Even if you discount the Bible as the inerrant Word of God, the Bible is singularly unparalleled as a source of ancient history. Dismissing its historical content simply because one disagrees with its teaching is disingenuous. There are also "secular" accounts of a Jewish man named Jesus who lived in Israel during the Roman occupation, during the rule of Herod Antipas, tetrarch of Galilee, and Pontius Pilate, governor of Judea. These accounts do not give a great deal of detail, but there can be no reasonable doubts as to the historical reality of Jesus. The extrabiblical historical accounts mention the death of Jesus' brother James at the hands of the Jewish Sanhedrin, and that Jesus was called "Christ" (as well as relating the imprisonment of John the Baptist).[2]

1. Phil 2:5–8.
2. Josephus, *Antiquities of the Jews* (xviii.5), in *New Complete Works of Josephus*, 973.

There is also some evidence (though significantly less than for Jesus) that there was an actual historical figure upon whom the Arthurian legends are based. Over the millennia, much of the Arthurian legend then developed as his exploits expanded with each retelling. Could the same be true of the historical Jesus? There are many who claim that Jesus was just a man. They will allow that He was a wise teacher perhaps, a great reformer and motivator, but just a man about whom legends have been developed over the millennia. What can we say about the historical Jesus, and, more importantly, what can we say about Jesus as Savior, Messiah, and Lord?

The Stories of Jesus as Myth or Legend

There has been much scholarship on the historical evidence in support of Jesus, and the evidence in support of the biblical account of His life. In the book *The Case for Christ*, Lee Strobel, *Chicago Tribune* reporter and former atheist turned evangelical Christian, recounts his own search into the claims of Christianity.[3] Among the chapters, each of which details an interview with a scholar from a particular field of study, are ones covering evidence in support of the authenticity of the four Gospels (the books in the New Testament that tell of the life of Christ), a summary of Old Testament prophecies concerning the Messiah and whether Jesus fulfilled them, and an overview of the archeological evidence in support of the historicity of the New Testament accounts of Christ. Similarly, J. Warner Wallace, a homicide detective and crime scene investigator, became a Christian (having been an atheist until the age of thirty-five) after investigating the Gospels as potential eyewitness accounts to the life of Jesus. He has argued that the scriptural accounts represent actual eyewitness accounts and would be upheld in any court of law.[4] These and other arguments provide a great deal of support for the biblical accounts of Jesus' life. Archeology has demonstrated time and again the accuracy and historicity of the Bible, including the accounts of the life of Jesus of Nazareth. John McRay, author of the textbook *Archaeology and the New Testament*, points out that although archaeology cannot prove that the Bible is the inerrant Word of God, or that the spiritual truths proclaimed by Jesus are true, it can demonstrate that the geographical and historical

3. Strobel, *Case for Christ*.
4. Wallace, *Cold Case Christianity*.

information in the Bible are accurate.[5] McRay affirms that "there's no question that the credibility of the New Testament is enhanced" by archaeology.[6] He has concluded that "archaeology has not produced anything that is unequivocally a contradiction to the Bible."[7] As noted in chapter 5, William Mitchell Ramsey, a leading scholar in the study of the New Testament in the late nineteenth and early twentieth centuries, began as a skeptic. Having set out as a skeptic to discredit the New Testament writings, he eventually became convinced of the accuracy and reliability of the biblical record.[8]

This is not to imply that independent archeological evidence has been found to support every historical detail in the life of Christ, but rather that in every case where archeological evidence is unequivocal, it supports the historicity of the Bible. Throughout the history of archaeology there have been those who claim that the New Testament accounts of the life of Christ are historically inaccurate, and therefore the entire New Testament itself must be doubted. In many cases the "evidence" for such claims is simply a lack of corroboration—that is, skeptics have claimed that since the Bible is the only source, it must therefore be untrue. This is in spite of the fact that the Bible is spectacularly more well authenticated that any other ancient text. It is often simply atheistic doubt and incredulity, rather than any actual contradictory evidence behind such claims. It would be foolish to stake one's moral and religious beliefs on a text with no evidence to support its accuracy, but in light of the absence of any clearly contradictory evidence, the fact that corroborating archaeological data does not exist to support every single historical detail in the New Testament is not evidence against it. In fact, the history of archaeology is replete with examples where a claim was made, based mostly on the lack of independent corroborating evidence, that the New Testament is incorrect regarding some detail, only to have that claim overturned by later evidence supporting the biblical account. For example, skeptics had long asserted that the town of Nazareth, where Jesus spent His childhood, did not actually exist during the time of Christ. This was based on the fact that there was reportedly no independent evidence for the existence of such a place until the fourth century AD. However, recent

5. McRay, *Archaeology and the New Testament*, 19.

6. Strobel, *Case for Christmas*, 41.

7. Strobel, *Case for Christ*, 100.

8. Ramsay, *St. Paul the Traveler*, 8.

data has provided evidence that Nazareth did indeed exist, that it was a very small (likely fewer than five hundred inhabitants) Jewish settlement during the Roman era.[9] In many similar examples, questions had been raised regarding specific details from the New Testament accounts of the life of Christ, only to be answered conclusively by new discoveries and further study. Among these are details surrounding the census ordered immediately before Christ's birth, the governor in Syria at the time,[10] the existence of Pontius Pilate (the governor of Judea who condemned Christ to death), and the pool of Bethesda (where Jesus healed a man who had been ill for thirty-eight years).[11] All of these were in question at one time or another. However, additional research and new discoveries have clarified the details surrounding censuses in Roman times,[12] confirmed the identity of the Syrian governor during the time when Christ was born,[13] demonstrated the existence of Pontius Pilate,[14] and actually discovered a pool from Roman times in Bethesda with the characteristic five porticoes reported in the Gospel of John.[15] Overall, the archaeological data overwhelmingly supports the reliability of the New Testament accounts of the life and death of Jesus Christ.[16] This includes confirmation that the early Christians considered Jesus to be divine. Although many skeptics have said that Jesus himself never claimed to be God (see the following section), and that the myth of his divinity developed much later, in a 112 AD letter to Roman emperor Trajan the governor of the province of Bithynia et Pontus, Pliny the Younger, noted that the Christians sang hymns "to Christ as to a god."[17]

Jesus Was Simply a Wise Teacher

Christians believe that Jesus had a dual nature, both fully man and fully God. Whether or not you believe Jesus was God incarnate, it is certain

9. Finegan, *Archaeology of the New Testament*, 46.

10. Luke 2:1–3.

11. John 5:2–8.

12. Wilson, *Jesus: The Evidence*, 67.

13. Boyd, *Boyd's Handbook of Practical Apologetics*, 185–86.

14. Strobel, *Case for Christmas*, 46.

15. Lutzer, *Seven Reasons*, 66.

16. See for example Montgomery, *History and Christianity*.

17. Carrington, *Early Christian Church*, 429.

that Jesus was a man. What kind of man was he? Jews might say that Jesus was a rabbi, a reformer, and something of a critic of the religious leadership during the time of the Roman occupation, but that He was ultimately a blasphemer, making heretical claims to be the Jewish Messiah and God incarnate.[18] Muslims would say Jesus, "Isa ibn Maryam" (literally "Isa son of Mary"), was a prophet and a messenger of God, but that accounts of His words and His teachings have been corrupted and are subordinate to the words and teachings of Muhammad.[19] However Muslims, like the Jews, reject the belief that Jesus was the incarnate God, and Islam does not accept that He was actually crucified. Theologically liberal Christians believe that Jesus was only a human man, though a man who served as a role model for achieving salvation by living a life of integrity, sincerity, and love. Many atheists and agnostics believe that Jesus was a wise teacher and a great man, perhaps one whose teachings are worth considering, but that He was ultimately only a man.

Was Jesus just a great teacher of profound moral truths, but ultimately just a human man? C. S. Lewis made perhaps the most famous critique of the idea that Jesus was only a great moral teacher. In *Mere Christianity* Lewis wrote:

> I am trying here to prevent anyone saying the really foolish thing that people often say about Him: "I'm ready to accept Jesus as a great moral teacher, but I don't accept His claim to be God." That is the one thing we must not say. A man who was merely a man and said the sort of things Jesus said would not be a great moral teacher. He would either be a lunatic—on the level with the man who says he is a poached egg—or else he would be the Devil of Hell. You must make your choice. Either this man was, and is, the Son of God, or else a madman or something worse. You can shut Him up for a fool, you can spit at Him and kill Him as a demon; or you can fall at His feet and call Him Lord and God. But let us not come with any patronising nonsense about His being a great human teacher. He has not left that open to us. He did not intend to.[20]

As Lewis argued, Jesus did not leave open the option of calling him a great moral teacher. Although skeptics commonly charge that Jesus never claimed divinity for himself—that the idea of Christ being God

18. Schäfer, *Jesus in the Talmud*, 106.

19. Qureshi, *No God but One*, 80.

20. Lewis, *Mere Christianity*, 55–56.

incarnate did not arise until Paul (who authored nearly half of the New Testament)—these people have either discounted the Gospels entirely or simply never read them. Even a cursory reading of the Gospels shows that Jesus did indeed claim to be God, and the Gospel authors also considered Jesus to be God incarnate. The Gospel of John begins with the words, "In the beginning was the Word, and the Word was with God, and the Word was God. He was in the beginning with God; all things were made through Him, and without Him was not anything made that was made."[21] "The Word" is one of the ways in which John refers to Christ (as evidenced by John's later statement, "And the Word became flesh and dwelt among us, full of grace and truth; we have beheld His glory, glory as of the only Son from the Father"[22]). Throughout the Gospels, in both the Synoptic Gospels (Matthew, Mark, and Luke) and in John's Gospel, Jesus frequently makes claims to divinity. Jesus claimed, "I and the Father are one."[23] He told the Jewish religious leaders, "I say to you, before Abraham was, I am"[24]—a play on words and on the name by which God had revealed Himself to Moses (When Moses asked God, "who shall I say sent me?," God answered, "I Am that I Am" and "Say to the people of Israel, 'I Am has sent me to you'"[25]). Jesus claimed to be "the Christ, the Son of God," a claim for which the high priest accused Him of blasphemy,[26] and for which He was ultimately executed. Furthermore, throughout the Synoptic Gospels (as well as in John) Jesus refers to Himself as "the Son of Man." This is not a way of declaring His own humanity, as some who are unfamiliar with the Bible have claimed. Rather it is a reference to a messianic prophecy in the Old Testament book of Daniel that says, "I saw in the night visions, and behold, with the clouds of heaven there came one like a son of man, and he came to the Ancient of Days and was presented before him."[27] In these instances Jesus always referred to Himself as "*the* Son of Man" (using the definite article, not simply *a* Son of Man), reinforcing this claim to being the unique Savior foretold in the Jewish scriptures. Among His uses of this designation, Jesus claimed, "the

21. John 1:1–3.
22. John 1:14.
23. John 10:30.
24. John 8:58.
25. Exod 3:14.
26. Matt 26:62–65.
27. Dan 7:13.

Son of man has authority on earth to forgive sins";[28] "The Son of man is Lord of the Sabbath";[29] "The Son of man will send His angels";[30] "the Son of man shall sit on His glorious throne"[31] "the Son of man will be delivered to the chief priests and scribes, and they will condemn Him to death";[32] and "they will see the Son of man coming on the clouds of heaven with power and great glory."[33] Jesus also said He forgave sins; for example, in healing a paralyzed man He said, "your sins are forgiven."[34] The Jewish religious leaders of the day thought that this statement was blasphemy. If you do something against me, I have the right to forgive you, but what right does someone else have to forgive a sin against me? Only the God who created me, and I myself, can forgive a sin committed against me. It was for blasphemy, a serious offense to the Hebrews, that the Jewish religious authorities delivered Jesus to the Roman authorities—if Jesus was just a wise teacher, would the Jewish authorities have delivered him up for crucifixion in contravention of several of their own religious laws? Jesus clearly made multiple claims to be God. Are these the claims of a sane man? If Jesus is not God incarnate, then as C. S. Lewis wrote, He was either insane (for He clearly believed Himself to be God) a deluded and diabolical pretender, a false prophet ranking with the likes of Jim Jones or David Koresh.

Along with His claims of divinity, Jesus made many other astonishing claims, which, if untrue, suggest a megalomaniac rather than a great and wise moral teacher. For example, Jesus said, "whoever is ashamed of me and of my words . . . of him will the Son of man also be ashamed, when he comes in the glory of his Father with the holy angels,"[35] suggesting that Jesus genuinely thought that everyone should proclaim Him as Lord. He said, "I am the light of the world; he who follows me will not walk in darkness, but will have the light of life";[36] "I am the vine, you are the branches. He who abides in me, and I in him, he it is that bears much

---

28. Matt 9:6; Mark 2:10; Luke 5:24.

29. Matt 12:8; Mark 2:28; Luke 6:5.

30. Matt 13:41.

31. Matt 19:28.

32. Matt 20:18; Mark 10:33.

33. Matt 24:30; Mark 13:26; Luke 21:27.

34. Matt 9:2–7.

35. Mark 8:38.

36. John 8:12.

fruit, for apart from me you can do nothing";[37] "I am the resurrection and the life; he who believes in me, though he die, yet shall he live";[38] and perhaps most famously, "I am the way, and the truth, and the life; no one comes to the Father, but by me."[39] Note again the use of the definite article, "the," rather than the indefinite, "a." As with the claims of divinity, these claims suggest that Jesus had a very high opinion of Himself—such vanity is not usually the hallmark of a great and wise teacher, but of an arrogant autocrat or someone not entirely in control of his mental faculties. Along with the fact that Jesus broke with every other religious teaching before His time and since in preaching salvation by grace and faith (specifically faith in Him) rather than salvation by works and morality, one can only conclude that if Jesus was not telling the truth in all of His remarkable claims, He was indeed either diabolical or deluded.

What Kind of Messiah Was Jesus?

As described in chapter 6, Christians believe that Jesus and God the Father are one, two different persons of the one triune Godhead, and that in taking on flesh Jesus in some way that is difficult to fully comprehend "emptied himself, taking the form of a servant, being born in the likeness of men."[40] Satan, being aware of Jesus' new humanity, tempted Jesus in the Judean wilderness.[41] No other religion has such a concept. What is there to have tempted Jesus with? If Jesus was already God, simply God made flesh, what could Satan possibly have offered to Jesus? For one thing, Satan would have wanted to suborn Christ's mission here on earth. Aware that Jesus was also fully man, perhaps Satan would have wished to exert his own will over this God-man. As at his original fall, Satan, whom the Bible tells us was once one of God's angels,[42] sought to overthrow God and take His place as the head of creation. What a coup, then, if Satan could make the very Son of God, the second person of the Trinity, pay homage to him?

37. John 15:5.
38. John 11:25.
39. John 14:6.
40. Phil 2:7.
41. Matt 4:1; Mark 1:13; Luke 4:2.
42. Ezek 28:11–19.

Text Box 12. Perhaps even more than belief in God, belief in Satan or the devil is widely regarded in popular culture as foolish and absurd. But Satan is very real. Jesus knew this and spoke often of Satan. The apostle Paul warned the church in Ephesus to "Put on the whole armor of God, that you may be able to stand against the wiles of the devil. For we are not contending against flesh and blood, but against the principalities, against the powers, against the world rulers of this present darkness, against the spiritual hosts of wickedness in the heavenly places."[43] Regardless, these days Satan has become for many people nothing more than a cartoon-like caricature. For example, every year during the Tour de France an elderly fellow dressed in tights and a cape and carrying a pitchfork makes at least one appearance, usually on a difficult mountain stage. In fact, the ridiculous little red cartoon-like character with horns and a pitchfork was an intentional insult against Satan's pride, common during the Middle Ages.[44] The Bible is clear that Satan is real and was the instigator of the fall and the author of much of the suffering in the world. It may be, as C. S. Lewis proposed in his allegorical novel *The Screwtape Letters*,[45] that Satan himself is the author of this unbelief. Trivializing or disbelieving in Satan makes it that much easier to disbelieve the Bible, and eventually God Himself.

The temptations recorded in the New Testament seem to show that Jesus was, in effect, being tempted to be a different kind of Messiah. The fourth chapter of the Gospel of Matthew records three specific temptations to which Christ was subjected by Satan.[46] After fasting for forty days, Satan came to Him and said, "If you are the Son of God, command these stones to become loaves of bread,"[47] to which Christ replied by quoting the scripture, "Man shall not live by bread alone, but by every word

43. Eph 6:12.
44. Sproul, *Adversary*.
45. Lewis, *Screwtape Letters*, 39–40.
46. Matt 4:1–11.
47. Matt 4:3.

that proceeds from the mouth of God."[48] Not to be outdone, Satan then quoted scripture back to Jesus in the second temptation, taking Him to the pinnacle of the temple in Jerusalem and saying, "If you are the Son of God, throw yourself down; for it is written, 'He will give his angels charge of you,' and 'On their hands they will bear you up, lest you strike your foot against a stone.'"[49] Jesus replied, "Again it is written, 'You shall not tempt the Lord your God.'"[50] Finally, Satan took Jesus to a very high mountain and showed him all the kingdoms of the world and said, "All these I will give you, if you will fall down and worship me,"[51] but Jesus replied, "Be gone, Satan! for it is written, 'You shall worship the Lord your God and him only shall you serve.'"[52]

In these three temptations Satan was surely tempting Jesus to more than a loaf of bread, a circus stunt, and a sovereignty that Jesus already had. In the first temptation, the temptation to turn a stone into bread, one may wonder why this is even a temptation to sin. After fasting for forty days Jesus most certainly would have been hungry, but in what way could eating bread possibly be considered sinful? In fact, later in His ministry, Jesus multiplied a few loaves of bread and a few fish to feed thousands.[53] It may be that Satan was actually tempting Jesus to limit Himself to being a different kind of Messiah than the suffering servant foretold in the messianic prophecies in the Old Testament. Jesus clearly had great love and compassion for the poor. Knowing this, perhaps Satan, in tempting Jesus with a loaf of bread, was in effect tempting Jesus to become a prophet of the poor, a sort of "savior" who preached social justice and charitable deeds. In fact, the liberation theology movement of the Catholic Church has emphasized the social justice aspects of the Gospels, sometimes to the exclusion of the primary faith- and grace-based message of the New Testament. Although Christ clearly had a great deal of compassion for the poor and preached often on matters of social justice, this was not His primary reason for taking on humanity and walking among us. In fact, Jesus once said, "you always have the poor with you, and whenever you

48. Deut 8:3.

49. Matt 4:5–6. The verses quoted by Satan are from Ps 91:11–12.

50. Matt 4:7. Jesus is quoting Deut 6:16.

51. Matt 4:8–9.

52. Matt 4:10. Jesus is quoting Deut 6:13.

53. The feeding of the five thousand is reported in all four Gospels: Matt 14:13–21; Mark 6:31–44; Luke 9:12–17; and John 6:1–14. The subsequent feeding of the four thousand is recorded in Matt 15:32–39 and Mark 8:1–9.

will, you can do good to them; but you will not always have me."[54] Jesus' primary reason for coming was "to seek and to save the lost,"[55] so that we "may have life, and have it abundantly,"[56] and so that "whoever believes in him should not perish but have eternal life."[57] Perhaps Satan knew that a Messiah focused exclusively on social justice rather than atoning for man's sins would present little threat to him. A Savior (and His church) focused solely on social issues and good works can offer no ultimate redemption for sinners—we are not saved by good works.

The second temptation that Satan tried was to tell Jesus to throw Himself from the top of the temple in Jerusalem, a strange thing with which to try to tempt someone. But perhaps Satan was again tempting Jesus to be a different kind of Messiah—a flashy miracle worker who would dazzle the masses with miracles and wondrous signs. Miracles were indeed a part of Christ's ministry, but not the focus. In several cases Jesus told those who witnessed the miracles, "Tell no one the vision, until the Son of man is raised from the dead."[58] A Messiah who performed flashy miracles would certainly draw a lot of attention, just like some tent revival televangelist, shaking and hollering and handling venomous snakes without getting bitten. Such a Savior would also likely draw a significant following. Indeed, early in His ministry there were apparently many who followed Jesus mostly for the "light show," but these fell away when His teachings got controversial and "hard."[59] However, had Jesus limited His ministry to a spectacular show of miracles and healings, without the greatest miracle of paying the price for our sins so that we can come before a Holy God clothed in the righteousness of Christ, all of the flashy miracles in the world would not have made a lasting difference in eternity. In fact, some skeptics have wondered why Jesus did not perform more miracles. That is, if Jesus could heal a leper, why not cure leprosy? If Jesus could heal a paralytic, why not cure paralysis? Again, this misses the point of Christ's ministry. Christ could indeed heal our infirmities (and

54. Mark 14:7, see also Matt 26:11 and John 12:8.

55. Luke 19:10.

56. John 10:10.

57. John 3:16.

58. Matt 17:9; Mark 9:9.

59. See John 6:60, 66. After introducing what was to become the sacrament of Holy Communion, John records that "Many of his disciples, when they heard it, said, 'This is a hard saying; who can listen to it?'" and "After this many of his disciples drew back and no longer went about with him."

one day will), but we would still be sinners, walking around in physically healthy bodies but still sinful and condemned to separation from the God who loves us.

The last of the three temptations recorded in the Gospel of Matthew may seem to be the easiest to understand. Satan offered Jesus rule over all the kingdoms of the world if only Jesus would bow down and worship Satan. Although the lure of such power might seem to be a great temptation, Jesus, as God incarnate, was already Lord over all creation.[60] Is this some sort of testimony, as some have charged, that Jesus was not in fact God incarnate, but just a man that could be tempted by worldly might? Not at all. This temptation was for Jesus to be the kind of Messiah that many Jews of His day were hoping for, the kind of Savior that Judas Iscariot and the other disciples no doubt expected Jesus to be. For hundreds of years prior the Jews had been ruled by one foreign power or another. From the time of the Babylonian captivity, starting around 605 BC, up to the Roman occupation from 63 BC onward, the Jews were hoping for a warrior Messiah who would free them from foreign rule and oppression, to restore them to the supremacy they had known during the Davidic kingdom. The temptation for Jesus to have been that kind of Messiah must have been great. Likely most or all of His followers would have expected this, even His closest disciples, who seemed never to have fully grasped the full nature of His ministry while He was with them. Although the temptation to rule the earth would have been inconsequential to Jesus (the Bible says He will rule the earth anyway upon His return),[61] the temptation to heed the hopes and expectations of His people and throw off the yoke of corrupt foreign rule may have been very real. Again, however, this type of Savior would ultimately not meet the real needs of humanity. In the history of Israel, Jesus' forebearer David had been a great earthly king and lord over the greatest kingdom of his time, but his strength could not atone for their sins, and the Israelites fell away from their God shortly after David's reign. Only a Savior who could serve as the one pure and final sacrifice for the sins of men could gain victory over sin and death, once and for all.

60. Col 1:15–20.
61. Rev 1:5.

The Last Temptation of Christ?

The Bible also says that Christ was tempted at other times and in other ways. The author of the book of Hebrews writes, "For we have not a high priest who is unable to sympathize with our weaknesses, but one who in every respect has been tempted as we are, yet without sin."[62] Although the Bible does not explain what other temptations Jesus may have faced, many have speculated on the nature of these temptations. Some years ago, the movie *The Last Temptation of Christ* generated a great deal of controversy within Christian circles. Based on the book of the same name written by Nikos Kazantzakis,[63] the movie delved into what the author speculated to be the last (and greatest) temptation of Christ. Part of the controversy around the movie was that it portrayed Jesus being tempted to have sex with Mary Magdalene. Jesus most certainly did *not* imagine having sexual relations with Mary Magdalene. Jesus Himself said that "everyone who looks at a woman lustfully has already commit-ted adultery with her in his heart,"[64] and Jesus was without sin. But the Bible does say that Jesus was "tempted as we are," and surely one of those temptations must have been to simply be a man, a husband, and a daddy. Jesus predicted the way in which He would die—He knew what lay ahead of Him as the kind of Messiah He would be when He emptied Himself of His divine attributes to live and walk among His creation, and when He resisted the temptations of Satan in the wilderness. In the garden the night before He was arrested and crucified He prayed, "Abba, Father, all things are possible to thee; remove this cup from me; yet not what I will, but what thou wilt."[65] He was said to have been in such travail that His sweat fell like drops of blood.[66] Surely at times like that the temptation to live a full life as a man—a revered teacher, a great religious leader, a beloved husband and a loving daddy—must have been great.[67]

62. Heb 4:15.

63. Kazantzakis, *Last Temptation of Christ*.

64. Matt 5:28.

65. Mark 14:36; see also Luke 22:42.

66. Luke 22:44.

67. It is worth noting, however, that Ravi Zaccharias believed that Kazantzakis got it "dead wrong," pointing out that "a home in Bethany would not exactly be an allurement to one whose dwelling was in heaven" (*Jesus among Other Gods*, 44). The argument is valid. No doubt Jesus did not succumb to any temptation in part because He knew the glories of heaven. But I believe, with Kazantzakis, that this temptation, simply to live as a husband and father, may still have been among the greatest.

Although the traditional belief (as portrayed in the book and movie versions of *The Last Temptation of Christ*) of Mary Magdalene as a prostitute has been widely refuted, the Bible does record that Jesus had driven out seven demons from her.[68] Because of this, Mary likely felt a sense of gratitude and devotion to Jesus. Regardless, Mary, like Jesus' other followers, likely understood little of the true nature of Jesus' ministry during His time on earth. Like the other disciples, she probably knew Him as a great teacher and a charismatic leader and hoped that He would be the sort of Messiah that they all expected Him to be. More than that, like the other disciples (and perhaps more than any of them), Mary knew Jesus was a kind man, a man to whom she owed her life. She no doubt loved Him, and perhaps harbored hopes that He might one day take her to be His wife. Did Jesus know this? Did He sense her love for Him? I am of course speculating here, but what could be more tempting to a man than a beautiful woman who loves Him? How great must have been the temptation to be the sort of husband that Mary may have hoped He would be. How satisfying to be a daddy, to bounce their children on His knee and hear their joyful voices at play. As a daddy myself, I can think of little more satisfying than spending time with my wife and our little boy, watching him grow and become. Although Jesus most certainly did not entertain lustful thoughts, it seems preposterous to presume that among all the temptations He faced, perhaps His greatest temptation would have been to come down from the cross and live a full life as a human man. Among the temptations Jesus overcame, in Kazantzakis's words, "He conquered the invincible enchantment of simple human pleasures."[69] Thanks be to God that Jesus chose instead to finish the work He began, ensuring that the bonds of sin and death would be broken and that all who so choose might come before a holy God.

> **Text Box 13.** Returning to the problem of evil, if, as Kazantzakis speculated, Jesus "conquered the invincible enchantment of simple human pleasures"[70] as His greatest temptation, what does this say about human life? Part of the atheists' charge against God deals with the evil and suffering in life. The atheists seek meaning and, absent God, they find none. Faced with

68. Luke 8:2–3.

69. Kazantzakis, *Last Temptation of Christ*, 3.

70. Kazantzakis, *Last Temptation of Christ*, 3.

the evil and suffering, and the absurdity and meaninglessness of life, the brave and honest among them then ask if life is worth living at all. Yet the created order, though undeniably fallen and imperfect, is still good, and being "in the flesh" is at the very least more good than bad. Kazantzakis believed that perhaps Jesus simply enjoyed being "in the flesh," and that this also was a temptation. In spite of all of the suffering and woe about which the atheists wring their hands, the fact remains that life is good, and most, including you, the reader, prefer life to death. That life should be, in the balance, good, follows from God's having created it and declared it "good." Even in its fallen state, the image of God, though tarnished, is not erased. It does not, however, follow naturally from an atheist perspective that life should be good—only that, for the success of the species, it survives.

The Jewish Messiah, the Risen Christ

Some theologically liberal Christians hold that Jesus was not God, but only a human man who served as a role model for moral living and achieving salvation through a life of moral integrity, sincere faith, and generosity. Muslims believe that Jesus did not actually die on the cross, teaching instead either that Allah replaced Jesus as the last minute with a look-alike or, alternatively, that He faked His death (this is often referred to as the "swoon theory"). Jews agree that He was not God and deny that He was the Jewish Messiah described in their scriptures (i.e., the Old Testament). But Jesus claimed to be the Messiah. Among the words of Christ recorded in the Gospels are overt statements in which He identifies Himself as the Jewish Messiah, and not simply a reformer. For example, after reading from a messianic prophecy in Isaiah, Jesus said to those present, "Today this scripture has been fulfilled in your hearing."[71] He said, "Think not that I have come to abolish the law and the prophets; I have come not to abolish them but to fulfill them."[72] He told His disciples, "These are my words which I spoke to you . . . that everything written about me in the law of

---

71. Luke 4:21. The passage Jesus read from was Isa 61:1–2.
72. Matt 5:17.

Moses and the prophets and the psalms must be fulfilled."[73] In predicting the manner in which He was to die, Jesus said, "For I tell you that this scripture must be fulfilled in me, 'And he was reckoned with transgressors;' for what is written about me has its fulfilment,"[74] and, "Thus it is written, that the Christ should suffer and on the third day rise from the dead."[75] Finally, when Jesus asked His disciples, "who do you say that I am?," Peter replied, "You are the Christ, the Son of the living God," to which Jesus answered, "Blessed are you . . . for flesh and blood has not revealed this to you, but my Father who is in heaven."[76]

Claiming to be the Messiah and actually fulfilling the biblical prophecies may be two entirely different things. While Jesus could have contrived to fulfill some of the prophecies (for example, the prophecy in Zechariah that He would come riding on the foal of a donkey),[77] the majority of these prophecies were beyond the control of a mere mortal claiming to be the Messiah. This includes the prophecies regarding the time, place, and circumstances of His birth, and of some of the details of His death. There are hundreds of specific details about the Messiah predicted in the Old Testament, and Jesus met each of them.[78] It has been estimated that the odds of any person fulfilling all of these prophecies merely by chance are astronomically small—much less than the number of people who have ever lived. In fact, one such analysis suggested that the odds are one in a number several orders larger than the total number of atoms in our universe.[79] The kinds of miracles Jesus performed were characteristic of the promised Messiah, as foretold in the Old Testament (notably Isaiah 35 and 42, and Psalm 22). For example, there are no other recorded instances in the Old Testament of restoring sight to the blind or hearing to the deaf—only in the messianic prophecies. Among the most compelling of the fulfilled prophecies was that Jesus Himself predicted that He would be raised from the dead. Although the biblical reports of this very thing happening are considered to be myth by non-believers, the disciples themselves claimed to be witnesses of this very fact. They

73. Luke 24:44.

74. Luke 22:37. In this passage Jesus is referring to the messianic prophecy in Isa 53:12, "[He] was numbered with the transgressors."

75. Luke 24:46.

76. Matt 16:15–17.

77. Zech 9:9.

78. See for example McDowell, *Evidence That Demands a Verdict*, 141–76.

79. Stoner, *Science Speaks*, 109.

believed and professed this truth at great personal cost. Ten of the original twelve disciples, and several other of Jesus' earliest followers, were executed for proclaiming the truth of Christianity.[80] As philosopher and theologian J. P. Moreland has pointed out, "People will die for their religious convictions if they sincerely believe they are true," but people will not die for an obvious lie.[81] The disciples and other followers of Jesus were in a unique position to know if the resurrection was true or if they had made it up. If they had known that the resurrection was a lie, they would never have been willing to sacrifice their lives. Yet the fact remains that something momentous happened on the third day following Christ's crucifixion. Following Pentecost—the fulfillment of Christ's promise that the Holy Spirit would come to the disciples[82]—these men both lived and died for Jesus. Men who had previously been simple fishermen (several of the twelve disciples had come from this vocation), most likely uneducated, suddenly found the courage, the wisdom, and the motivation to take up the reigns of a revolution that has changed our world.

Jesus not only claimed to be the Jewish Messiah; He claimed to be God incarnate, the second person of the Trinity. The Old Testament prophecies concerning the Messiah all came true in Jesus of Nazareth, providing a witness to the truth of His claims. Alternate theories raised by skeptics regarding Christ's death and resurrection have been addressed and found wanting.[83] If Jesus, the so-called Son of God, was just a man and not an equal part of the triune Godhead, then God is guilty, as some have charged, of divine child abuse, and Christ's death can no more cover my sins that the death of a bull or a lamb. If He was not God incarnate, Jesus really was guilty of blasphemy, and He was either a fool or a crazy man, having provoked and antagonized the religious leaders of His day,[84] and gone knowingly to the terrible death that He Himself predicted in advance.[85] As Timothy Keller has argued, "Throwing your life away need-

---

80. See McBirnie, *Search for the Twelve Apostles*.

81. Strobel, *Case for Christmas*, 89.

82. In Acts 1:5, after Jesus had risen from the dead and appeared multiple times to more than five hundred followers over a period of forty days, Jesus told His disciples shortly before they witnessed him ascending into the heavens, "for John baptized with water, but before many days you shall be baptized with the Holy Spirit."

83. See for example Qureshi, *No God but One*, in particular chapters 6 and 7.

84. See for example Matt 23:27; Mark 7:9 and 11:15–19; and John 8:44.

85. Mark 8:31; 9:31; and 10:33.

lessly is not admirable . . . Jesus's death was only a good example if it was more than an example."[86]

If, however, Jesus is God, His death demonstrates plainly the result of sin, as well as God's answer to sin and evil. Christ's death shows that sin results in suffering and death. Christ was sinless, yet He still suffered and died. He was found innocent by two courts (Pontius Pilate and Herod Antipas).[87] If, as He claimed, He really is God, then Jesus was also innocent of the charge of blasphemy, yet He was still executed. As God knew from the beginning, the result of sin entering the world at the fall is suffering, separation, and death, and not only for the sinner but for all of creation. The evidence confirms both Jesus' claims and the Bible itself. As Josh McDowell has written, the evidence "demands a verdict."[88] What if everything that the early church and evangelical Christians believe today is true? Jesus Christ, God incarnate, died for your sins. Sin is not just something we do; it is a state of separation from God. We are all in rebellion against God's rule, we all want to do what the flesh demands, and ignore what God's Word commands. We are all spiritually dead in our sin. There is no "goodness ratio" that we can tweak by doing a few more good works to earn our way to heaven. Unlike relationship and love, judgement is not an eternal part of the essence of the eternal triune God. Since sin and rebellion did not exist within the trinity, there was no need for judgement before sin entered into creation. But holiness and purity are part of God's integral essence, and He cannot permit impurity, imperfection, and sin, just as an earthly king cannot be in a loving relationship with one who rebels against his rule. We are in debt to God,[89] but not a debt of money. One could imagine repaying even a very large monetary debt, but ours is a debt of purity and holiness, and we have none. Fortunately, in His divine love and mercy, God took on human flesh, lived a perfect life, and paid the price for our sins. Jesus lived the life we should have lived and died the death we should have died so that we can gain eternal life with Him. As John Stott has written "the essence of sin is we human beings substituting ourselves for God, while the essence of salvation is God substituting himself for us."[90] To gain this salvation

86. Keller, *Reason for God*, 200.

87. Luke 23:14–15.

88 McDowell, *Evidence That Demands a Verdict*.

89. Rom 8:11–16. In Rom 8:12 Paul writes, "we are debtors, not to the flesh," but to Christ, who died for our sins.

90. Keller, *Reason for God*, 202.

is both costly and totally free. It is costly because Jesus calls us to die to ourselves,[91] to lose our lives so that we can find them,[92] to put aside our selfish desires and to instead desire Him and life in and with Him. But it is totally free because there is nothing we can give to earn it. It is freely given to all who claim Jesus Christ as Lord, for "the wages of sin is death, but the free gift of God is eternal life in Christ Jesus our Lord."[93] Jesus said, "For God so loved the world that he gave his only Son, that whoever believes in him should not perish but have eternal life."[94]

Additional Reading

For more reading regarding the historicity and divinity of Christ, consider these excellent works: In *The Case for Christ* author Lee Strobel builds a convincing case for the divinity of Christ through journalistic interviews of acknowledged experts from various fields around the world.[95] In *Cold Case Christianity* author J. Warner Wallace relies on his experience as a homicide detective and crime scene investigator to demonstrate that the Bible contains reliable eyewitness testimony to the life, death, and resurrection of Jesus Christ.[96] In *Evidence That Demands a Verdict* author Josh McDowell investigates the evidence, including hundreds of Old Testament prophecies, that demonstrates that Jesus was the Jewish Messiah and the Son of God.[97]

91. In Rom 8:13 Paul writes, "for if you live according to the flesh you will die, but if by the Spirit you put to death the deeds of the body you will live."

92. Mark 8:35.

93. Rom 6:23.

94. John 3:16.

95. Strobel, *Case for Christ*.

96. Wallace, *Cold Case Christianity*.

97. McDowell, *Evidence That Demands a Verdict*.

8

Organized Religion Is Evil

Many of us saw religion as harmless nonsense . . .
September 11th changed all that.

—RICHARD DAWKINS[1]

A HALLMARK OF POSTMODERN thought, along with the idea that all truth is relative, is the nearly universally accepted belief that submitting one's individuality to authority is, at best, selling out. At worst, it is to be a part of something that is unhealthy, and even a source of evil and injustice. Western thought and literature of the nineteenth and twentieth century is crowded with a celebration of the individual and criticism of authority and of submission of the self to organized religion or political parties. From Walt Whitman ("Resist much, obey little"), Ralph Waldo Emerson ("Whoso would be a man, must be a nonconformist"), and Henry David Thoreau ("Disobedience is the true foundation of liberty. The obedient must be slaves") to Timothy Leary ("Think for yourself and question authority") and virtually every contemporary rock musician, obedience and conformity are considered to be evidence of moral and intellectual inferiority. In the past this sentiment sprang from the words and warnings of thoughtful men from the Enlightenment and beyond, as tyrants were

1. Dawkins, "Has the World Changed?"

overthrown and representative forms of government born. Their words may serve to remind individuals of their responsibility to "not be hindered by the name of goodness, but . . . explore it if it be goodness."[2] To that end Benjamin Franklin stated, "it is the first responsibility of every citizen to question authority."[3] These and other exhortations served as a valuable encouragement to rank-and-file citizens, who may tend to be intellectually lazy. Accepting things without thinking them through and uncritically believing anything given to them by any recognized authority, too many have settled for the promise of personal peace and affluence and will not challenge the status quo so long as their own comfort is not disturbed.[4] In this capacity such wisdom is indeed true, and worthy of consideration.

However, in this present age of vapid individualism, going your own way, and standing out from the crowd, submitting to any group is seen as "selling out." Sadly, much to the likely dismay of Franklin, Whitman, Emerson, and Thoreau, most people have simply changed which authority they blindly follow. There can be little doubt that "nonconformity" is simply the new way to conform, whether it be wearing mass-produced T-shirts ("Why Be Normal?"), displaying mass-produced bumper stickers ("Question Authority"), spouting vapid slogans ("Keep Austin Weird"), or showing one's "non-conformance" by one of the currently acceptable ways (hair styles, hair color, piercings, clothing styles). The French poet Charles Baudelaire is said to have walked the streets of Paris in the 1850s with his hair dyed green—dying one's hair an unusual color has not been particularly unique since then. We have gone from legitimate rebellion against mindless conformity to being a nation of rebels without a clue. Meanwhile, ever vigilant for ways to capitalize, advertisers cash in on the non-conformity craze with slogans meant to appeal to the "non-conforming" masses, and lame attempts to convince them that the color of their cell phone case is a means of expressing their personality and individuality.

2. The quote is from Ralph Waldo Emerson's 1841 essay entitled "Self-Reliance" (in Myerson, *Transcendentalism*, 318–39).

3. A maxim attributed to Benjamin Franklin.

4. Schaeffer, *How Should We Then Live?* See in particular chapter 11, in which Schaeffer argues that as the "Christian-dominated consensus in [the West] weakened, the majority . . . adopted two impoverished values: personal peace and affluence. It is against the mindless acceptance of these (decidedly un-biblical) doctrines of modern Western civilization that much legitimate rebellion has arisen."

Against such a backdrop of mindless conformity to advertising slo-gans and pop culture "personalities," identifying with a group of "judgmen-tal" and "narrow-minded" Christians seems the height of conformance to a corrupt authority. Permutations of the oft-heard phrase "I'm spiritual, I just don't believe in organized religion" suggests that organized religion, regardless of the nature of the religious belief, is a certain path to hypoc-risy, ignorance, and narrow-mindedness. Sadly, the history of mankind is replete with examples of the abuse of power, including abuses perpetrated by every organized religion, including the Christian church (and, lest we be fooled, by every atheistic regime as well). Among the more famous infractions by the Christian church are the crusades against Muslims in the Middle Ages, the Salem Witch Trials of the early 1690s, the African slave trade, imperialist subjugation of native peoples, and a history of pe-riods of anti-Semitic attitudes and behaviors. But smaller and more rou-tine examples of ignorance, narrow-mindedness, injustice, and violence occur every day at the hands of those who call themselves "Christian." Does this not demonstrate clearly that organized religion is a force for evil, and that we all should "turn on, tune in, and drop out,"[5] or is there some "saving grace" in organized religion? Is the church, as has been claimed, the last best hope for humanity?[6] A fair and even evaluation of the basic teachings of Christianity and the fruits of the church itself may provide a surprising defense of the Christian faith. As numerous sociologists and historians have demonstrated, much of the advancement of the human race has occurred directly because of the efforts of organized religion.[7] Just one example of this is found in the example of institutes of higher learn-ing, many of which were begun by and for the church. Erroneous quotes from ill-informed atheists to the contrary, the church has a long history of supporting education and scholarship. As Mike Bryan noted, "Harvard was . . . dedicated to the education of Puritan ministers. Princeton, Dart-mouth, and Brown were founded during the Great Awakening, a series of Christian revivals in the mid-1700's, by evangelical denominations with sectarian goals. Columbia . . . was in essence a religious institution: its first president was an Episcopalian clergyman, and classes were held in the

5. A phrase popularized by Timothy Leary, said during a speech at the "Human Be-In" in Golden Gate Park, San Francisco, 1967.

6. Hybels, *Courageous Leadership*, 12.

7. See for example Schmidt, *How Christianity Changed the World*; Sunshine, *Why You Think the Way You Do*; and Mangalwadi, *Book That Made Your World*.

schoolhouse of Trinity Church on Wall Street."[8] Closer to my home in the Dallas–Fort Worth area, Southern Methodist University, Texas Christian University, and Baylor, though now secular to varying degrees, were all founded with the support of Christian denominations. Throughout Europe as well nearly every great university was founded and initially staffed by the church.

Once again Dawkins's claim that "religion . . . teaches us that it is a virtue to be satisfied with not understanding"[9] is demonstrably untrue. Given the number of Christians there are and have been in all areas of academic pursuit, including the sciences, only one who is willfully ignorant could accept such a claim. The study of God's creation is actually encouraged in Scriptures. In fact, throughout most of the past two thousand years math and science in the Western world was performed and taught almost exclusively at Christian institutions. Gregor Mendel (the father of modern genetics and an Augustinian friar) and George Lemaître are but two recent examples of Christians who have pushed forward the frontiers of scientific inquiry. Sociologist Rodney Stark has said, "The success of the West, including the rise of science, rested entirely on religious foundations, and the people who brought it about were devout Christians."[10] In addition, Islam in the eighth to the twelfth centuries AD had a proud tradition of advances in math and science, including Alhazen (who made contributions to the scientific method) and Al-Kwarizmi (known for his contributions to algebra and the introduction of Arabic numerals). Saying that religion "teaches us to be satisfied with not understanding the world" is so patently false as to call into question the objectivity of anyone who could make such a claim.

I do not mean to suggest that institutions, even those with noble and sacred goals, are entirely immune from corruption, deceit, and misdeeds. This should come as no surprise to Christians, who believe in original sin and the fallenness of humanity and human institutions. However, to many moderns and atheists who put their faith in man's wisdom and the supposed self-improvement produced by a progressive, secular education, this may be surprising. Institutions are made up of people and led by people. Christianity has preached all along that people are fallen, corrupted and corruptible. It was Auguste Comte, Karl Marx, and Herbert Spencer,

8. Bryan, *Chapter and Verse*, 10.

9. Dawkins, *God Delusion*, 152.

10. Stark, *Victory of Reason*, 10.

early heroes of atheism, who suggested that societies, governments, and the human species were on an inexorable course of evolving into greater and greater stages of enlightenment. Throughout history virtually every great cause has given rise to a mixed litany of successes and failures, gains and losses, victories and defeats. The Russian revolution in 1917 ended the Tsarist autocracy, with the victorious "Red" (Bolshevik) Russian party eventually devolving into Stalin's atheistic regime, seeing the murder of millions of Russian citizens, followed by decades of corruption and economic underachievement, bringing the fall of the USSR and the resulting kleptocracy left behind. The Cuban revolution of the 1950s overthrew one oppressive regime only to have it replaced with another, even more oppressive regime led by the very men who championed the revolution. The Protestants, persecuted at the hands of the Catholic Church, turned around and persecuted the Anabaptists. Charitable organizations are not immune from such outcomes either. The fairer question, then, would not be why do so many human institutions go wrong, but rather why have so many of them gone well for as long as they have or, for that matter, why were so many noble efforts and institutions even begun in the first place?

Christianity as a Force for Good?

One significant way in which Christianity has beneficially impacted individuals and society is through charitable organizations. The Bible clearly commands Christians to acts of charity and service.[11] Even a brief review of the most well-known and long-standing charities shows that the Christian faith was a primary motivation for their founding. In many ways charity is the handprint of a kind and loving God.[12] This is seen in overtly Christian missions, as well as in more secular groups, many of which were initially founded on fundamentally Christian principals by Christian men and women. In ignoring or discounting the good works that have been performed by overtly Christian charities, one is left with the misperception that they exist only to push religion and impose their

11. See for example Heb 13:2–3, "Do not neglect to show hospitality to strangers . . . remember those who are in prison, as though in prison with them; and those who are ill-treated, since you also are in the body."

12. In 2 Cor 9:6–7 Paul writes, "The point is this: he who sows sparingly will also reap sparingly, and he who sows bountifully will also reap bountifully. Each one must do as he has made up his mind, not reluctantly or under compulsion, for God loves a cheerful giver."

worldview on the unsuspecting and uneducated poor. If the beliefs of that particular religious group are actually true (that is, if the eternal salvation that they offer is real), this is not such an ignoble pursuit. But allowing for a moment the atheist position that religious belief may be false and has little value in and of itself, it is simply not true that all overtly religious charities do no lasting social or moral good. This misperception can be easily discredited with only the slightest effort. To be sure, many great evils have been performed in the name of organized religion—Christianity included. But so too have many good and generous deeds been performed by and expressly in the name of organized religion, and among these Christianity stands out. Any honest appraisal will demonstrate that Christian charity is at the forefront of making this world better for people who are not empowered to do it for themselves. An honest evaluation of the history of Christianity will show that it is a religion of charity and social justice. Following are just a few examples.

Perhaps the most famous example of Christian charity that does much more than simply push a Christian worldview on poor people is Mother Theresa and the Sisters of Charity. Mother Teresa (1910–997), born Agnes Gonxha Bojaxhiu, heard a call at the age of twelve and entered a convent in her native Albania.[13] She spent her life ministering to the poor in India while living among them. Her Missionaries of Charity built homes for orphans, nursing homes for lepers, and hospices for the terminally ill in Calcutta. As the mission grew in size, the organization also engaged in aid work in other parts of the world. In 1979 Mother Teresa received the Nobel Peace Prize, recognizing her decades of working among the poorest of the poor in the slums of Calcutta.[14]

Mercy Ships travels around the world providing free medical care to poor people in desperate need of even the most basic health care services. Their web site declares plainly that "Mercy Ships follows the 2,000–year-old model of Jesus to provide hope and healing to the world's forgotten poor."[15] The organization provides free basic healthcare, transformative surgeries, and access to first-rate medical professionals, state-of-the-art medical and surgical facilities, and healthcare training to communities throughout the developing world.

13. Kolodiejchuk, *Mother Teresa*, 14.

14. http://www.nobelprize.org/nobel_prizes/peace/laureates/1979/.

15. http://www.mercyships.org/home/.

World Vision International is one of the largest Christian relief and development organizations in the world.[16] It was founded in 1950 by a young American Baptist minister and relief worker named Robert Pierce. Among the impacts of this organization are provision of clean drinking water to individuals and schools throughout the developing world, the treatment of severely malnourished children, protection of pregnant women and their children from malaria, training of teachers, and provision of microloans. World Vision also fights against human trafficking, working to free those enslaved by sex and labor trafficking. Since the group's inception, they have also led numerous emergency responses serving nearly fourteen million people in fifty-six nations. It is also possible to sponsor a child through World Vision. World Vision and Catholic Relief Services (begun during World War II to serve migrants and refugees)[17] are two of the largest private organizations in the world dedicated to caring for the poor and hungry.

Also founded by Robert Pierce, Samaritan's Purse is a non-denominational evangelical Christian organization providing aid around the world.[18] Since its founding in 1970, Samaritan's Purse has helped victims of war, poverty, natural disasters, disease, and famine. Nearly 90 percent of every dollar raised goes directly to projects, with only ~4.3 percent spent on administrative costs (the Better Business Bureau's Wise Giving Alliance requires that charities spend at least a mere 65 percent of their total expenses on their charitable missions). Among its ongoing programs are Operation Christmas Child, which delivers more than ten million shoebox gifts to poor children in more than one hundred countries each year, and World Medical Mission, which sends doctors, equipment, and supplies to underprivileged countries.

Wycliffe Bible translators provides the Bible to people who might otherwise have no opportunity to hear or read that word in their native tongue.[19] Although the primary goal of Wycliffe to translate the Bible into other languages may seem less than admirable to those for whom the Bible is just unfounded religious propaganda, the group does not force its beliefs on anyone. It simply seeks to provide Christian Bibles, along with reading and writing education, to people all over the world so that they

---

16. https://www.wvi.org.

17. https://www.crs.org.

18. http://www.samaritanspurse.org.

19. http://www.wycliffe.org.

might hear the word and choose for themselves if it's true. In their work with many remote people groups, Wycliffe missionaries have generated written forms of languages that had previously only been handed down in oral traditions. A key to the ability to advance oneself is an education, and a fundamental component of an education is learning to read and write. The anthropologic benefits of this work are self-evident. Studying and understanding a culture and its language and oral traditions, codifying the language, creating and recording a grammatical structure and vocabulary, and teaching people to read and write has benefits over and above the sharing of religious beliefs.

Both the Salvation Army[20] and the Gideons began as "holiness groups," offshoots of larger Christian denominations founded by devout Christians. The Salvation Army was founded in 1852 by British Methodist preacher William Booth. The focus has evolved to include hunger relief, housing and homeless services, prison ministries and adult rehabilitation, combatting human trafficking, and thrift stores. The stated mission of the Salvation Army is "to preach the gospel of Jesus Christ and to meet human needs in His name without discrimination." Dietrich Bonhoeffer, the Lutheran pastor, theologian, and anti-Nazi dissident who was hanged by the Nazi regime shortly before the end of World War II, was influenced by hearing General Bromwell Booth of the Salvation Army—it may have been a watershed moment in his life.[21] It has been suggested that "the Salvation Army alone does more for the homeless and destitute in most areas than all secular agencies combined."[22]

The Gideons International was founded in 1899 by Christian businessmen John H. Nicholson, Samuel E. Hill, and Will J. Knights. Although most famous for placing Bibles in hotel rooms, hospitals, convalescent homes, domestic violence shelters, and prisons, the Gideons[23] is an association of Christian businessmen and professionals devoted to service and personal testimony.

Just as Christian charitable groups provide compassion and service to those in need, so too do countless individual Christians. Everything Mother Teresa did in service to the desperately poor of Calcutta (and beyond) was in response to her faith in Jesus Christ. William Wilberforce,

20. http://www.salvationarmyusa.org.

21. Metaxas, *Bonhoeffer*, 39.

22. Colson and Pearcey, *How Now Shall We Live?*, 137.

23. http://www.gideons.org.

the English politician and evangelical, played a significant role in the abolition of the British slave trade.[24] Wilberforce was born into the privileged class, and lived a life of gambling, drinking, gluttony, and excess. Early in his life he had actually denounced the deity of Christ. However, in 1775 Wilberforce, by that time a successful Parliamentarian, gave his life to Christ. After visiting John Newton (a former slave trader, famous for writing the well-known hymn "Amazing Grace" after converting to Christianity), Wilberforce was convinced that he could do the most good by remaining in Parliament. Wilberforce and his Clapham Sect (a group of evangelical social reformers based in Clapham, London) championed many worthwhile causes, most notably the campaign for the complete abolition of slavery. That campaign led to the Slavery Abolition Act of 1833, which abolished slavery in much of the British Empire. There are also untold numbers of less famous individual Christians serving their fellow man in the name of Jesus Christ. At the time of this writing my wife and I are privileged to help support a number of Christian missionaries around the world. This has included a young woman providing physical therapy to the poor in Arequipa, Peru, and training locals to take over her role as physical therapist through Medical Missions International;[25] a gentleman (now passed away) who was involved in building and improving dormitories for orphans and freed sex-trade workers in Nepal;[26] a young married couple with two children finding and providing alternative employment opportunities for freed sex trade workers in Calcutta, India, and Chiang Mai, Thailand, through Serge (formerly World Harvest Missions);[27] and a family providing language and healthcare education in Northern Africa through Africa Inland Mission.[28] These individuals

24. See for example Belmonte, *Hero for Humanity*.

25. http://www.medministries.org.

26. This individual and the organization of which he was a member (whose work is on-going) wished to remain anonymous. It seems that the many members of the majority Hindu religion in that region will not abide "Christian missionaries," even if they are providing beneficial services to needy people that are considered beneath contempt and unworthy of service by the majority of the population, giving the lie to the oft-repeated mantra that the Eastern religions are more open-minded than Christianity.

27. https://serge.org.

28. http://www.aimint.org. Note that this family is working in a majority-Muslim nation where their lives could be endangered if attention were to be drawn to their presence and their identity as Christians. For this reason, the country in which they are working is not stated.

and countless others throughout the history of the Christian faith work in anonymity, serving their fellow humans simply because they see those people through the eyes of the Christian God, as persons of value, dignity, and worth.

Charitable Groups Founded on Christian Values

Along with the countless overtly Christian charities that provide for the sick and needy, there are also numerous charities, organizations, and institutions that benefit humanity which, although no longer overtly religious, were started as explicitly religious organizations by distinctly Christian founders. The YMCA is one such example. In 1844 twenty-two-year-old farmer-turned–department store worker George Williams joined a handful of friends to organize the first Young Men's Christian Association (YMCA), a refuge of Bible study and prayer for young men seeking to escape the hazards of life on the streets. As the YMCA website notes, "Although an association of young men meeting around a common purpose was nothing new, the . . . organization's drive to meet social needs in the community was compelling, and its openness to members crossed the rigid lines separating English social classes."[29]

The International Red Cross was founded by Jean Henri Dunant.[30] Dunant engaged in religious activities in his early life, including a period of full-time work as a representative of the YMCA in Europe. It is written of him that "passionate humanitarianism was the one constant in his life, and the Red Cross [was] his living monument."[31] In its more than one-hundred-year history, the Red Cross has vaccinated 1.1 billion children against measles and rubella and helped untold millions in over seventy countries through disaster response, community-based programs, and measles vaccination campaigns. Although the Red Cross claims its symbol is based on the Swiss flag (with the colors reversed), Muslim countries have refused to recognize the organization. The Red Crescent, the symbol for which was first used during armed conflict between Russia and the Ottoman Empire in 1877–1878, is a subsidiary of the Red Cross.

The Boy Scouts was initially a British youth organization founded in 1907 by General Robert Baden-Powell, whose father was a reverend and

29. http://www.ymca.net.
30. Red Cross, http://icrc.org/.
31. https://www.nobelprize.org/prizes/peace/1901/dunant/biographical/.

professor of geometry at Oxford University.[32] The Boy Scouts of America is one of the largest private youth organizations in the United States. Although focused on non-sectarian values such as building character, citizenship, and personal fitness, the organization was founded on Christian principals, with early policies prohibiting atheists and agnostics from leading troops of boys and young men.

Among the causes that William Wilberforce (noted above for fighting to end slavery in Great Britain) championed from his position as Parliamentarian was the Society for the Prevention of Cruelty to Animals (SPCA).[33] The American Society to Prevent Cruelty to Animals (ASPCA) was founded by Henry Bergh, enlisting support from businessmen, politicians, and religious leaders (including his minister, Henry Whitney Bellows of the First Congregational Church of New York City). Bergh gave a lecture in New York in 1866 citing statistics and examples of animal abuse, and laws granting a charter for the society and punishing cruelty to animals was passed by the state of New York two months later. In 1874 Bergh was approached by a Methodist missionary named Etta Wheeler, who sought his help in rescuing a child named Mary Ellen Wilson from her abuser. After the child was rescued, other cases were brought to his attention. In response, Bergh, along with polo star Elbridge Gerry and philanthropist John Wright, formed the New York Society for the Prevention of Cruelty to Children (NYSPCC) in 1875.[34]

Alcoholics Anonymous (AA)[35] was founded in 1935 by stock speculator Bill Watson and surgeon Bob Smith. Both were members of the Oxford Group, a Christian organization founded by the missionary Frank Buchman, whose stated purpose was to lead a spiritual life under God's guidance and to carry their message to others so that they could do the same. A number of the tenets of the Oxford Group were incorporated into AA's Twelve Steps. Although the organization generally respects the privacy and anonymity of its members, making numbers difficult to determine, countless millions who struggle with alcohol addiction have benefited from involvement with the organization.

The truth is, contrary to what some outspoken atheists would have us believe, the world owes much to the charitable activities of the Christian

32. http://www.scouting.org.

33. http://www.aspca.org.

34. http://www.nyspcc.org/nyspcc.

35. https://www.aa.org.

church. There are many more examples of charitable organizations and institutions that were founded by Christians and with overtly Christ-centered motivations that have provided much benefit to society. In his 2007 article in *USA Today*, Don Feder noted that "there are no secularist counterparts to Pope John Paul II, Mother Teresa, William Wilberforce, Martin Luther King Jr., or the Christians—from France to Poland—who rescued Jews during the Holocaust."[36] In addition, countless individual Christians throughout the world donate generously to charities serving in every corner of the earth. Charity is a fundamental principle in the teachings of Jesus Christ; after telling a story of a Samaritan man who crossed cultural barriers to provide aid to a crime victim unknown to him, Christ said, "Go and do likewise."[37] Dinesh D'Sousa relates a story in which a group of young Indian men walked by Mother Teresa as she was hugging a poor leper. One of the fellows commented to his friends, "I wouldn't do that for all the money in the world," to which Mother Teresa replied, "Neither would I. I am doing it for the love of Christ."[38]

Harmful Impacts of the Church

To be sure, Christianity has much to account for, as do all organized religions and religious organizations. As has been pointed out by countless critics, and by no small number of Christians reformers, supporters of the faith, and church insiders, a great many terrible deeds have been performed by or given support from both individual Christians and the church. As noted earlier, among the more well-known infractions that have been charged against Christianity are the Crusades against Muslims during the eleventh to thirteenth centuries, the Salem Witch Trials of the early 1690s, the African slave trade, imperialist subjugation of native peoples, and periods of anti-Semitism in the church. Although the full truth behind the simplistic narratives taught today is much more complex, the church's hands are still stained. Furthermore, less systematic but unfortunately more routine examples of narrow-mindedness, injustice, and violence occur every day at the hands of those who call themselves "Christian." Can the evil deeds done by and in the name of the Christian religion be reconciled with the claims of Christianity, or the claim that

36. Feder, "Atheism Isn't the Final Word."

37. Luke 10:30–37.

38. D'Souza, *Godforsaken*, 253.

the Christian God is a God of love? In light of the nefarious deeds of persons claiming to act in God's name, and groups espousing morally reprehensible ideas while claiming to adhere to Christian principles, God may seem all too silent.

In trying to address this question, it is important to differentiate between things done directly by God or as the direct result of God's command versus those done in God's name. Misguided individuals have done any number of things ostensibly in the name of or to honor someone or something else. But this does not mean that the one in whose name the nefarious deeds were done supported it or wished it to be done. In March of 1981 John Hinckley Jr. attempted to assassinate President Ronald Reagan in an effort (he claimed) to impress teen actress Jodie Foster. Of course, no one has suggested that Foster share in the blame for these crimes. While the church and individual Christians have done regrettable deeds while claiming to be acting on the will of God, or to honor God, it may be that such actions were not actually sanctioned by God.

There have been many over the centuries who have claimed to speak authoritatively, sometimes even exclusively, for the Christian God, but this does not guarantee that God Himself has given His sanction, either to the group or individual claiming divine authority or to the message claimed to be authoritative. If God were to come down to earth and speak, He might have a different message, and He might also identify some would-be authorities as frauds. In fact, in Christian belief, God did come down to earth, in the form of Jesus Christ, and His words have come to us in the form of the Bible. The acts of the church and of individual Christians must be compared to the message of the Bible, and in many cases this clearly demonstrates that the church has not always acted in accord with God's will. In some such cases where groups claim to be acting on God's behalf, even a cursory comparison of their beliefs with those put forward in the Bible shows that they are clearly at odds. The Ku Klux Klan, which claims to "bring a message of hope and deliverance to white Christian America," is not endorsed by any recognized Christian church or denomination and is obviously at odds with the teachings of Jesus Christ and the New Testament. There are other examples among the more lunatic fringe of the religious right (often claiming to be the only true adherents to the Christian faith), such as those who hold placards at public events that read, "God hates fags." Such sentiment raises the ire of critics of the church, as indeed it should. It also rightly raises the ire of those within the church. In fact, the Bible does not say any such thing.

The Bible does state that God hates sin, and sin is antithetical to God's very being, but the apostle Paul reminds us that "God shows his love for us in that while we were yet sinners Christ died for us."[39] We must be careful when interpreting statements made by those who claim to be speaking for God, and compare what they are saying to what God has already said for Himself, through the words of Jesus Christ and those who wrote the inspired words of the Bible. Simply accepting that the words of someone claiming to speak for God actually come from God is akin to believing that Jodie Foster's work as an actress somehow encouraged and approved of a criminally insane person's attempt on Reagan's life.

Just as it is important to distinguish between acts done directly by God or as the direct result of God's command with those done in God's name, so too it is critical to distinguish between deeds done by or with the explicit support of the church from those done by individuals. Although some Christians may act "holier than thou" and wear an attitude of smug superiority, few Christians or Christian organizations have claimed to be perfect. While most Christians would affirm that there is a clear difference between those who are saved and those who are lost, the difference is entirely by the grace of God. There is nothing innate about us that makes us better than anyone. Christians are not perfect they are forgiven. Although called to seek holiness and to try to emulate their Savior, as mere human beings Christians are guaranteed to make mistakes, as any human being will do. There is certainly no actual evidence that Christians are any worse than any other group, anecdotal impressions of anti-church polemicists aside. It has also been said that "the church is a hospital for sinners rather than a museum for saints," and in fact confession of sins has been an integral emphasis of Christian tradition through the centuries. Individual Christians can and have made mistakes: mistakes of interpretation, mistakes of social justice, and mistakes of belief and behavior. Such cases of wrong behavior, whether due to simple human failure or due to mistaken beliefs and interpretations, should not immediately be assumed to reflect the will of God or the teachings found in God's Word.

Similarly, just as individual Christians err, so too Christian institutions have erred. There is no reason to expect that the church (or any large group of human beings) is or ever can be perfect—contrary to what secular humanism supposes. No sensible group has made such

39. Rom 5:8.

a claim. That religious authorities can be in error with respect to the interpretation of God's Word and God's will is evident in the fact that Jesus saved some of His most damning criticisms for the religious leaders of His time. This is not to say that Jesus was an anarchist, or that He sought to tear down organized religion. He Himself is referred to in the Bible as the head of the church, with the church being described as His "body."[40] Instead, Jesus sought (among other things) to correct wrong ideas concerning the nature of God and our relationship with Him. He sought to reconcile us to God. Just like any large organization can go astray—departing from the initial plan put forward by its founder—the church can, and has, made mistakes. Unlike many other organizations, the church has also undergone frequent (often internally directed) corrections, in the form of church reforms, public apologies, and changes of direction and position.

Bearing in mind the fact that the church is not (and does not claim to be) inerrant and that not everything that is claimed to be done for God, whether done by an institution or an individual, is actually sanctioned by God or supported in His Word, it may be worthwhile to revisit some of the darker episodes in church history. In many such cases, the loudest criticisms of these terrible actions came from within the faith. For example, the German Lutheran Pastor Dietrich Bonhoeffer was among the earliest and most vocal opponents both to the injustice and anti-Semitism in Nazi Germany and to the complicity of the nationally sanctioned German church, a fact for which he was martyred. The English politician and evangelical William Wilberforce played a significant role in the abolition of the British slave trade. Some of the actions performed by the church itself, such as the Crusades (which were not entirely immune to criticism by some courageous theologians and religious leaders of the time), were outside of the will of God as revealed in the Scriptures. The church has since admitted as much, and apologized. Similarly, the church has also apologized and sought forgiveness for periods of anti-Semitism, including regrettable silence and inactivity during the period in which the Nazis were systematically exterminating Jews in the Holocaust. The Christian church was not unique in this sin of inactivity; no government, including the U.S. government and the atheist regime in Stalinist Russia, spoke out on behalf of the Jewish people prior to World War II. However, there were many

40. That is, the global church, the sum total of Christ-followers throughout the world and history, is referred to as the "body" of Christ in Eph 5:23 and Col 1:18 and 24.

individual Christians who were unparalleled in their support for and aid of Jews under Nazi regimes during this time. The Salem Witch Trials, in which nineteen men and women were hanged (a twentieth was "pressed to death"), were an example of extremism, though other Christians of the time were among the most outspoken critics of the behavior of those who carried out the farcical legal proceedings.[41] To claim that the African slave trade was a fault unique to the Christian church is entirely unfounded. To be sure, Christians owned African slaves, and to their shame many within the church justified slave ownership with biblical passages taken out of context, but to claim that the African slave trade was a unique enterprise entered into by Christians is not supported by even a casual investigation. Slavery has been present in nearly every culture throughout recorded history. Prior to the Crusades, Muslims frequently raided the lands of Christendom and took Christians as slaves.[42] For most of its history slavery was not a racial issue, and most slaves did not differ racially from their masters.[43] For example, Europeans enslaved Europeans (the word "slave" is thought to derive from the European people group known as the "Slavs," who were a common victim of slavers), South American natives enslaved South American natives, Asians enslaved Asians, and Africans enslaved Africans. African slaves were often captured by other Africans, since the Europeans were susceptible to African diseases and were thus afraid to venture into the interior of the continent.[44] It was individual Christians and Christian congregations (notably the Quakers in the U.S.) who were the most outspoken opponents of slavery. Similarly, imperialist subjugation of native peoples, though done under a thin veneer of "Christianity," was performed for nationalist and decidedly secular goals. Bradley P. Holt writes that during the imperialist periods of the European powers, even so-called mission work supported by the state religion was often "an ancillary arm of nationalist imperialism, so that control by Spain or Portugal, or gaining wealth by gold or slaves, was higher in priority than proclaiming the Savior."[45] The leaders of the imperialist nations, though appealing to the Christian God (and claiming to be adherents of the Christian faith), had actual motivations that included personal and corporate financial

41. Moody, *Saltonstall Papers*, 48–50.
42. Qureshi, *No God but One*, 130.
43. Sowell, *Black Rednecks and White Liberals*, 113.
44. Medved, *Ten Big Lies about America*, 54.
45. Holt, *Thirsty for God*, 95.

gain and national military power. As with the African slave trade, there were individual Christians and Christian groups that challenged the actions of the imperialist governments and regretted the impact upon the indigenous peoples. Among these Holt notes that the writings of Christian missionary Bartholomew de las Casas remain among the most severe indictments of the Spanish treatment of Native Americans.

There are of numerous other examples of crimes, injustices, and terrible atrocities done in the name of religion. One might wonder on which side God was during the sectarian fighting in Ireland between Catholics and Protestants. It may also be noted that both Germany and the Allied Nations of Western Europe claimed to be Christian nations during World War I, and indeed Christian individuals fought on both sides of that and other wars. Many people have bemoaned the fact that so many wars have been fought over religion. But religion is often a scapegoat for less noble motivations. Given that throughout the history of Europe in the past millennium the rank and file have been mostly religious, leaders on both sides of many conflicts have claimed to be acting in the name of God and accordance with Christian values. In fact, their actual motivations often had little to do with the will of God or the words of Jesus Christ. Jesus never commanded us to seek economic or geopolitical advancement. His commands are to love the Lord with all our heart, soul, mind, and strength and to love our neighbors as ourselves;[46] to seek justice, love kindness, and walk humbly with our God;[47] and to go and make disciples of all nations.[48] Just as Jodie Foster cannot be blamed for the misguided deeds of John Hinckley Jr., neither should God be blamed for deeds allegedly done in His name that go directly against His commandments. An evaluation of the words of Jesus Christ and of the Bible will demonstrate that many of the misdeeds performed in God's name are directly opposed to God's will and commands.

What of Overtly Atheist Ideologies?

As noted, the legacy of the church and of groups claiming to act in the name of the Christian God is mixed. Perhaps it is worth considering the track record of some of the alternatives to Christianity. The fact is,

46. Mark 12:30–31 and Luke 10:27.

47. Mic 6:8.

48. Matt 28:19.

comparatively few charitable groups as impactful as those described above have sprung from other religious traditions. More to the point, one must ask, what has atheism produced in the way of relieving human suffering and what are the fruits of unbelief? D'Souza has noted, "Atheist resentment seems not to produce very much charity . . . Inveighing against it is so much easier than doing something about it."[49] In an essay on atheism Don Feder asks, "What would a world without God look like?" and answers that in a world without God "morality becomes, if not impossible, exceedingly difficult."[50] Feder notes that "A universe that isn't God-centered becomes ego-centered. People come to see choices through the prism of self: what promotes the individual's well-being and happiness. Such a worldview does not naturally lead to benevolence or self-sacrifice." What is the track record of overtly atheist movements— groups led by those who have rejected any belief in a creator God or any kind of divine authority?

One particularly telling example is found in Nazi Germany. Although Christianity remained the nominal religion in Germany before, during, and following the rise to power of the Nazi regime, there can be little doubt that the Nazi leadership was not Christian. Hitler himself said that Nazism was a secular ideology founded on science and that "Science would easily destroy the last remaining vestiges of superstition."[51] Joseph Goebbels wrote that "the Fuhrer passionately rejects any thought of founding a religion. He has no intention of becoming a priest. His sole exclusive role is that of a politician."[52] There is a great deal of nonsense and misinformation on the matter, such as opinions on atheist websites like atheism.about.com, which states that Nazi Germany was an implementation of a Christian agenda. Such dishonest drivel has the intellectual credibility of the Holocaust denial movement. Hitler explicitly appealed to Christianity on a regular basis, but this was a political stunt of an astute (if deranged) politician to appeal to the stated religious beliefs of his people—beliefs that an evaluation of Hitler's own claims would show he did not share. The sin of the church was that it remained all too silent in the face of the Nazi regime's lies and atrocities. As for Hitler's beliefs, although brought up as a Roman Catholic, he rejected Christian beliefs

49. D'Souza, *Godforsaken*, 253.
50. Feder, "Atheism Isn't the Final Word."
51. Evans, *Third Reich at War*, 547.
52. Taylor, *Goebbels Diaries 1939–41*, 76.

as an adult. He used vague references to God in his speeches, but he rued his misfortune that Germany had the "wrong religion," declaring, "Why didn't we have the religion of the Japanese, who regard sacrifice for the Fatherland as the highest good? The Mohammedan religion too would have been much more compatible than . . . Christianity with its meekness and flabbiness."[53] Hitler also forwarded other reasons as to why Christianity should be rejected, including his views that Christianity protected the weak; that it was Jewish and Oriental in origin; that the Christian tenets of forgiveness of sin, resurrection, and salvation were "plain nonsense"; that the idea of mercy was dangerous and "un-German," and that the Christian idea of equality protected the racially inferior, the ill, the weak, and the crippled.

What were the fruits of this atheist regime? The Holocaust, the systematic state-sponsored murder of Jews led by Hitler and the Nazi party, resulted in the death of approximately two-thirds of the nine million Jews living in Europe before World War II. This included approximately one million Jewish children. The Nazi's also murdered millions of Romani (sometimes called "Gypsies"), people with disabilities, homosexuals, and prisoners of war. Concentration camps were outfitted with gas chambers for the mass extermination of "undesirables" and perceived enemies of the state. In addition, medical experiments were performed on unwitting human subjects. Among the most notorious of these were those performed by Dr. Josef Mengele working in the Auschwitz concentration camp. His experiments included placing subjects in pressure chambers, freezing them, attempting to change eye color by injecting chemicals into the eyes of children, and various amputations and other surgeries.[54]

> **Text Box 14.** The atrocities committed by the Nazis were a direct logical result of their atheistic worldview. If one presupposes an impersonal beginning, and accepts the Darwinian conjecture that we evolved from lower organisms and that only the fittest will (or should) survive, Nietzsche's "will to power" is the obvious philosophical fruit. Absent the concept of the image of God in all men, there is no reason why we should not try to stamp out competitors. The Nazi death camps and the eugenics movement in America both have their philosophical

53. Metaxas, *Bonhoeffer*, 165.
54. Harran, *Holocaust Chronicles*, 384.

roots in the secular humanism that arose as a result, in part, of the Darwinian creation myth that was seen as an alternative to a divine Creator. Even the subtitle of Darwin's *On the Origin of Species by Means of Natural Selection, or the Preservation of Favoured Races in the Struggle for Life* predicts the fruits of this worldview. The strong survive while the weak and the defective go extinct. That the Nazis sought to bring about the extinction of the Jews (along with Gypsies, homosexuals, and the physically and mentally handicapped) is, by this metric, a virtue— they were simply accelerating what nature would eventually make inevitable. As John Stonestreet, president of the Colson Center for Christian Worldview, is fond of saying, "Ideas have consequences. Bad ideas have victims."

The Nazi regime was not alone in committing atrocities during World War II. The Imperial Japanese Army built Unit 731 (officially named the Epidemic Prevention and Water Supply Department), a covert biological and chemical warfare research unit. The camp was the site of horrific human experiments carried out during the Second Sino-Japanese War and World War II. For nearly a decade, scientists at Camp 731 infected between three thousand and twelve thousand men, women, and children (both war prisoners and Chinese and Russian civilians) with plague, anthrax, and other biological agents and conducted vivisection (experimental surgeries on live subjects) without anesthesia.[55] Mistreatment of prisoners of war was not limited to Unit 731; in the *New York Times* bestseller *Unbroken*, Laura Hillenbrand recounts the story of Olympic athlete Louis Zamperini, who crashed into the Pacific during World War II and was captured and imprisoned by the Japanese.[56] The story details accounts of Zamperini's perseverance through years of physical and mental torture. It is interesting to note that, likely to the chagrin of vocal atheists who complain about God's injustice from their comfortable ivory towers, Zamperini professed faith in the Christian God.

Stalinist Russia is another example of an overtly godless regime. Though raised in the Georgian Orthodox Church, Stalin became an atheist and regarded religion as an opiate of the masses. Under Stalin, the

55. See for example Williams and Wallace, *Unit 731*.
56. Hillenbrand, *Unbroken*.

forced collectivization of Soviet agriculture led to widespread famine that contributed to the death of millions, and millions more were killed during purges in the 1930s and beyond.[57] The purges' victims included political rivals, party members, and military members who were seen as being disloyal (or just potentially disloyal) to Stalin, and anyone who dared speak out against Stalin's regime, as well as countless farmers and ordinary people who refused to cooperate with Stalin's five-year plans. It is widely believed that the purges within the military severely weakened the armed forces, contributing to the rapid conquests made by Hitler's Germany in Russia early in World War II.[58] People in all professions and of every background were purged during Stalin's rule, including millions who were sent to labor camps (many never returned), and perhaps as many as a million who were executed outright. By some estimates, Stalin was responsible for as many as twenty million deaths during his brutal rule.[59]

Mao Zedong's regime in China is thought to have caused as many as four times the number of deaths as Hitler's rule in Nazi Germany. Historian Frank Dikötter delved into Chinese archives and likened the systematic torture, brutality, starvation, and killing of Chinese peasants from 1958 to 1962 (when Mao was enforcing his "Great Leap Forward") to the Second World War in its magnitude. Dikötter estimated that at least forty-five million people were worked, starved, or beaten to death during these four years alone.[60] It has been reported of Maoist China that:

> State retribution for tiny thefts, such as stealing a potato, even by a child, would include being tied up and thrown into a pond; parents were forced to bury their children alive or were doused in excrement and urine, others were set alight, or had a nose or ear cut off . . . People were forced to work naked in the middle of winter; 80 per cent of all the villagers in one region of a quarter of a million Chinese were banned from the official canteen because they were too old or ill to be effective workers, so were deliberately starved to death.[61]

Mao Zedong is universally regarded as the principal architect of the China that emerged from the inception in 1921 of the Chinese Communist

---

57. See for example Kershaw and Lewin, *Stalinism and Nazism*.

58. McLoughlin and McDermott, *Stalin's Terror*, 6.

59. Rosefielde, *Stalinism in Post-Communist Perspective*, 959–87.

60. Dikötter, *Mao's Great Famine*, x (preface).

61. Akbar, "Mao's Great Leap Forward."

Party to Mao's death in 1976—a China that continues to effectively out-law Christianity. Only churches with government-paid pastors (and who deliver government-approved sermons) are permitted, and children un-der eighteen are barred from church attendance. The majority of Chinese Christians meet illegally in house churches, against which the govern-ment has launched crackdowns resulting in church leaders being placed under house arrest, and church members being fired from their jobs and evicted from their homes. Meanwhile, the legacy of disregard for human rights is further evidenced by the genocide perpetrated upon the mostly Muslim Uyghurs by the current regime in Beijing.[62]

Pol Pot led the Khmer Rouge in a brutal attempt to establish an agrarian utopia in Cambodia. Part of Pol Pot's education was in Marxist-Leninist theory in Paris in 1949–1953, where he read the atheistic writings of Marx, Nietzsche, Stalin, and Rousseau. In typical Marxist/communist fashion, Pol Pot declared his disastrous "agrarian revolution" to be "an extraordinary measure . . . that one does not find in the revolution of any other country."[63] Instead of a utopia, Pol Pot created what has become known as the "Cambodian Genocide" (also called "The Killing Fields"), which resulted in the deaths of one to two million Cambodians (out of a total population of approximately eight to ten million). These crimes against the Cambodian people "were organized by a group of Franco-phone middle-class intellectuals known as the Angka Leu (The Higher Organization) . . . [who] had studied in France in the 1950's where they had not only belonged to the Communist Party, but had absorbed Sartre's doctrines of philosophical activism and 'necessary violence.'"[64]

All of these mass murderers were the ideological children of twentieth-century atheism and secular humanism. They are just some of the more memorable examples of the fruit of atheism's poison tree. As Historian Glenn Sunshine points out, an honest assessment is that communism, which is "an explicitly atheistic system [is] a far greater killer than any force in history, including religion."[65] The total cost of communism, placed at ninety-four million innocent lives lost in the twentieth century,[66] does not include the twenty-first-century horrors of

62. See for example "Who Are the Uighurs?," *BBC News*, https://www.bbc.com/news/world-asia-china-22278037.

63. Short, *Pol Pot*, 288.

64. Zacharias, *Shattered Visage*, 58.

65. Sunshine, *Why You Think the Way You Do*, 176.

66. Courtois, *Black Book of Communism*, 4.

the Ughyur genocide in China,[67] the Rohynga genocide in Burma,[68] or the government-imposed starvation and suffering in atheist North Korea.

Common Grace

As we have seen, given their own track record, atheists have little right to complain about the failings of the Christian church. Neither do they have any great humanitarian successes to compare with the blessings given by Christianity. Within Christianity there exists the concept of *common grace*, the grace of God that is common to all humankind because its benefits are experienced by, or intended for, the whole human race without distinction. Common grace includes benefits experienced by everyone, whether or not they are Christians—such as the benefits of living in a free society like the United States of America, which was founded under overtly and intentionally Christian propositions by the overwhelmingly Christian founding fathers. This is not to say that America is God's chosen nation, or that America is infallible. The USA and every other human institution are marred by the fact that humans are sinful and fallen. We cannot legislate morality; nor can we guarantee that all of our motives are selfless. However, common grace includes the benefits that arise from Christianity that are given to Christians and non-Christians alike. Charity is one such example.

This is not to say that only Christians perform charitable deeds (though there is much evidence that, as a group, Christians are more charitable than other religious groups, including atheists[69]). Rather, there is no good reason for charity to have evolved in the absence of a good and loving God. Researchers have tried to arrive at a theory for why charity and altruism might have evolved in human populations, but no one has succeeded in identifying a gene that might contribute to this trait. Nor are there any plausible explanations for why such a trait would have evolved. Some have tried to propose evolutionary advantages to being charitable. To date there has been little success. R. A. Fisher, a leading proponent of Darwinian evolution, categorically denied selection at levels higher than the individual organism. There can be imagined an advantage to

---

67. https://www.breakpoint.org/genocide-in-china/.

68. https://www.breakpoint.org/breakpoint-genocide-burma/.

69. https://www.philanthropy.com/article/religious-americans-give-more-new-study-finds/.

a species with a strong herd instinct if there were a prominent genetic predisposition to help others in the herd, although there is not a great deal of evidence that humans (or any of the great ape species that are genetically most closely related to humans) are particularly prone to herding. Most primates live in small family groups, and these groups tend to be fairly exclusive. Fighting is more likely to break out between different troops than cooperation, and sacrificing resources solely for the benefit of an unrelated member of an out-group is virtually unheard of in the animal kingdom. It seems as if humans, to a greater or lesser extent depending on individual makeup, have a bent toward altruism that goes beyond any obvious advantage to the species. This proclivity can express itself in unusual ways. For example, what possible evolutionary advantage would be gained by trying to help save a beached whale? The beneficiary of such effort is not even the same species. A story appeared on NPR some years ago regarding efforts to save a very large, very old bur oak in rural Missouri.[70] The story told of a 350-year-old tree that was succumbing to a particularly bad summer drought. When the story of the tree's situation reached the local paper and then made it onto the internet, people around the nation sent money and offers of help. What possible evolutionary advantage could this be to our species? One might speculate that charity and altruism provided some evolutionary advantage early on, but that the trait is now exaggerated or even misdirected toward evolutionarily non-productive ends (like helping other species). The fact remains that there is really no clear evolutionary advantage to charity. Even if altruism were unproductively expressed in some members of the population to the benefit of others or of an out-group, there is little reason to suppose that this sacrifice would have benefitted that individual and provided the one with the altruism gene with additional reproductive success. Yet this trait (that is, the evolutionary inappropriate sacrificial provision of support and resources to others) seems to have survived in remarkable numbers of individual humans. Conversely, if there is a good God, a God in whose image we were created, then charity may well be just one little glimpse of the likeness of the divine within us. There are other examples of what might be called "common grace" that come from religion and provide benefit to the religious and non-religious

70. "The Big Tree" appeared on *Around the Nation*, National Public Radio, April 2, 2013.

alike. Ideas such as human dignity, freedom, humility, access to educa-tion, and "inalienable rights" all have their roots in religious soil.[71]

Religion certainly has a bad name in some circles. In part this bad name has been earned by the errors and sometimes willful mistakes of religious leaders and religious people over the centuries. Even within the church there is a widespread acceptance of (and most often repentance for) the fact that the church is imperfect and has committed grave sins, and that being religious is not the same as (or even nearly as good as) be-ing good. The history of the church has been a bittersweet story, combin-ing deeds of heroism with deeds of shame. This mixed legacy may have led John Stott, a well-known evangelical leader, to write in his book *Why I Am a Christian* that he had "no particular wish to defend 'Christianity' as a system or 'the church' as an institution. But we are not ashamed of Jesus Christ, who is the center and core of Christianity."[72] But the Christian church is not unique in getting things badly wrong from time to time. Simply going to church does not make one a true Christian. As the old adage says, "You can put your shoes in the oven, but that don't make them biscuits." In a culture where Christianity is the underlying faith (as in Western culture of the past millennium), most of the population at-tended church, but this is no guarantee that they were all truly Christian. Jesus Himself often condemned the religious authorities of His day for being hypocritical, while commending those who actually lived out the faith prescribed in the Scriptures. Christians are not perfect, nor do they claim to be, nor do their Scriptures claim this for them or for their insti-tutions. If you would find fault with the actions of the church, please do. Often throughout the history of the church the most vocal critics and the most encompassing corrections have come from within, from self-right-ing and renewal that is almost certainly the work of the Holy Spirit. But rather than only bemoaning the failures of the Christian church, I would invite you to consider the failures of every human endeavor, whether religious or otherwise, then come to the words of Jesus Christ and find peace, comfort, and hope.

71. See for example Schaeffer, *How Should We Then Live?*; and Sunshine, *Why You Think the Way You Do.*

72. Stott, *Why I Am a Christian*, 4.

Is Religion Just a Crutch?

Karl Marx, the founder of Marxist socialism wrote that "Religion is the sigh of the oppressed creature, the heart of a heartless world, and the soul of soulless conditions. It is the opium of the people."[73] Marx believed, in effect, that religion is "the wrong answer to the right question."[74] This was not a critique of religion so much as a critique of the world as it exists, and of philosophy, which sought only to interpret rather than actually change the world. While Marx was no friend of organized religion in any of its forms, he set out primarily to address what he (wrongly, as it turns out) saw as the root problem—social and capital inequality. Although there really is no single definitive Marxist theory, and it is by no means clear that Marx would have approved of many of the ways in which Marxist socialism has been put into practice, people reciting this "opium of the people" quote are typically saying in effect that religion is a fiction created to placate the ignorant, the uneducated, and the poor. They are claiming that religion is only a way that the wealthy and powerful can manipulate the masses, by playing on irrational fears and superstitious notions of retribution and divine reward.

Is religion really just a drug to lull the simple-minded into complacence? Or is it, as some of the angrier atheists claim, dangerous nonsense that "immunize[s] people against all appeals to pity, to forgiveness, to decent human feelings,"[75] and allows "millions to believe what only lunatics or idiots could believe on their own"?[76] As has been discussed, much has been done in the name of religion, both good and bad. Dismissing all religion as a fiction created to comfort the downtrodden and placate the ignorant does a disservice to the positive force that religion has been in society and in the lives of countless individuals for millennia. To criticize religion for the errors made by its adherents without also crediting it for the vast treasures that it has provided is unfair and dishonest. The benefits that have been provided by Christianity and by Christian individuals and institutions have been underappreciated, while much of the worst evils done in the name of God, Jesus, and the Christian faith have been done by those who are either outside the faith or by those who have misunderstood the will and words of God. Even if you do not accept that

73. Marx, *Deutsch-Französische Jahrbücher*.

74. Thompson, "Karl Marx."

75. Dawkins, *Selfish Gene*, 331.

76. Harris, in "Sam Harris Extended Interview."

Christianity is true, the social justice and service to the poor that has been done in the name of Christianity is sufficient to defend genuine Christian faith as a net force for good in this broken world. And, of course, if Christianity is true, then perhaps its greatest sin is that it has not been more obedient in sharing the truth and love of Christ to a broken world.

There will be those who criticize this view as biased—that I credit every good thing to real Christians, while discounting much of the bad as not true Christianity—but this is not some sneaky way of cooking the books. If you are a citizen of a particular nation and you honestly evaluate the history of your nation, you would no doubt find many not-so-good things that have been done by the citizens, government, leadership, or legally instituted military of your nation. This does not necessarily make your nation evil; nor does it make the entire idea of nation states evil. Nor would it cause you to renounce your citizenship and adopt anarchy. Instead, you might investigate the motives of a particular leader or citizen group to show that, although they claim adherence to the laws and constitution of the nation, either their actual beliefs and practices were in conflict with those laws, or they were simply pretending loyalty to the nation in order to manipulate circumstances in their favor. This would not be a dishonest attempt to justify an evil nation, as opponents from other nations might charge; it would simply be an honest attempt to understand the errors of the nation you love and to evaluate your nation's behavior against the standards that it has set for itself (in its laws and its constitution). Christianity should be afforded the same opportunity to evaluate its own fruits, and in fact Christians over the millennia have routinely asked the same hard questions of themselves that modern atheists ask today.

By contrast, what if the atheists are correct? What if religion is, at best, an opium for dulling the senses of any who might stand up to tyranny, or, at worst, an evil enterprise that seeks to ensure its own survival and advancement by asking people, as Dawkins charges, "to switch off their own minds, ignore the evidence, and blindly follow a holy book based upon private 'revelation'"?[77] If we truly believe that in the balance religion has caused more evil than good in the world, we should by all means abolish all religion. We should not just hope that the inexorable march of human reason will one day result in the natural death of religious belief. We should allow no weak-willed nonsense about letting

77. Dawkins, quoted in "Richard Dawkins Hits Back."

religion die quietly, knowing that in another couple centuries Christianity, like the polytheistic religion of Greek mythology, will no longer exist except as a study of the irrational motivations of certain historical figures. If Christianity really is a net cause of evil, it should be stamped out, and Christians should be made to recant. Immediately. Does this sound like Stalinist Russia, or communist North Korea, or Sharia law as imposed by some of the more militant Islamic regimes? How have the rank-and-file masses faired in those regimes? We must insist that the atheists also honestly evaluate the fruits of their own systems and beliefs. It is not difficult to see that true atheism is unlivable, and that the fruits of this broken belief system are universally destructive to life and happiness. Countless philosophers have drawn this conclusion, including several honest atheists such as Albert Camus ("There is but one truly serious philosophical problem and that is suicide"[78]) and Jean-Paul Sartre ("Man is a useless passion, condemned to freedom"[79]).

Perhaps instead you will acknowledge that organized religion, Christianity in particular, has given us some good and some bad, and that it is not so evil that it needs to be actively stamped out. Perhaps you also believe that through education people will eventually be convinced that religious belief is irrational and unfounded and in time it will have gone the way of belief in a flat earth and an earth-centric universe. But what will be left in its place? As detailed by the examples in this chapter, the death of religion might leave us with little hope for charitable deeds in the future. Jesus' followers have loved and served the ill, the weak, and the disabled because Christ first loved them. Those served were seen to have value because they were created in God's image. Christians set up organizations to try to benefit more of our fellow men than one individual could do alone—admittedly human organizations that are therefore fallen and broken just as individuals are fallen and broken, but organizations that aim to share God's love by serving those who are less fortunate. Christianity's legacy is indeed mixed, as is the legacy of any human institution. But an honest assessment shows that, by the grace of God, it has provided more good than harm—quite a bit more if we discount the deeds of those who were obviously using religion for their own selfish ends. There may not be a gene for altruism, but there certainly does appear to be one for

78. Camus, *Myth of Sisyphus*, 3.
79. Sartre, *Being and Nothingness*, 744.

selfishness. Christianity is humanity's last best hope to confront the self-ishness of the human heart.

Finally, at least one of the benefits of charity is that it also benefits the one serving as well the recipient of that service. This is a point that the atheists seem to miss. When serving others, we are most like Christ, the suffering servant foretold in the Old Testament book of Isaiah. Service and charity are at least as much about making us right as it is about making the world right. This is absolutely not to say that charitable service earns our salvation. Rather, God has promised to set His creation straight, to restore all things, and He often chooses to do that through His people. He also does this in His people when they do His will. His will, summarized by Jesus Christ as the two great commandments, is that we love the Lord with all our heart, soul, mind, and strength and love our neighbors as ourselves.[80] An omnipotent God does not need our service, but one of the ways that we can obey the first commandment is by obeying the second commandment. Through service in God's name, Christians become more Christlike, changing both the world and their own heart. This is demonstrated amply in the lives of great Christians throughout history, and not least of all in my own wife. As a young woman my wife chose a career in physical therapy intentionally, as a means to serve God. Her vocation included two years spent in Kenya with Africa Inland Missions[81] providing physical therapy (free of charge) to children with profoundly disabling birth defects whose parents could never have afforded to pay for such care. My wife, whose willingness to serve is evidence of her beautiful heart and Christian virtue, is made more beautiful and virtuous by her hunger to love God through her service to His precious children.

Love Is the Answer

Therein lies the answer. Charity is both the evidence of our love for a creator God and part of the evidence for the creator God Himself and His love for His creation. This love is a gift of God, common grace made available to all, for which materialistic determinism has no answer. There have been those who have tried to explain love using genetics. To the materialists, love is nothing more than neurochemistry and electrical impulses that animate the human brain. It cannot be more than this to the

---

80. Mark 12:30–31 and Luke 10:27.

81. http://www.aimint.org.

materialists, because to them there is no transcendence. To the atheist, who does not accept or believe in anything that cannot be explained by physics and chemistry, the only difference between what you feel when you are desperately and hopelessly in love and what a dog feels when it licks itself is the number and type of receptors that are activated and the number of neural connections present in the brain. At the risk of being paternalistic, for such as these I have only pity. What a sad, pathetic comment on their worldview that something as beautiful and transcendent as love is dismissed as nothing more than neurochemistry.

Western culture is flush with allusions to love, and although it often badly misses the point, this is in some ways evidence of the common grace of God. Eastern culture, influenced by pantheistic religions and impersonal gods, could not have arrived at such a point. Historian C. John Sommerville has argued that many critics of Christianity are actually basing their arguments against the faith on premises given to them from the Judeo-Christian faith itself.[82] Specifically, Sommerville differentiates between honor/shame-based cultures, which depend upon a self-regarding ethic, and the Judeo-Christian tradition, which relies on an other-regarding ethic.[83] He asks his students to consider a little old lady carrying a fat purse down a darkened alley. In an honor-based culture, one would not mug her and steal her purse because picking on the weak is shameful, and nobody would respect you if you did this. In fact, defending the woman from attackers would garner you much more respect. This is an ethic based on the self, and on honor versus shame. In the Judeo-Christian way of seeing the world, one does not rob the old lady because it would be wrong, and one might even defend her because it is right. This is an ethic based on the well-being of others; it is driven by absolute morality derived from a good and just divinity, and charity is a natural product of such a worldview.

The Bible says that "God is love,"[84] and as such love really is the answer. Missing the point entirely, Western culture makes astonishing claims of love. While increasingly embracing atheism (without, apparently, understanding that atheism preaches materialism, in which love must be dismissed as simply a poorly understood adaptive mechanism), our culture routinely claims that love is all we need, and that love is the

82. Sommerville, *Decline of the Secular University*, 63.
83. Summarized in Keller, *Reason for God*, 62–63.
84. 1 John 4:8.

answer. Our culture is replete with such claims, from popular music to myriad references in film and pop culture. But what is this love that moves mountains and the human heart? Is it the love routinely portrayed in films that develops after a few dates and a particularly heated sexual encounter? Such "love" is little different than the mating practices of most mammals—no wonder so many people can so easily believe that we evolved from a common ancestor shared with our pet dog. But just as most mammals do not mate for life, the love that we see portrayed in film and in our culture often does not endure. With divorce rates, hopelessness, and suicide ever increasing, can anyone seriously believe that the "love" of our broken human understanding is "the answer" to anything? Even if you regard love as an "emergent phenomenon," more than simply neurochemistry and electrical impulses in your brain, it must be admitted that human love is failing—has failed. This world too often knows little of real love and has not recognized it when confronted with it. True love, love that can transform the human heart and human society, comes from a higher source, from a God who is love. "Greater love has no one than this: to lay down one's life for one's friends."[85] Love, charity and fellowship, gifts given from God, are both evidence of Him and a part of His answer to the evil in this world. Love and relationship are part of the nature of the personal triune God, and this God, unlike the god of any other religion, calls you to be in a loving relationship with Him.

Additional Reading

For more evidence in support of the unparalleled blessings provided by Christianity and the church, please see these excellent books. *How Christianity Changed the World* by Alvin J. Schmidt[86] is a thorough treatment of all of the ways in which Christianity has benefitted Western society and the wider world. *The Victory of Reason* by Rodney Stark[87] is a thoroughly documented study on the many bequests of freedom, opportunity, and advancement from Christianity to Western civilization and to the world. Finally, Vishal Mangalwadi's *The Book That Made Your*

---

85. John 15:13 (NIV).
86. Schmidt, *How Christianity Changed the World.*
87. Stark, *Victory of Reason.*

World[88] describes ways in which the Bible and biblical principles have shaped nearly every aspect of Western culture and civilization.

---

88. Mangalwadi, *Book That Made Your World*.

9

Christians Are Closed-Minded

An open mind, like an open mouth, does have a purpose:
and that is, to close upon something solid. Otherwise, it
could end up like a city sewer, rejecting nothing.

—G. K. CHESTERTON[1]

A HALLMARK OF CONTEMPORARY postmodern thought (along with the
belief that there is no ultimate or absolute truth) is the ubiquitous view
that religious belief is a personal matter, not to be discussed in public, and
certainly not to be shared as if it were true. Theologian Francis Schaeffer
commented often on this split in our modern culture, which is described
variously as public/private, facts/values, or rationality/faith.[2] Underlying
this artificial rift is the notion that only empirically verifiable scientific
facts are absolute, and that values are never absolutely true but are
relative to the time and circumstances. American evangelical author
Nancy Pearcey has called this division "the single most potent weapon
for delegitimizing the Biblical perspective," noting that upon accepting
this idea, "Secularists can then assure us that of course they 'respect'
religion, while at the same time denying that it has any relevance to the

---

1. Quoted in Zacharias, *Shattered Visage*, 2.
2. Schaeffer, *Escape from Reason*, 234.

public realm."[3] If the Christian religion is mentioned at all, it is usually only to list a series of misdeeds attributed to religious ideologues. Implicit in this (through the absence of any serious mention of the vast benefits wrought by the Christianity and in the name of Christ over the past two thousand years) is the notion that Christians who believe that they are right and who are willing to speak their views must be judgmental and closed-minded.

Removing all mention of Christianity from the public square is a mistake. Christianity is worth studying and discussing, not just because of the vast benefits that have been wrought in Western civilization by the tenets of the Judeo-Christian worldview, but because Christianity has influenced every aspect of Western art, literature, music, philosophy, and culture. Even avowed atheist Richard Dawkins allows that the Bible ought to be taught "because it underlies so much of our literature and our culture."[4] Studying Christianity does not force a Christian worldview on people. In fact, when treated only as anthropology at liberal universities, in the same way that Greek mythology is taught, it may do more to harm the Bible's influence in spiritual matters. However, an understanding of Christianity would help to make sense of the beliefs and motivations of our forefathers, even if we do not agree with those beliefs. It is impossible to truly understand the motivations of many of the great men and women in Western history (great scientists included) without understanding their deeply held religious convictions, just as it would be impossible to understand all of the allusions and references in contemporary literature without being familiar with the earlier literature to which it refers. Twentieth-century literary critic and Christian apologist G. K. Chesterton noted that "real development is not leaving things behind, as on a road, but drawing life from them, as from a root. [For example] the ancient English literature was . . . something more than European. A most marked and unmanageable national temperament is plain in Chaucer and the ballads of Robin Hood . . . That note is still unmistakable in

3. Pearcey, *Total Truth*, 21.

4. Attributed to Richard Dawkins. Dawkins has stated several times that the Bible should be taught, though, given his repudiation of Christianity, he stresses "emphatically not as reality. It is fiction, myth, poetry, anything but reality. As such it needs to be taught because it underlies so much of our literature and our culture." The Bible should be taught as a means of understanding English idiom, Western literature, and European history, which is "incomprehensible" without an understanding of Christianity and the Bible.

Shakespeare, in Johnson and his friends, in Cobbett, in Dickins."[5] The idea here is that English literature is what it is today because of what it is built upon. Similarly, one might say that Western civilization is what it is because of its overtly Christian foundation. One cannot truly study and understand American culture and history without studying and understanding the Judeo-Christian values upon which it was so obviously based. It is not closed-minded for Christians to oppose politically correct attempts to expunge all mention of or reference to Christianity in our public schools, or to ask that students be literate in the Bible and the tenets of the Christian faith. A truly honest and inclusive curriculum that would seek to educate the uninitiated into the rationale behind many of the decisions taken by the founding fathers might dispel the simple postmodern knee-jerk charge that Christians are closed-minded. To say that we can ever understand Western culture and Western history without understanding Christianity is to close your mind against an obvious and verifiable truth.

Is Believing Something Closed-Minded?

Regardless of whether or not we agree in all of our opinions and beliefs, understanding why we believe what we claim to believe can often build a mutual respect between opposing parties. This is often not possible in today's "cancel culture." An oft-heard criticism leveled against individuals of many creeds and associations is, "He is so narrow-minded" or, "People who believe [fill in the blank] are so closed-minded." Such epithets are often leveled against anyone who happens to disagree with the person leveling the criticism, and this criticism seems most often to be laid at the feet of religious conservatives. Is believing something strongly or with certainty "closed-minded"? If so, then is the opposite—being open-minded—simply believing nothing, or not believing anything at all very strongly? Or perhaps, if believing the same thing all of one's life is "closed-minded," then changing one's mind is a harbinger of open-mindedness. Taken to the extreme, this means that the most open-minded person in the world is one who believes everything he reads, and believes most strongly the last thing he read, changing his mind with each new argument or opinion. Chesterton commented that "the object of opening the

5. Chesterton, *Victorian Age*, 12–13.

mind, as of opening the mouth, is to shut it again on something solid."[6] Chesterton also wrote:

> "Man can hardly be defined . . . as an animal who makes tools; ants and beavers and many other animals make tools, in the sense that they make an apparatus. Man can be defined as an animal that makes dogmas . . . When he drops one doctrine after another in refined skepticism, when he declines to tie himself to a system, when he says that he has outgrown definitions, when he says that he disbelieves in finality . . . then he is by that very process sinking slowly backwards into the vagueness of the vagrant animals and the unconsciousness of the grass. Trees have no dogmas. Turnips are singularly broad-minded."[7]

What if a person who believes fundamentally the same thing all of his life just happens to have been right? That is, what if a person grew up in a Christian home, challenged the fundamentals of their beliefs openly and intellectually, and then came to the eventual realization that where he finished is not that distant from where he started (G. K. Chesterton was such a person)? Such a person is not "closed-minded" in any meaningful sense of the word. Many issues in the Christian worldview have been addressed before—right there in the Christian scriptures. For example, the Old Testament book of Job dealt unflinchingly with the problem of pain and suffering millennia before secular man thought to level challenges against God's goodness and sovereignty. There is, in fact, very little in this or any other book that is entirely new. If Christianity were based on fundamentally flawed logic and easily picked apart, it would not have spread and persisted in spite of significant challenges and even outright hostility against the purveyors of this great faith. If someone challenges their assumptions with an open mind and a modicum of intellectual honesty, and that person ends up concluding that Christianity is true, is this such a great surprise given twenty centuries of criticism, struggle, apologetics, and enquiry?

For everyone there are some beliefs that they hold sacred. This is true of open-minded people and closed-minded people alike. The real difference between open-mindedness and closed-mindedness is not what is believed, but how that belief is arrived at. The difference is that open-minded people think about the things that they hold sacred, challenge

6. Chesterton, *Autobiography*, 137.
7. Chesterton, "Concluding Remarks," 288–89.

their basic assumptions and presuppositions, consider alternatives, and arrive at a more defensible view, though perhaps not necessarily a completely different belief than the one with which they started. Closed-minded people typically do none of this, or at least they do not do it with any significant degree of intellectual honesty. A closed-minded individual will believe something even if they cannot defend their views, and even if some of their beliefs are contradictory to other of their beliefs or to their actions. In this regard, Christians do not hold the corner on the market on closed-mindedness. To be sure, there are many closed-minded people who claim to be Christians. In a culture where Christianity is the standard, such as the culture of the United States through much of its history, the greatest number of hypocrites and narrow-minded fools will be nominally Christian. This does not mean that Christians are always narrow-minded hypocrites. If we were to visit a Muslim nation in the Middle East, or atheist communist China, or the faculty of an elite liberal university, we would find the majority of the closed-minded (as well as a majority of the open-minded) people to be Muslims, atheists, or secular humanists, respectively. To conclude that all Muslims, atheists, or secular humanists are closed-minded based on this evidence alone would be specious; it would be closed-minded. In fact, accusing every member of any group of individuals of being closed-minded is a particularly closed-minded opinion. Unless you know someone personally, you cannot know if they have ever honestly and thoroughly challenged their beliefs. Unless you personally know a majority of, for example, opponents to abortion, you simply cannot say, "Anti-abortionists are so closed-minded" (as this author has heard some exclaim). Any such blanket statement is itself bigoted.

There Is No Absolute Truth

A sweeping generalization often made regarding religious belief is that it is a personal matter, and not to be foisted onto others. Implicit in this view is that religious belief, unlike science, is a matter of personal preference or opinion. The idea is that no one religion is true to the exclusion of other religions—that all religious beliefs are equally legitimate (or illegitimate). Underlying such opinions is a troubling belief, namely, that there is no absolute truth. Truth is relative, this view holds, and what is true for you may not necessarily be true for me. Many will confess this opinion outright, and even when this is not admitted, there are many who live as though this were true. A somewhat softened version of this fallacy is the notion that only empirically verifiable scientific facts are absolutely true—that values are never absolutely true but are relative to the time and circumstances. Such notions are considered to be the height of open-mindedness. Armed with this presupposition, the only people who can be called "wrong" are those who say that they alone are right. How absurd that in this day and age those who claim to be right are held to be wrong, while the only ones who are deemed right are those who profess that no one knows what is absolutely right and wrong. A detailed logical and philosophical defense of absolute truth is beyond the length and purview of this book, and has been undertaken elsewhere;[8] however, a brief discussion is warranted. First, it must be pointed out that the very statement "There is no absolute truth" is itself the statement of an absolute. If the statement "There is no absolute truth" is absolutely true, it contradicts itself and becomes untrue. But if the statement is not absolutely true, then it is false, meaning that absolute truth can (and does) exist. The very statement contradicts the faulty logic upon which it is based. Moreover, it is not difficult to conceive of several moral truths that are shared amongst virtually every culture, regardless of their degree of isolation from every other culture that might have influenced them. Specifically, every culture has held that rape and child abuse are morally evil. These truths have been arrived at independently in numerous cultures throughout history, almost as if they are an inborn bequeath from a higher power. In addition to these truths, it can be agreed that every culture shares in the truth that at least some people have innate value, and that killing without justification (that is, murder) is morally wrong. It is also universally true that stealing (at least from one's own in-group) is morally wrong.

> **Text Box 15.** By writing above that "at least some people have innate value," I do not mean to suggest that I believe that some do not have innate value. The Judeo-Christian tradition uniquely teaches that every human is created in God's image and has value. Rather, there have been cultures that did not believe everyone has equal value. One such culture was the Wuaorani tribe in the Amazonian jungle of Ecuador, which believed that men, but not women, have souls.[9] As such, the

8. See for example Schaeffer, *Escape from Reason*, 225–36.

9. The story of the first missionaries to reach the Wuaorani is told in Hitt, *Jungle*

women were treated as beasts of burden and as property. Presumably in such a culture killing or raping a woman would have been considered a crime as it related to stealing or damaging something of value to the man who "owned" the woman in question. Christian missionaries have a history of advocating for change when faced with such obviously immoral cultural practices. But if one holds that there is no absolute truth, one could not criticize a culture that found value in a woman only as the property of a man. One has no moral basis to criticize the use and misuse of children, child marriage, female circumcision, or any of a number of other obvious evils that many (including some atheists) have spoken against. When nihilist Jean-Paul Sartre signed the 1960 Algerian Manifesto declaring the Algerian War unjust, he was contradicting his own assertions that there was no ultimate truth or moral absolutes.[10] By what criteria could he expect anyone to accept his declaration that the war was unjust?

It is also interesting to note that virtually every culture has shared in certain absolute moral standards in spite of the fact that these standards are not always adhered to. That is, every culture seems to have an innate sense of right and wrong that is above and beyond what is routinely achieved. Every culture honors (or at least pays lip service to) fairness, virtue, and justice (however defined). As C. S. Lewis pointed out in his classic *Mere Christianity*, it is a fact that people all over the earth (and throughout time) "have this curious idea that they ought to behave a certain way," but it is also universally true "that they do not in fact behave in that way."[11] This second fact does not disprove the first fact; rather it gives credence to the biblical view of the fallenness of man, a concept that humanism rejects. The existence of this moral standard is just one more signpost giving testimony to the existence of a moral standard–giver. World-renowned geneticist Francis Collins has said, "the Moral Law stands out for me as the strongest signpost of God."[12]

Pilot; and Elliot, *Through Gates of Splendor*.

10. Schaeffer, *How Should We Then Live?*, 167.

11. Lewis, *Mere Christianity*, 21.

12. Collins, *Language of God*, 218.

If we agree that there is no absolute truth, we cannot judge anyone as being right or wrong. We cannot say that rape is wrong—the rapist may simply say that he had needs, and his belief system holds that women do not have souls. Without absolute truth we cannot accuse the Nazi's or Stalin or Pol Pot of any crime. In recognition of this, one of the legal defenses given by some of the vilest leaders of the Nazi regime was that they had broken no laws that had been ratified by their government, implying that morality is not inherently and universally true, but must be agreed upon and legislated. We reap what we sow—if we reject the possibility of absolute truth, we reject any rational basis for calling any belief wrong or any action evil. In fact, the very evils that atheists march out as evidence against the existence of God cease to be evil in the absence of absolute truth. We ourselves may value a person who was a victim of a crime and therefore seek revenge on the perpetrator of the crime, but that relies on our own personal sense of right and wrong—we cannot sensibly speak of the perpetrator being "wrong" or "evil" in any absolute sense, nor can we expect others (who may not have valued the victim as we do) to join in our sense of injustice or to even care. Without moral absolutes, it really is "each man for himself," and "survival of the fittest." Herbert Spencer, an avowed Darwinian and the one who coined the phrase "survival of the fittest," said that the "poverty of the incapable . . . starvation of the idle and those shoulderings aside of the weak by the strong . . . are the decrees of a large, far-seeing benevolence."[13] In the morality of the Darwinian, poverty, starvation, and exploitation of the weak by the strong is called "benevolence."

Finally, if there is no absolute truth, no absolute right and wrong, the concept of earning our way to heaven becomes even more nonsensical, and indeed everyone—Jeffrey Dahmer, Joseph Stalin, Richard Speck, and Pol Pot included—can get into heaven. Their moral truth may have held that they had a right to seek personal happiness at any cost. They were simply being "true to themselves." Every deed becomes a good deed; none are evil. If there is no absolute truth and no absolute right and wrong, the very idea of heaven as any sort of paradise becomes moot. There is no god, or at least not one with any sort of absolute power or morality in such a worldview, so any god that may exist would be weak and ineffectual—unable to impose his idea of right and wrong onto the rabble that made it into whatever afterlife may exist. Dying at the hands of Stalin, you "wake up" in "heaven" to be marched into Hitler's gas

13. Quoted in Schaeffer, *How Should We Then Live?*, 150.

chambers. This is no heaven—in fact, absent an all-powerful God and the resulting absolute moral code, any life after death that might exist would be just as hopeless as life before death.

More practically, what are some other implications of moral relativism on this side of the grave? Logically speaking, one of the fruits of a belief that there is no absolute truth is the end of logic. Saying that there is no absolute truth is itself a statement of absolute truth, revealing the absurdity of such a belief. Absent an absolute moral truth, there can be no courts of law. We may ratify laws by mutual agreement within a community (that is, by the power of a simple majority), but there is no logical basis for refuting one who claims to be outside or above those laws. Throughout history kings in many nation states have held that they ruled by divine fiat—that in effect they are in power because God placed them there. Corollary to this was often the view (put forward by the ruler) that they were not subject to the same laws and restraints as were those that they governed. Short of either disproving the existence of God or producing God to give testimony against the monarch, the rank and file had no recourse to discount the king's claims. It was truly a situation of "might makes right," in which the king did whatever he pleased. It was against such tyrants, men who believed that they were above the law, that the founding fathers of the United States rallied, claiming that "We hold these truths to be self-evident."[14] Note that the founding fathers did not appeal to the might of the colonies (no one at the time would have predicted that the colonies could win a war of revolution); nor did they appeal to any majority. They appealed to the divine authority of the Christian God. In a secular state such as ours, it may appear that it is a simple majority that determines the law, but again the founding fathers recognized a higher authority than human opinion. If morality is determined by the majority (rather than power), then the minority has no logical basis to call something "wrong" or "immoral." When Martin Luther King Jr. wrote his "Letter from a Birmingham Jail,"[15] the majority of America was not yet on his side, but King did not appeal to the majority. Nor did he appeal ultimately to any human-derived opinion regarding truth—he appealed

14. From the US Declaration of Independence. For the complete text of the document, see http://www.archives.gov/exhibits/charters/declaration_transcript.html.

15. https://kinginstitute.stanford.edu/king-papers/documents/letter-birmingham-jail.

to the Word of God. King quoted Augustine that "an unjust law is no law at all," and based justice squarely on the law of God.

It was against claims of one man's truth being superior to another's that the great thinkers quoted at the beginning of chapter 8 were speaking. Walt Whitman ("Resist much, obey little"), Ralph Waldo Emerson ("Whoso would be a man, must be a nonconformist"), and Henry David Thoreau ("Disobedience is the true foundation of liberty") were not putting forward some vapid notion of individualism and moral relativity; rather they were speaking out against the right of any one man to claim that he was above another. What the transcendentalists did not seem to recognize is that when every man's truth is relative, individual rights disappear. The truth that no one man can claim to be above another is based solely on the God-given rights of each individual. The founding fathers recognized this. George Washington, first president of the USA, said in his farewell address, "It is impossible to govern the world without God and the Bible" and ". . . let us with caution indulge the supposition that morality can be maintained without religion."[16] Our second president, John Adams, wrote that "Our Constitution was made only for a moral and religious people. It is wholly inadequate to the government of any other."[17] The founding fathers recognized that with God-given rights comes responsibility. We are each responsible to uphold these moral absolutes and are accountable to each other. Absent a belief in absolute truth, we can but descend into a chthonic maelstrom of decadence, depravity, and moral decay. And so we seem to be doing.

As is often the case, the Christian Bible considered the matter of absolute truth and moral relativism millennia before the humanists thought to give the idea a name. In several places in the Old Testament book of Judges, the author notes, "in those days there was no king in Israel; every man did what was right in his own eyes."[18] The book of Judges details a period in ancient Jewish civilization when the people vacillated between regard for the Mosaic law and times of apostasy and disregard for morality and God. During those periods when the people had fallen away, the book details numerous sins and crimes, some of which are astonishing in their depravity. It almost seems as though the book of Judges in the Old Testament should come with a warning label,

16. Lee, *In God We Trust*, 28.

17. "From John Adams to Massachusetts Militia, 11 October 1798," Founders Online, National Archives, https://founders.archives.gov/documents/Adams/99-92-02-3102.

18. Judg 17:6 and 21:25.

like CDs that contain explicit lyrics. For example, a traveler who fears for his own well-being when the men of a town in the tribe of Benjamin seek to rape and harm him instead sends his wife (who is also referred to as his concubine) out to them.[19] In a land where "every man did what was right in his own eyes," this seems to be a reasonable and ethical course of action—she is after all "only" a woman. They mistreat her throughout the night, and in the morning she is found dead at the door of the house where her husband is staying. The man, who feels wronged at the death of the woman he sent out to the violent mob, cuts her into twelve pieces and sends a piece of her body to the leaders of each of the twelve tribes. The book of Judges tells other alarming stories of theft, idolatry, folly, and generally immoral behavior, and is clear in blaming the people's rejection of the absolute truth of God's law as the source of this moral and social decay. If truth is relative, who are we to judge?

Closed-Minded Liberals?

At the risk of broaching a potentially divisive topic in a book whose purpose is most definitely not political, it is also apparent that the term "closed-minded" is most often leveled at conservatives, whether political or religious. The charge here may have nothing to do with how open to alternatives either side of the debate may be; nor does it account for if or how much the individuals have struggled to arrive at their position—instead "closed-minded" is simply the automatic charge laid at the feet of those who speak out against permissive views. This is not a new state of affairs. G. K. Chesterton wrote a century ago that in "modern Europe a free-thinker does not mean a man who thinks for himself. It means a man who, having thought for himself, has come to one particular class of conclusions, the material origin of phenomena, the impossibility of miracles, the improbability of personal immortality and so on."[20] "Open-minded" and "progressive" are not synonymous, just as "closed-minded" and "conservative" are not synonymous. Perhaps the more conservative person simply does not agree with what the other is progressing toward. Neither is being intolerant the same as being strict. Being open-minded does not imply that, following open and fair consideration, nothing can be adopted as truth. If there is absolute truth, and if that absolute truth stipulates that

19. Judg 19:25.
20. Chesterton, *Orthodoxy*, 131.

a particular belief or practice is right while another is wrong, it is not closed-minded to believe that. Conversely, a permissive worldview may actually be the more closed-minded view—one might wonder if the person with the permissive view has ever given fair and open consideration to opposing views or are they simply following the anti-theistic dictum "If it feels good, do it." Christians who decry practices that they believe to be immoral are routinely considered to be closed-minded, without regard to whether or not they have considered the alternatives, in an example of extreme bigotry on the part of the more "open-minded" (but actually only more permissive) holder of the liberal view.

When the Fox News network began providing news, people lost no time in decrying the detestable conservative bias in their reporting. Yet the other three main broadcasting companies (as well as PBS) are undeniably biased in the other direction. In his book *Bias*, Bernard Goldberg, a CBS insider and self-proclaimed liberal, relates specific examples of how liberal bias in "the big three" (ABC, CBS, and NBC) affected and sometimes even distorted the news.[21] Ideally the big three and PBS would have learned to provide a more balanced coverage of the news and current events, but absent that development, the existence of an equally biased network coming from the opposite angle is in some ways a welcome (though certainly not ideal) outcome. Unfortunately, individuals on both sides of the aisle increasingly seek out media outlets that match their already well-established preconceived ideas regarding politics, morality, and religion, instead of challenging themselves to listen with an open mind to individuals who hold different views and engage them in meaningful (and respectful) debate. This is just as true of those on the liberal side as on the conservative side, in spite of misrepresentations from the left-leaning media.

Education too, under the guise of pluralism, is hopelessly biased in favor of materialism and secular humanism. As Allan Bloom posited a generation ago in his influential book *The Closing of the American Mind*, higher education has failed democracy and impoverished the minds and souls of students by focusing upon the "open-mindedness" of moral, cultural, and political relativism.[22] Kent R. Hill, executive director of the Institute for Religion and Democracy, agrees, commenting that "Religion and values have been pushed further and further to the periphery in order

21. Goldberg, *Bias*, 2.
22. Bloom, *Closing of the American Mind*, 26.

to advance an allegedly neutral agenda of pluralism," while "The task of dispelling common myths about Christianity has been made more difficult as contemporary education has become increasingly vacuous."[23] In one of the most intellectually honest attempts at dispelling these myths and giving "closed-minded" evangelical Christians a fair hearing, reporter and author Mike Bryan wrote candidly of his experiences as a guest student enrolled in the religiously conservative Dallas evangelical Bible school Criswell College. Bryan openly stated his intentions to the college administration, who opened the doors to the school with no strings attached. What Bryan found, as reported in his excellent book *Chapter and Verse*,[24] was not a haven for fundamentalist hypocrites and their feeble-minded dupes, but rather a group of caring and loving but steadfast and unwavering followers of serious, reasoned religious tenets who were determined to hold the line against accommodation. Bryan's remarkable book is a most fair and open-minded treatment of evangelical Christianity by someone who is not a professing Christian.

Judge Not . . .

Perhaps the only Bible verse everyone today seems to want to live by is, "Judge not, that you be not judged."[25] In this day and age, being "intolerant" is the one unforgivable sin. Terms such as "judgmental," "intolerant," and "closed-minded" are used indiscriminately against anyone who does not fall in line with "progressive" ideals of unquestioning permissiveness. It is an unfounded knee-jerk accusation and being judgmental is not limited to the religious right. Those holding more extreme positions on either side of the political fence routinely pass judgment openly and loudly against adversaries across the aisle. This includes individuals of both political parties blaming every conceivable ill on the opposing political party. Political, social, and fiscal ills and complicated political issues that clearly started years (even decades) before today are simple-mindedly attributed entirely to the present policies of the opposing political party. Although this is done by both sides, no one seems to use the word "judgmental" more freely than liberals (political or religious) hurling accusation and blame at conservatives. Similarly, when the entertainment

23. Hill, "Sweet Grace of Reason," 226.
24. Bryan, *Chapter and Verse*.
25. Matt 7:1.

industry routinely and intentionally paints unflattering and inaccurate images of conservative Christians on sitcoms and in movies, the cries of "judgmental" and "closed-minded" are strangely absent. Conservative Christianity is reduced at best to a punch line, portrayed as being peopled by small-minded prudes, well-meaning simpletons, and loud-mouthed hypocrites, and at worst as the source of all of society's woes and a bar to the advancement of a liberated and liberal-minded populace. If Christianity is mentioned in even a remotely positive light, it is a weak, watered down, and liberal brand of the faith, spewing non-confrontational feel-good truisms and soft universalist pabulum.

But the history of the Judeo-Christian religion is one of confronting the errors of the world, and particularly moral errors and political misdeeds. In the ancient Jewish monarchy in Israel, the king was separate from the religious authority. It was the responsibility of the king to govern, but it was the responsibility of the priests and the prophets to speak on behalf of God to both the people and, if need be, the king. When King David committed adultery and then arranged for the woman's husband to be killed in battle, it was the prophet Nathan whom the Lord sent to convict David of his sins.[26] This relationship between religious leaders and rulers is critical in ensuring that the ruler does not develop a sense of being above the law, and indeed in instances throughout history where there was no priest, where the priests (or religious leaders) were in charge, or where the priests were silent or silenced, great crimes against humanity were committed. This is perhaps the primary reason for the grave sins (e.g., the Inquisition, the Crusades, burnings at the stake) committed in the name of the church during the Middle Ages—a time when the church was as much a political power (that is a king) as it was a spiritual power. It is interesting that many who criticize the church for the sins committed during its political reign (such as the Inquisition and the Crusades) also criticize the church for not doing enough to condemn the Nazis. It is quite true that the church was sadly silent during the Holocaust, a sin for which Pope John Paul II famously apologized in 1998 and asked forgiveness of the Jewish people.[27] Perhaps the church was not "judgmental" enough. The Nazi regime was so obviously an outgrowth of atheist ideology and Nietzsche's "morality" of the will to power that

26. 2 Sam 12:1–15.

27. Issued by Pope John Paul II in 1998 during his "Day of Pardon" mass and in an accompanying letter, "We Remember: A Reflection on the Shoah," and again publically in 2000 during a visit to Israel.

history has rightly judged the church for not speaking out more strongly against it. But it is hypocritical to criticize the church for not speaking out then while accusing it of being judgmental for speaking out against continued moral decay in the present. As Lesslie Newbigin has pointed out, the church is at its best when it is confronting evils in society. Newbigin writes, "missionaries have not hesitated, in their encounter with strange cultures, to attack forms of behavior, whether private or public, that they deemed incompatible with God's will revealed in Christ. Thus, in the Indian society which I know, missionaries have attacked such deeply entrenched elements of public life as caste, dowry, child marriage, and the immolation of widows. In Africa they have similarly thrown their weight against polygamy and the slave trade."[28]

It is also useful to note that there is a difference between being judgmental and being discerning. Imagine for a moment that you are the parent of a pretty sixteen-year-old girl. One Friday evening she informs you that she is going on a date, just moments before a motorcycle roars up in front of your house. A man about twenty-five years old comes to your door, and you notice tattoos of the Nazi swastika, various skulls and death heads, and satanic symbols. The man informs you that he is going to take your daughter out, and they likely won't be home until late. Seeing the dubious look on your face, the man exclaims, "Don't judge me!" In the spirit of being open-minded and non-judgmental, you should obviously let the man take your daughter out, right? Perhaps you see your financial advisor at the local racket club and overhear him saying some troubling things to a friend. With some concerns regarding his character, you investigate him a bit more and discover that he had been a lawyer but was disbarred for inappropriate conduct, and that he was also dismissed from one financial company for dubious dealings. Is it judgmental of you to decide to take your money elsewhere? Do you not have the right, when it is concerning your family, your finances, and even your well-being, to exercise a bit of discernment before making any major decisions? Now, imagine for a moment that you are a Christian. You were born in a nominally Christian family, but you made a serious commitment to follow Christ as a youth. Over the ensuing years you have weighed the arguments and evidence and have decided that you firmly believe in the divinity of Christ, the uniqueness of His claims as Savior, biblical inerrancy, and the fallen nature of humanity. You truly believe that no one

28. Newbigin, *Foolishness to the Greeks*, 95.

can be saved except through faith in Christ. With these beliefs making up an important part of your worldview, you discover that the local elementary school is teaching moral relativism that you fear will endanger and possibly even harm your child and the hundreds of other impressionable children in his or her class, and you speak out publicly against what you see as a wrong-headed curricula. "You are so closed-minded!" is the charge that will be made against you, and "What is true for you is not necessarily true for me." Perhaps. But what if, in the example above, you discover that the elementary school is teaching that African Americans and Mexican Americans are racially inferior? Not speaking up in this situation would almost certainly incur the ire of the same people who accused you of being closed-minded in the first circumstance. Why the difference? Since there is no absolute moral standard, and "what is true for you is not necessarily true" for that elementary school teacher, the only possible reason for this discrepancy is that "closed-minded" was actually code for someone who does not agree with the current politically correct "progressive" agenda.

Consider another example. Imagine you have a friendship with a coworker who routinely regales you with tales of his or her drunken ruts, involving the use of alcohol and illicit drugs, sexual exploits with multiple partners, and dangerous behaviors including public drunkenness, unprotected sex, and driving under the influence. You like this coworker and are genuinely concerned that they do not know Christ and will not be with Him in eternity if they were to die tomorrow. If you share the gospel with this person, if you even occasionally scold them for their inappropriate actions, are you not acting out of love, or are you simply being a narrow-minded and judgmental prude? Obviously sharing the gospel can be done in a distasteful manner, with a "holier than thou" attitude. But it can also be done with admirable intentions; done in love, rather than in judgment. This was the experience of Mike Bryan during his time among evangelicals at Criswell College. For the most part Christians are no more narrow-minded or judgmental than anyone else. Of course, there is a continuum of open- versus closed-mindedness, just as there is a range for any virtue or character flaw in any population of individuals. As Bryan was told, there is no "character within us that makes us superior to anybody."[29] Nearly every Christian I know would agree. Christians are not perfect; they are just saved. As a pastor of mine used to

---

29. Bryan, *Chapter and Verse*, 313.

remind his congregation frequently, "The church is a hospital for sinners, not a museum for saints." The church is most often at its best when it is doing the very thing for which its opponents criticize it: speaking out against and seeking redress for social injustice, moral decay, and political corruption—not because the church is perfect or infallible, but because it is commanded to do so.[30] It is meant to faithfully represent the kingdom of God, a task that it is doomed to do imperfectly, at best, but still one that is expected of it by its founder (Jesus Christ).[31] N. T. Wright has written that "The church is never more in danger than when it sees itself simply as the solution-bearer and forgets that every day it too must say 'Lord, have mercy on me, a sinner,' and allow that confession to work its way into genuine humility even as it stands boldly before the world and its crazy empires."[32] This is no doubt true, but the danger is only slightly less when the church is cowed into silence in the face of shallow accusations of "closed-minded" and "hypocrite."

To be sure, there are some within the Christian faith who are judgmental, and whose motives may seem disingenuous or hypocritical, but as with so many sins that have been laid at the feet of Christianity, Christians are not unique in this regard. People of all faiths, creeds, and backgrounds are just as guilty of this seemingly unforgivable sin. In his song "Good People," musician and former professional surfer Jack Johnson bemoans that lack of any good people on television shows.[33] The artist complains that instead we have a lot of what we sow, in reference to the biblical metaphor that we reap what we sow.[34] The song is a valid and cogent bit of criticism of our entertainment culture and of the mindless, unoriginal, and insipid sitcoms and "reality shows" that pass for entertainment. But has anyone accused Jack Johnson of being judgmental? Knowing that your author is a Christian, when you read my criticism of reality TV in the last sentence, did you think, "What a judgmental idiot" (or something worse), when in fact I didn't say anything very different or any less damning than Jack Johnson did? Not knowing either Jack Johnson or me, is it not judgmental of you to assume

30. Mic 6:8 says, "He has showed you, O man, what is good; and what does the LORD require of you but to do justice, and to love kindness, and to walk humbly with your God."

31. Matt 28:18–19.

32. Wright, *Evil and the Justice of God*, 99.

33. Johnson, "Good People."

34. see for example Prov 22:8; Hos 8:7; 2 Cor 9:6; and, most notably, Gal 6:7–8.

noble motives for him but more narrow-minded motivations for me as a Christian for judging the content of contemporary television?

Yet this is how much of the politically correct "progressive" world judges Christianity. The Midwest and the Deep South are often called the "Bible Belt," and the liberal elite on either coast routinely dismisses people from these areas as narrow-minded, uneducated, and ignorant. This part of the country is derisively referred to as "flyover country," with the implication being that there can be no really worthwhile experiences there, and certainly no meaningful opinions from people who live in these regions. Without taking the effort to know or engage them, it is simply assumed that "We know what they think, why they think it, and why they're wrong" before even giving people a chance to express and defend their views. To be sure, there are many in the Midwest and the South who hold a similar ungenerous view of the liberal elites on the coasts, but that does not make either position defensible; nor does it render those in "flyover country" uniquely guilty of the crime of narrow-mindedness. Being closed-minded is almost synonymous with being human. Most people need to be challenged to walk a mile in the shoes of those they neither know nor understand. Politically correct liberal curricula in our public schools make a great show of considering other cultures and other points of view. Sadly, they also often exhibit outright hostility toward the predominant worldview that shaped the political and religious freedom in which they live and work—namely, Christianity. Yet Christians are the ones who are singled out as "closed-minded."

The Moral Necessity

Many non-scientists, misunderstanding Einstein's theories of special and general relativity, try to extrapolate the concept of relativity to truth and morality. "What is true for you is not true for me," they might say. As a scientist, I used to object to this misuse of Einstein's theories. I considered it to be a misunderstanding and inappropriate extrapolation of Einstein's theory of relative motion to a convenient notion that they are not bound by other people's rules. But they are, in a sense right. Einstein's theories show (among other things) that motion is relative. If I am standing still, I can rightly say that I am motionless—relative to the earth. But relative to the sun, I am not motionless; instead I am moving, at once revolving and rotating. Relative to the center of the Milky Way galaxy, I am hurtling through space. My motion is relative to some defined point. I have come to think that the same is true with morality. If not defined relative to some fixed point, truth and morality really are relative. With Sartre we must conclude that "if a finite point does not have an infinite reference point, it is meaningless and absurd."[35] But the Judeo-Christian tradition has always related moral and epistemological truth to the divine absolute.

Aside from the logical flaw that lies behind the self-contradictory statement that "There is no absolute truth," this belief is unlivable. No one can truly believe the postmodernist notion that truth is relative. Certainly no one can truly live according to this ridiculous notion. The most self-professed "open-minded" and "progressive" individuals in the public square spew vitriol and condemnation against conservative Christians; but if truth is relative, if morality is a social construct, if nothing is ultimately absolutely true, their indignation is at best misguided and at worst hypocrisy. No. Their outrage is in fact moral outrage, based upon their own beliefs about what is absolutely right and wrong, what is absolutely true and false.

Francis Schaeffer used the term "moral motions" for the sense that everyone has that there is a difference between right and wrong.[36] This term "moral motions" is to distinguish this moral sense of right and wrong from specific norms (which can vary from culture to culture) and even from underlying principles (e.g., honesty and bravery are good and right, dishonesty and cowardice are bad and wrong). Schaeffer also noted that there are two basic views for human origins: impersonal and personal. In what may be called the "impersonal view," we evolved from an earlier non-sentient organism, which itself evolved from inanimate matter (atheism), or we sprang from energy (as in the pantheistic Eastern religions). The personal view of origins is that we were created by a personal God. As noted in chapter 3, if, as the atheists and agnostics charge, Christians have the problem of evil to explain, atheists have the problem of good. That is, why are so many good deeds done that benefit neither the individual nor their genetic in-group? But the atheists must still deal with the evil too—they simply cannot justify calling it evil. Although humans can and have done much good, man is also capable of great evil. Even a cursory reading of history demonstrates that humans are capable of terrible acts of cruelty and evil. Starting from an impersonal beginning (Eastern pantheism, or

35. Quoted in Schaeffer, *He Is There*, 291.
36. Schaeffer, *He Is There*, 293.

inanimate matter/energy), we can neither explain why humans are capable of both remarkable acts of kindness as well as great cruelty, nor derive any universal basis for good and evil. As author and literature professor Gene Veith stated, "If there are no absolutes, if truth is relative, then there can be no stability, no meaning in life. If reality is socially constructed, then moral guidelines are only masks for oppressive power and individual identity is an illusion."[37] Starting from an impersonal beginning, we can speak of what society does and does not like, of what is socially acceptable and what is antisocial. We can speak of what is expedient (beneficial to the individual or to the species) or what is pragmatic (what works for bringing about a desired outcome). But there is no good or evil. There is only survival of the fittest. In the pantheistic Eastern religions, good and evil fall away. Individuality is an aberration; the individual is out of line with the oneness of the universe, so ultimately the only sin or tension is failing to accept that your individuality is an illusion.

From a personal view of origins, however, right and wrong are possible. With Schaeffer we can conclude that "the infinite-personal God has a character from whom all evil is excluded . . . it is God Himself and His character who is the moral absolute of the universe."[38] We are created in the image of God. We are beings with individuality and will, created by a God with individuality and will. But unlike our infinite-personal God, man is finite. Our character is not without blemish, but we are also beings with value and worth, bearing the image of God, and about whom God declared "very good."[39] Knowing whose we are, we also know who we are.

As mentioned in chapter 5, the biblical story can be seen as a story in four parts: creation, fall, redemption, and restoration. Much has been written on origins (of the universe, of life, etc.), and how the creation bespeaks a Creator. Much less has been written on the fall. In a sense evil fell out of favor in academic circles in the Enlightenment (is it any wonder that now good is also falling out of favor?). Rousseau rejected the Christian idea of original sin, replacing it instead with the idea of man's innate goodness. Although even the most cursory examination of this premise would clearly and irrevocably refute any idea of the innate goodness of mankind (G. K. Chesterton wrote that original sin "is the

37. Veith, *Postmodern Times*, 72.

38. Schaeffer, *He Is There*, 300.

39. Gen 1:31.

only part of Christian theology which can really be proved."[40]), most people do at least consider themselves to be fundamentally good (even while calling out all manner of evil, real and perceived, in others and in the systems of which we're a part). In an insightful and unflinching critique of Rousseau's ideology, Camille Paglia noted:

> Rousseau's idea . . . of man's innate goodness led to social environmentalism, now the dominant ethic of American human services, penal codes, and behaviorist therapies. It assumes that aggression, violence, and crime come from social deprivation— a poor neighborhood, a bad home . . . But rape and sadism have been evident throughout history and, at some moment, in all cultures . . . aggression comes from [our human] nature . . . getting back to nature (the Romantic imperative that still permeates our culture from sex counseling to cereal commercials) would give free reign to violence and lust.[41]

The Enlightenment thinkers, beginning with Jean-Jacques Rousseau, denied original sin, thereby denying the fall. Instead, we have Rousseau's concept of the "noble savage." When they deny original sin, secular humanists must blame all evils on society (including organized religion). "Man is born free, and everywhere he is in chains."[42] But this view is untenable. First, society is made up of humans. If humans are born innocent and noble, how did society, made up of humans, become so corrupt? Furthermore, if evolution merely provides for survival of the fittest, the fact that society values some more than others can hardly be called "wrong." Second, the "noble savage" is a myth, unsupported by an honest reading of human history. The Huaorani in the jungles of Ecuador was a violent tribe that struck fear in other nearby tribes before any contact with modern society. In one of their first contacts with Westerners they committed five murders.[43] Other primitive cultures have had slavery and human sacrifice. The "noble savage" is verifiably a myth, wishful thinking, as artist Paul Gauguin discovered to his dismay.[44]

It is not just atheists who have tried to deny original sin. When liberal theologians (such as those of the so-called higher criticism in late-eighteenth-century German academic circles, and contemporary

---

40. Chesterton, *Orthodoxy*, 9.

41. Paglia, *Sexual Personae*, 2.

42. Rousseau, *Social Contract*.

43. Hitt, *Jungle Pilot*, 277.

44. Described in Schaeffer, *How Should We Then Live?*, 159.

"progressive" Christians) deny the fall, they too lose the ability inveigh against the brokenness and sin in our society. As Schaeffer points out, if man, capable of great acts of cruelty, is now as he has always been, we cannot escape the conclusion that the god who created him is also cruel. This is the god left to us by the deists. It is for this reason that the nineteenth-century French poet Charles Baudelaire declared, "if there is a God, He is the devil."[45] Denying the fall, we are left with an "unbroken line between what man is now and what he has always intrinsically been."[46] The humanist notion of the perfectibility of man is a myth. When the atheists deny the existence of God, and theological liberals deny the fall of man, they both lose the ability to complain about evil or to hope for salvation wrought by human hands because the evil is hard-wired into human nature.

Additional Reading

For additional reading on how the Christian worldview provides personal and public blessings in ways in which atheism and postmodernism cannot, please see these excellent books. *He Is There and He Is Not Silent* by Francis Schaeffer is a classic work of theology arguing that God is there and that He has spoken (in the form of the Bible).[47] This book can be read as the third in a trilogy of books in which Schaeffer argues thoroughly and convincingly for existence and presence of God. *How Should We Then Live?* by Francis Schaeffer is the culmination of Schaeffer's thought and ministry, detailing the practical implications for living out the Christian worldview.[48] *How Now Shall We Live* by Charles Colson and Nancy Pearcey is an outstanding treatise on how the Christian worldview should (and has) influenced the life and ministry of every Christian.[49]

45. Schaeffer, *He Is There*, 296.
46. Schaeffer, *He Is There*, 300.
47. Schaeffer, *He Is There*.
48. Schaeffer, *How Should We Then Live?*
49. Colson and Pearcey, *How Now Shall We Live?*

10

Everyone Goes to Heaven

Whatever path men travel is my path: No matter
where they walk it leads to me.

—LORD KRISHNA[1]

As MENTIONED PREVIOUSLY, SOME of the Eastern religions believe that
paradise can be reached by many paths, while many nominal Christians
think that a loving God should allow everyone to get to heaven.
Conservative Christians who claim that Jesus is the only way to heaven,
and that those who have not accepted Him will not get there, are seen as
closed-minded and bigoted. Is there reason to believe that heaven is an
exclusive club, or does it make more sense that a loving God would allow
admittance to all? Would a God who keeps some people out of heaven—
people that He Himself created—be a just God?

Probably everyone has seen the "COEXIST" bumper sticker. The
image was originally created by a Polish graphic designer named Piotr
Młodożeniec for an art competition sponsored by the Museum on the
Seam for Dialogue, Understanding, and Coexistence and displayed during U2's Vertigo Tour of 2005–2006. The original design had the Muslim crescent for the "C," the Jewish Star of David for the "X," and the

---

1. Bhagavad Gita 4.11, 51.

Christian cross for the "T." The most common version on bumper stickers also has the hippy peace sign for the "O," a variant of the male and female symbols on the "E," the pagan pentagram as the dot on the "i," and the yin and yang of Taoism for the "S." Although many have bought it and display it proudly on the bumper of their car, probably just as many have taken exception to it on social media. Why? Who could possibly disagree with the idea of dialogue and harmony? The original intention was likely simply one of getting along and engaging in frank and open discussion across the philosophical and religious lines that often separate us, something worthy of consideration in today's postmodern "cancel culture." Unfortunately, too few people on all sides of any issue take the time to listen to those with opposing views. But the implication of the "COEXIST" symbol is not simply one of getting along—the implication is that every belief is equally viable, equally true. Those who proudly display the bumper sticker have most likely never considered the conflicting truth claims of the different beliefs of the religions represented. As described in chapter 6, they can't all be true. Claiming to believe everything is akin to believing nothing at all.

Mike Bryan, in *Chapter and Verse*, makes just this point. It is not logically possible for every religion to be true. Bryan tells of American artist Mark Rothko. Mark Rothko was of Russian Jewish descent, having been born as Marcus Rothkowitz in what is now Latvia before the Bolshevik Revolution, emigrating with his family to the USA in 1913.[2] His upbringing was more secular than religious, though his father did send him to Cheder, where he studied the Talmud, at the age of five. Rothko did well in high school and attended Yale for two years before dropping out following his sophomore year. Under the tutelage of cubist artist Max Weber, Rothko began to view art as a tool of emotional and religious expression. Among the more significant influences on his life and art was his reading of Friedrich Nietzsche's *The Birth of Tragedy*. Rothko claimed that his art had the goal of relieving modern man's spiritual emptiness. He believed that this emptiness resulted partly from the lack of mythological images, symbols, and rituals. Today, it is possible to visit the Rothko Chapel in Houston, Texas, a shrine of universalist spirituality located on the campus of the University of St. Thomas. Bryan described Rothko Chapel as "the perfect embodiment of a godless world, the array of God-seeking texts [the Koran, Bhagavad Gita, Upanishads, Torah and

---

2. Breslin, *Mark Rothko*, 18–19.

Bible] on display notwithstanding, or actually proving the point: belief in everything—belief in nothing."[3] On February 25, 1970, Rothko's assistant found Rothko lying dead, covered in blood, on the floor in front of the sink in his kitchen. He had sliced his arms with a razor found lying at his side, and the autopsy revealed that he had also overdosed on antidepressants. Given their often stark contradictions, if every religion is true, then all of them are false. Trying to fill modern man's spiritual emptiness with empty symbols and religious words devoid of truth or meaning is doomed to compound the spiritual emptiness it was meant to alleviate.

Is God Good?

What then of the Christian way? A charge leveled by many is that the God of the monotheistic Abrahamic religions is a capricious and pitiless tyrant. To be sure, the wrath of the God (or gods) of any religion is a thing to be feared, but characterizing the Christian God as an angry and tyrannical God does not consider all of the attributes displayed by Him throughout the Bible, attributes such as grace, mercy, patience, and love. Misunderstanding God can lead to misunderstanding our relationship with Him and of His expectations of us. In contrast, there has also been throughout the history of Christianity those who lean too heavily on God's grace, mercy, and love. They say that because God is a God of love, He will not condemn anyone, or perhaps He will not condemn anyone who tries to do good and has generally good intentions. Such beliefs lead to cheap grace and a vague sense that because of God's grace all we need to do is try, and God will understand. Our good intentions will lead God to give us blessings in this life and then let us into heaven in the next life.

Both of these extreme views of God, as a cosmic Santa Claus who finds all little boys and girls good or a vengeful tyrant eager to smite evil doers, are vastly inadequate. Yes, God is a God of mercy, grace, and love, as many have claimed, "not wishing that any should perish."[4] Jesus said, "Come to me, all who labor and are heavy laden, and I will give you rest. Take my yoke upon you and learn from me; for I am gentle and lowly in heart, and you will find rest for your souls. For my yoke is easy, and my burden is light."[5] But Jesus also said that the Father "has given him

3. Bryan, *Chapter and Verse*, 70.

4. 2 Pet 3:9.

5. Matt 11:28–30. Note, as Dane Ortlund points out, this is the only place in the Scriptures where Jesus describes His own heart (*Gentle and Lowly*, 17).

[the Son] authority to execute judgment, because he is the Son of man."[6] God is a righteous God who does not abide sin, saying, "Behold, I will bring you to judgment for saying, 'I have not sinned.'"[7] God is a God of relationship, saying, "you shall be my people, and I will be your God,"[8] but He is also a God of purity and holiness, a Heavenly Father who will judge "everyone according to his ways, lest iniquity be your ruin."[9] He knows that the sins that we do hurt His other children and hurt us as well. As such, evil must be addressed, and crimes must be paid for. An innate sense of justice is part of the universal moral code with which humans are imbued and is in part the reason why generations of Christians (and several biblical authors) have wrestled with the amount of pain and suffering in the world. Following the first recorded murder in history, when Cain slew his brother Abel in a fit of jealousy, Cain asked indignantly, "Am I my brother's keeper?" God effectively answered Cain, "Yes," saying, "The voice of your brother's blood is crying to me from the ground."[10] The very existence of injustice cries out for redress, and to those seeking to work out a solution to the problem of evil, "Because I said so" is simply not a satisfactory answer. If we agree that man, through his own will, owns at least a portion of the blame for evil, justice is not done if that evil is not somehow paid for. This does not make God pitiless and cruel, any more than you would be cruel to expect a criminal to receive a just punishment for stealing from you or hurting a member of your family. God must balance His perfect justice with His perfect love. God does not sit in heaven with a "smite" button, waiting for you to mess up so that He can gleefully punish you for the slightest infraction. Neither does He ignore the hurt that your disobedience and sin cause to others, to yourself, and to the creation of which we are called to be stewards. God desires that we be in relationship with Him, but His holiness demands that sin cannot be in His presence.

Perhaps an analogy, albeit a weak one, is in order here. God is in some way like the very largest possible prime number. Prime numbers are whole numbers greater than 1 that can only be divided by 1 and themselves and result in another whole number. Thus, the numbers 7, 13,

6. John 5:27.
7. Jer 2:35.
8. Jer 20:22.
9. Ezek 18:30.
10. Gen 4:10.

and 109 (among many others) are prime numbers, in that dividing them by any number other than 1 or themselves results in a fraction, whereas 4, 49, and 169 (which can be divided by 2, 7, and 13, respectively, to generate whole numbers) are not prime numbers. The largest prime number known at the time of this writing is a number equal to $(2^{57885161} - 1)$, a number with 17,425,170 digits that was discovered in 2013.[11] As noted in chapter 6, God would have to cease being God to allow Himself to be in relationship with one who has sin in their life. If God is imagined as the largest prime number (again, this analogy breaks down in that God is infinite, whereas the largest known prime number, though very large, is still finite), then being in relationship with one of us would be like adding 1 to that largest prime number. With the exception of the number 2 (which is only divisible by one and itself), even numbers are never prime numbers, since they can be divided by 2 and yield a whole number. For this reason, the largest prime number must be an odd number, and adding our "1" would make it even and therefore no longer prime. The apostle Paul writes, "But he who is united to the Lord becomes one spirit with him,"[12] and warns the church in Corinth that "your bodies are members of Christ. Shall I therefore take the members of Christ and make them members of a prostitute? Never!"[13] Though God seeks spiritual union with His children,[14] His justice and holiness simply cannot abide sin. Just as a king cannot be married to someone who denies that he is the king and rebels against his kingdom, so God cannot have a true union with someone who rebels against His lordship. He must therefore find a way to balance His attributes of mercy, grace, and love with holiness and purity, all of which are integral attributes of His divine nature.

11. Chris Caldwell, "Largest Known Primes—A Summary," http://primes.utm.edu/largest.html#largest.

12. 1 Cor 6:17.

13. 1 Cor 6:15.

14. Note that this union is not like the Eastern sense of union with the universe resulting in a loss of self. The union with our heavenly Father spoken of in the Bible is a joining together of two distinct parts. The individuality of each is retained, like in a marriage. It is no coincidence that the global church, the sum total of all those who are or will be saved, is referred to as the "bride of Christ."

What Would Heaven Be Like?

What would heaven be like if everyone got in? Imagine that you were to die and go to heaven and Ariel Castro, the Cleveland man who kidnapped three women between the ages of fourteen and twenty-one and held them in captivity, subjecting them to imprisonment and rape for ten years, is there to greet you. Next to Castro stands Richard Speck, who systematically raped, tortured, and then killed eight student nurses in Chicago in 1966, welcoming you with a big smile. They lead you to a room to be sized for your new halo by none other than Charles Manson and Pol Pot, while Adolf Hitler and the founders of the KKK fit you for your new wings. In response to your obvious shock and disappointment, they explain to you that when they died, they explained to God that they were "really sorry." Although there is no reason to believe that we'll need to be fitted with wings and a halo should we get to heaven, this little bit of foolishness leads me to ask, do you really want such people in heaven? If the crimes of such people can go unpunished, unpaid for, can we really say that God is just, or even good? Perhaps only the really bad are excluded from heaven, but as was discussed in chapter 6, what is the cut-off in the goodness ratio that will permit entry into heaven? Has God set the bar low enough that we all will get in, and if so, how much like our idea of heaven will the real thing be like if Jeffrey Dahmer and Pol Pot are right there with us? Or if the bar is set higher, what of those who miss the mark by just one or two good deeds less than the requirement? What of someone who misses heaven by only a single bad deed, or someone who makes it in by just one good deed over the requirement? How can God be so arbitrary? Who then can earn his way to heaven? If God's justice is perfect, it seems that it ought not be arbitrary. Justice must be absolute, or it is not justice at all. God's justice must allow no exceptions.

Perhaps you do believe that we earn our way to heaven through good works that outweigh the bad things that we've done over the course of our lives, and the arbitrariness of such a system does not trouble you. But if you really do believe this, just how good are you really? I ask this not by way of judgment, for I am not the judge, but the question is one worth considering. Many people have a vague idea of being a good person (in comparison to the really terrible people we hear about in the news). If heaven is the default destination when we die, and some miss it by being bad, in all honesty you must admit that you have done some bad things in your life, and you must therefore also do at least some good things to balance out the bad deeds.

Of course, if heaven is not the default destination but must be earned by good works, again, an accounting of how good you've been is in order. So how good have you been, and in truth, what really constitutes good? Perhaps you think that you're good enough because you tried hard to be a good spouse and parent, worked hard (most of the time), didn't cheat on your taxes (at least nothing as big as the guys at Enron), and generally tried to do the right thing. Is being a good parent and spouse good?Presumably Adolf Hitler was a good husband to Eva Braun. She was an attractive young woman who could have chosen from a lot of men, but she stayed with Hitler until the very end, so perhaps he was good to her. Should being good to one's family count toward one's goodness ratio? Consider for a moment the fictional character Mrs. O'Brien from the British television show *Downton Abbey*.[15] In the third season Mrs. O'Brien shows kindness to her nephew Alfred, helping him to get a job as a footman in the house, and she is always looking out for her friend Thomas. So perhaps she is not all bad. Yet anyone familiar with the show will know that Mrs. O'Brien is a petty, scheming individual, who is continually trying to manipulate people and situations for her own gain. Perhaps you would like to have someone like her as your neighbor in heaven. It is also worth considering, when deciding if helping one's family members counts as a good deed to be included on the good works side of the ledger, that in many cultures nepotism (favoritism granted to relatives) is considered a crime. If the academic dean at a college where you or your child was denied acceptance was found to be giving positions to his family and friends, would you think his deeds good? Recall the college admissions scandals of 2019, in which several Hollywood stars bribed colleges and standardized testing services to obtain preferential treatment for their college-aged children.[16] Perhaps being a good spouse and parent (much less just trying to be) should not count for very much in your goodness ratio.

Perhaps you think volunteering your time or giving to charity counts toward your good deeds and will help to earn your place in paradise. To be sure, charitable giving is a great act of kindness and is to be lauded. But how much does it count toward the hypothetical goodness ratio? Note that the three major monotheistic religions require a lot more giving than the vast majority of people actually give. The third pillar of Islam is mandatory charity, or *zakat* (which means literally "purification"), and

---

15. *Downton Abbey*, created by Julian Fellowes (Carnival Films).

16. Kates, "Dozens Charged."

requires the giving of 2.5 percent of one's net worth each year. In the Jewish and Christian tradition, one must tithe 10 percent of one's gross income. Yet the average American gives less than 5 percent of their income to charity each year and only about a quarter of Americans volunteered their time in 2012.[17] Even within the church, about 20 percent of regular attenders give nothing at all, and 70 percent give 2 percent or less.[18] In the book of Malachi in the Old Testament the prophet, speaking for God, says that giving less than the tithe is stealing from God,[19] so even if you're impressed with your 2 percent or 5 percent, what if God does not consider this to be either good or good enough? Even giving the tithe may not be particularly good if you're giving out of abundance. In the Gospel of Mark there is a story recorded where Jesus witnesses wealthy people giving their tithes, followed by a poor widow who places in the equivalent of a penny. Jesus tells His disciples, "Truly, I say to you, this poor widow has put in more than all those who are contributing to the treasury. For they all contributed out of their abundance; but she out of her poverty has put in everything she had, her whole living."[20] Jesus seems to require more giving than we expect of ourselves, so perhaps your idea of how much charity is enough should be reconsidered. When asked what he must do to be saved, Jesus told a rich young ruler, "Sell all that you have and distribute to the poor, and you will have treasure in heaven; and come, follow me."[21] The young man went away sad, because, the Bible says, "he was very rich." Although it may be harder for a rich man than for a poor man to give away everything, it is certainly not harder, or at least it is not as much of a hardship, for a rich man to tithe. When Bill and Melinda Gates or Paul Allen (the founders of Microsoft) give large sums of money to charitable organizations, it makes the headlines, but even tithing when one's net worth is counted in the billions may be more about tax write-offs than about sacrifice. To be perfectly honest, how impressed are you when someone as rich as Gates or Allen gives a few million dollars out of their billions? Now consider just how impressed a starving person in India or Nepal living on pennies a day would be to hear that you gave a few percent of your five- (or six-) figure gross income last year.

17. https://www.charitynavigator.org.

18. Groeschel, *Christian Atheist*, 187.

19. Mal 3:8–10.

20. Mark 12:41–44.

21. Luke 18:18–27.

By these standards giving a few percent of your income may not count very much toward your hypothetical goodness ratio. If any portion of that giving went to a political party, what if God is a member of another party, and that giving is not credited to your goodness ratio at all? Given the untruths and backbiting supported by both political parties in the USA, it is not clear that giving to any political organization should be counted as a particularly good deed.

Even if the theologically conservative reading of the Bible is wrong, and we work our way to heaven, be careful when assessing your own odds. Before you smugly convince yourself that you are a good person and will therefore gain access to God's favor when you come before the judgment throne, consider all of the things you've done, as well as the motives for having done them. Nineteenth-century philosopher and anthropologist Herbert Spencer, who coined the phrase "survival of the fittest" after reading Darwin's *On the Origin of Species*, believed that there is essentially no truly altruistic act. He and other adherents to the theory of psychological egoism believed that humans are always motivated by self-interest and that true altruism does not really exist. There can be no doubt that truly selfish acts abound—we see them happening every day and from every person we know. If, as discussed above, God is not just a kind and loving God, but also a holy God, then no amount of evil can be in His presence. Rather than simply making up for bad deeds by doing good works, we must be justified. God's justice must be satisfied, as in a court of law. There must be justice, and that means that our debts must be paid. Justice must be done for the wrongs that we have committed. If the head of a charitable group that has done much good is found to have profited unfairly through his role at the charity, are his crimes ignored because of the good done? If a man steals from you, but you're assured that he is otherwise a good man, is justice done even if you never get your money or property back? How many good deeds can cancel crimes, and who gets to decide the exchange rate? God is perfect, and His justice is perfect; it must be absolute or it is not justice at all.

Text Box 16. The Bible is not long on details concerning what heaven will be like. Even those passages that deal with heaven are somewhat opaque. The evidence in the Old Testament is so scant that the Sadducees, a powerful religious faction during

Jesus' life, did not believe in an afterlife at all.[22] However, the
New Testament (and Jesus Himself) mentioned heaven frequently. Randy Alcorn has speculated that, given the presence of animals before the fall, there will likely be animals in
heaven.[23] By the same logic, most theologians agree that there
will be work in heaven. Adam and Eve were given work to
do in the garden before the fall,[24] and Isaiah 65 (which many
interpret to be speaking of the "New Jerusalem") states that
"They shall build houses and inhabit them; they shall plant
vineyards and eat their fruit."[25] It is clear from the biblical accounts of the afterlife that we will be aware, and we will retain
our individuality. Any sort of heaven one can imagine (other
than the depressing Eastern notion of the dissolution of self)
seems bound to get boring if we're there for eternity, though
Peter Kreeft argues why heaven will not be boring.[26] What is
clear, however, is that we will be in the presence of an infinite
God, so we will never exhaust our awe and wonder at His
beauty and glory. And He invites to go further up and further
in, because "the inside is larger than the outside."[27]

Who Needs a Savior Anyway?

There is another issue with the belief that everyone goes to heaven, or
the belief that we can work out our own salvation by being good enough.
If either of these ideas are true, one must ask, why did Jesus die? As
discussed in chapter 7, many say that Jesus was not God incarnate, but
simply a great leader. Lewis's counterargument was that Jesus must not be
called just a "great moral teacher"—if Jesus was not God, He was either
insane or evil. Whether or not you believe that Jesus is God, if there were

22. Luke 20:27.
23. Alcorn, *Heaven*, 374.
24. Gen 1:28.
25. Isa 65:21.
26. Kreeft, *Heaven*, 84–96.
27. Lewis, *Last Battle*, 207.

any other way that we could get to heaven, you would have to conclude that He was also an incredibly pathetic fool. If salvation is indeed based on works (or on "good intentions"), Jesus' pain and suffering on the cross were for nothing. The pain of crucifixion was so terrible that a new word was invented to describe it—"excruciating," which means literally "out of the cross." Yet out of His love for us Jesus went willingly to such a death. What a pitiful and pathetic fool He was if He suffered this fate for no reason. If Jesus was indeed God's Son, and God had provided other paths to salvation, allowing Christ to die this death was horribly cruel. Under such circumstances, if God allowed this, God Himself is either an ineffectual and dithering old fool, or a murderer, sending Jesus to die for nothing. Faced with the historical fact of Christ's crucifixion and the inescapable evidence that He did indeed die,[28] there are several possible interpretations. Jesus may have been a man who was simply wrong—a heretic who claimed to be the Jewish Messiah and God incarnate, either crazy or evil as C. S. Lewis has noted, and the resurrection was just a hoax; or He may have been just a man, but a particularly holy man who earned God's favor and was thus brought back to life as evidence for the way for us to gain salvation; or else Jesus was exactly who He said He was—God incarnate—and He died to pay the price for the sins of humanity.

If Jesus was just a man who was simply wrong (and either deluded or depraved), then all of the evidence for His resurrection would have had to have been invented by a group of ~120 men and women.[29] Of course the hundreds of people who were claimed to have seen the risen Christ were all lying and were in on the scam, and none of the Jewish or Roman authorities at the time thought to refute the evidence in support of the resurrection. There is no record, until well after the death of the eyewitnesses, of anyone claiming that Jesus did not really die on the cross, or that the tomb of Joseph of Arimathea still contained the body of Christ. There is no record of anyone claiming that the people healed by Christ had actually faked their diseases, or that the hundreds of people who witnessed the risen Christ were making it up for personal gain. This would have required a conspiracy that not even Chris Carter (creator of the popular television show *The X Files*) could have written. But surely, if all of this were a huge invention, at least one of the disciples who loved Jesus would have wondered what it had all been for. Perhaps Thomas,

28. Edwards et al., "On the Physical Death of Jesus Christ," 1461.

29. Acts 1:15.

often called "doubting Thomas," or cynical Nathaniel (who upon being told by his friend Philip that they had found "him of whom Moses in the law and also the prophets wrote, Jesus of Nazareth, the son of Joseph," replied, "Can anything good come out of Nazareth?"[30]), or even Peter, who wept bitterly after denying Christ three times on the night of His crucifixion, would have finally questioned a God who would allow His faithful followers to be slaughtered needlessly, and blown the whistle on any such conspiracy. But none of them did. Instead, these men dedicated their lives to the mission of Christ, preaching forgiveness of sins and eternal, abundant life through faith in Christ.

Many skeptics have claimed that there is little extrabiblical support for much of the detail in Christ's life, and in particular for His resurrection—they claim that since the Bible is a "biased source," it cannot be trusted without additional corroborating evidence from external sources. They are arguing not from any evidence against the New Testament accounts of Christ, but rather from the absence of corroborating evidence supporting those accounts. They then argue in favor of extenuating circumstances—for example, that Christ's body was stolen by well-meaning but ultimately deluded followers—in the complete absence of any evidence at all. And yet Christians are accused of believing fairy tales and nonsense. The accounts in the Gospels are not entirely without extrabiblical historical support, but the most important corroborating evidence is seen in the lives (and deaths) of His followers. They gave up much and gained little—in an earthly sense. They suffered scorn, imprisonment, poverty, pain, and torture. Ten of the twelve original disciples gave their lives for the cause.[31] If they knew that the crucifixion was a fabrication, at least one of them would have recanted, if not while being imprisoned or tortured, then to save themselves from being martyred for preaching Christ crucified.

Perhaps you believe that Jesus was raised from the dead not because He was God made flesh, but because He lived such a good and virtuous life that He was favored by God. By this reasoning, Jesus was just an exceptionally good and wise man that God brought back to life after an untimely (and exceptionally brutal) death as a sort of role model for humanity. If it is true that people earn their way to heaven and Jesus was just a man, one must wonder why He was allowed to die such a horrible

---

30. John 1:45–46.
31. McBirnie, *Search for the Twelve Apostles*.

death in the first place. Either He made a serious miscalculation and died a horrible death needlessly or, again, God is as sadistic or disinterested as the atheists and deists accuse Him of being. If Christ is only a role model of an exemplary life, He need not have died at all, and certainly not in the horrible and inhumane way in which it happened. Furthermore, if you accept this view, what sort of role model is Christ? A slightly crazy man who blasphemed (He claimed, "I and the Father are one"[32]) and was tortured to death—not a particularly inspiring role model. As noted previously, Tim Keller has pointed out that "Throwing your life away needlessly is not admirable . . . Jesus's death was only a good example if it was more than an example."[33] If we earn our way to heaven and Jesus was simply a man who showed the way, how are you doing in your walk as compared to that of Jesus? Perhaps you're doing better than your neighbor who cheats on his wife, or your boss who cheats on his taxes, but if we earn our way to heaven and Christ is the model, are we not all falling woefully short? If Jesus the virtuous human being had to give up His dignity and His life, suffering such a shameful death, what have you given up? I do not ask this in judgment, because compared to Jesus I too am doing very poorly. If it is true that people earn their way to heaven and Jesus was just a man and a role model, one must wonder what His life, and the manner of His death, say about how good we must be to earn our way to heaven. Perhaps we too must follow His path to work out our own salvation, apparently by forfeiting our wealth and our very lives to earn approval from a God who would exact such payment from each of us.

Finally, what if Jesus really was exactly who and what He said He was? If Jesus really was God incarnate, at all times filled with the Holy Spirit,[34] then we must admit that at the very least He knew (and knows) more than we do. He knows the way to heaven, and if we earn our way to heaven by good works, He would have known that His suffering on the cross was unnecessary. Some might say that God's grace is such that Christ's sacrifice on the cross is His free gift to all (whether they believe and accept it or not), but such cheap grace does not address the requirements of God's justice to be met and, again, it is no virtue to allow evil men into heaven and their crimes to go unpunished. None of these alternative possibilities makes sense. God's justice demands recompense for

32. John 10:30.
33. Keller, *Reason for God*, 200.
34. Luke 4:1.

sin. Fortunately, God's love caused Him to pay that price—we are "bought for a price."[35] "Christ redeemed us from the curse of the law"[36] so that we do not have to live up to God's holy standard of perfection; we have only to accept in faith the free gift of God's grace, living in relationship with a kind and loving Savior who suffered and died for us, so that we can have abundant and eternal life. Although at first glance the concept of justification by faith seems unbelievable—as Paul wrote "a stumbling block to the Jews and foolishness to the Greeks,[37]—in the end it is the only way that makes sense. It is the only way in which God's attributes of holiness, justice, love, and mercy can remain, and is evidence for God's love for His creation and a beginning to an answer to the problem of evil.

Some will cry foul, exclaiming, "That's not fair." Some will still blame God—even those who do not believe in Him—since by the biblical account He made us and ought to have known that we would fall. With Jean Paul Sartre they exclaim that there is "No Exit."[38] Even the great twentieth-century apologist C. S. Lewis wrote of his life before Christianity

> I was . . . feeling it something of an outrage that I had been created without my permission. To such a craven the materialist's universe had the enormous attraction that it offered you limited liabilities. No strictly infinite disaster could overtake you in it. Death ended all. And if ever finite disasters proved greater than one wished to bear, suicide was always possible. The horror of the Christian universe was that it had no door marked "Exit."[39]

But it is of course not true that there is no exit. God did not leave us with no way out; He left us with *the* Way.[40] As Sally Lloyd Jones writes in *The Jesus Storybook Bible*, after the flood, when God promises to never again destroy the earth by flood, He puts His war bow in the sky, and it is "pointing up, into the heart of Heaven."[41] If you want to blame God for creating you for

35. 1 Cor 6:20.
36. Gal 3:13.
37. 1 Cor 1:23.
38. *No Exit* is a 1944 play by Jean-Paul Sartre in which the three protagonists are placed into a room in hell to make each other miserable for all eternity.
39. Lewis, *Surprised by Joy*, 171.
40. John 14:6.
41. Lloyd-Jones, *Jesus Storybook Bible*, 44.

eternal life without your permission, go ahead and blame Him. Although the guilt for our own sin is ours, He has already paid the cost.[42]

What Did Jesus Say?

Jesus knew who He was, and He knew what He was about. He was (and is) one with God, an equal partner in the Trinity, present at the creation and "Ancient of Days."[43] Jesus said, "I am from above; you are of this world, I am not of this world. I told you that you would die in your sins, for you will die in your sins unless you believe that I am he."[44] He said, "I am the vine, you are the branches. He who abides in me, and I in him, he it is that bears much fruit, for apart from me you can do nothing,"[45] and He said that God had given Him "authority to execute judgment, because he is the son of man."[46] Jesus also knew the manner in which He was to die, and the inestimable benefits that would come of that terrible death. He said, "I am the resurrection and the life; he who believes in me, though he die, yet shall he live"[47] and, "I came that they may have life, and have it abundantly."[48] The word Jesus used here, "abundantly" (*perissos* in the Greek), implies an excess or overflowing, as a cup overflows when filled with more water than is needed or it can hold. This is the life Christ wants for you, a life that is overflowing. He does not require that you are perfect, or that you earn your way to heaven through good works—for which of us could? Nor does He require nothing at all. Although His "yoke is easy, and [His] burden is light,"[49] He told His disciples, "If any man would come after me, let him deny himself and take up his cross and follow me."[50] Although salvation is a free gift for all those who confess that Jesus is Lord and believe that God raised him from the dead,[51] Jesus

42. John 19:30 records Jesus' last words from the cross. "He said, 'It is finished;' and he bowed his head and gave up his spirit." The word translated as "it is finished" is *tetelestai*, a legal term meaning "paid in full."

43. Mic 5:2.

44. John 8:23–24.

45. John 15:5.

46. John 5:27.

47. John 11:25.

48. John 10:10.

49. Matt 11:28–30.

50. Matt 16:24.

51. Rom 10:9.

said, "If you love me, you will keep my commandments."[52] It is one thing to believe that the ice on a frozen lake is thick enough to support our weight, but it takes a step of faith to walk out onto the ice. Similarly, it is one thing to believe in God—James the brother of Jesus wrote, "even the demons believe that and tremble with fear"[53]—but it is quite another thing to entrust your life and submit your will to Him. It is one thing to believe that Jesus was a real man who really lived in Roman-occupied Judah two thousand years ago, but it is another thing entirely to pattern your life after the example that He set of radical obedience to God and set about the work that He gave us to do.[54] Jesus said, "For whoever would save his life will lose it, and whoever loses his life for my sake will find it. For what will it profit a man, if he gains the whole world and forfeits his life? Or what shall a man give in return for his life?"[55] Faith must go hand in hand with faithfulness. This is not so that we can earn our salvation, for we never could; rather, it is a demonstration of the authenticity of our faith, love, and gratitude for what Christ has done for us. It is a step of faith to believe that Jesus Christ is exactly who He said He is, and to accept Jesus at His word when He says, "I am the way, and the truth, and the life; no one comes to the Father, but by me,"[56]

The Gospel of Matthew records a parable that Jesus told His disciples after Peter asked Him about forgiveness.[57] In the parable, Jesus tells of a servant who owes an exorbitant amount (ten thousand talents) to the king. This amount (a talent was about twenty years' wages) has been estimated to be nearly $3.5 billion in today's money. Such an amount was inconceivable to the hearers of the parable. Jesus' point was that no one could ever earn their way to heaven. No one could pay the debt or buy their way to a right relationship with a perfect God. Given the super-rich we read about today, perhaps this amount is not inconceivable to you. Let me give a slightly modified analogy. One of the attributes of God is holiness. God's purity is unblemished by any sin or flaw. How much holiness and purity do you have? How much purity can you scrape together to pay the debt? In a slightly earthy variant of this parable,

52. John 14:15.

53. Jas 2:19 (ISV).

54. Eph 2:10 says. "For we are his workmanship, created in Christ Jesus for good works, which God prepared beforehand, that we should walk in them."

55. Matt 16:25–26.

56. John 14:6.

57. Matt 18:21–35.

imagine that you are the biological parent of several children, and you are thrown into prison. Instead of money, your bail is set as your virginity. Like purity and holiness, you either have your virginity or you do not. You can't have a little bit of virginity. You can appeal to me (I have a little boy of my own) and to all of your friends in your parenting group, but none of us have any virginity that we can gather up to meet your bail. Although it may in theory (though hardly in practice) be possible to scrape together $3.5 billion, all the biological parents in the world could never gather together any virginity to pay such a fee. Nor can any human being gather any purity or holiness to pay the fee. We are all unclean, and "all our righteous deeds are like a polluted garment."[58] Only God Himself has the righteousness, the holiness, and the purity to pay the debt of holiness owed for us to have union with Him. Jesus is not the only way to salvation because God seeks to be exclusionary; Jesus is the only way to salvation because He is God, and only God can pay the debt of holiness owed. If Jesus is not God, or if we seek to gain salvation by our own good works or good intentions, that debt will remain unpaid.

Additional Reading

For additional reading on the Christian view of heaven (and how to get there), please consider the following books. Randy Alcorn's *Heaven* is a definitive evangelical treatise on the biblical concept of heaven.[59] *Heaven, the Heart's Deepest Longing* by Peter Kreeft expounds upon the traditional Christian hope that death is not the end, but rather the beginning of new life in Christ.[60] Finally, *The Great Divorce* by C. S. Lewis is a classic allegory on good and evil and heaven; Lewis proposes that the gates of hell are locked from the inside.[61]

58. Isa 64:6.
59. Alcorn, *Heaven*.
60. Kreeft, *Heaven*.
61. Lewis, *Great Divorce*.

11

The Greatest Foolishness

How faint the whisper we hear of Him

—JOB 26:14

IF YOU'VE GOTTEN THIS far in the book, perhaps you have not completely discounted the possibility that the Judeo-Christian God is the one true God. Perhaps you've observed that any other belief system, including (and especially) atheism, requires at least as much of a leap of faith to believe in as Christianity. Admittedly there are still unanswered questions—more things than can be dealt with in a single book. Although there are within this book references to other more thorough treatments of many of these questions and topics, as noted in the foreword, Christianity ultimately requires a step of faith. But in saying that Christianity requires faith I most certainly do *not* mean fideism (blind faith). This faith is not believing in spite of evidence, nor even believing because of overwhelming evidence. It is more than that. This faith is taking God at His Word. When a person makes a marriage vow, they are putting their faith in the person they are marrying. They do not need faith to be convinced that their spouse exists; it is not that kind of faith. This step of faith is putting faith in the other person: that they are who they say they are, and that they will remain faithful to the promises that they are making. It is no coincidence then that New Testament refers to the church, the combined body of all who profess faith in Jesus Christ, as the "bride" of Christ. Jesus even used marriage language when He told His disciples, "Let not your hearts be troubled; believe in God, believe also in me. In my Father's house are many rooms; if it were not so, would I have told you that I go to prepare a place for you?"[1] This language of "I go to prepare a place for you" reflects marriage practices in Israel in Jesus' time.[2]

It has been said that apologetics is a means, not an end unto itself. The intention of this book has not been to prove empirically that God exists, that Jesus Christ is the Jewish Messiah and God incarnate, or that Christianity is the one true religion. Such a proof, in purely empirical terms, is not possible. Rather, it is an attempt to show that Christian beliefs provide the best explanation of reality. It is an attempt to show that Christianity is quite reasonable, and in fact more reasonable and rational than the alternatives. It is an attempt to dispel the incorrect notion that only gullible, uneducated, or ignorant people could ever be religious. Contrary to what Dawkins has claimed, the Christian faith is not the great cop-out; nor is it an excuse to evade the need to think and evaluate evidence. Christian faith is not the belief in spite of or because of the lack of evidence. In fact, in many ways, some of which I have tried to describe in the preceding chapters, Christianity makes more sense than the other religions to which you may have been exposed, and most certainly more sense than atheism. Viewed fairly and with an open mind, the Christian worldview coheres with reality in a way that the alternatives, including materialism and atheism, do not. Although Christianity requires faith, so too does a belief that, against all the laws of science, nothing blew up into everything and then organized itself by random chance into the exceptionally ordered universe we see before us. As G. K. Chesterton put it a century ago, "It is absurd . . . to complain that it is unthinkable for an admittedly unthinkable God to make everything out of nothing, and then pretend that it is more thinkable that nothing should turn itself into

---

1. John 14:1–2.

2. This language of "I go to prepare a place for you" reflects marriage practices in Israel in Jesus' time, when the bride groom would make arrangements with the bride's father, including paying the marriage price (the *mohar*), after which she was considered his betrothed. Before the bride and bridegroom would come together, the bridegroom would promise to come back for her, and until then he would go to his home to prepare a place for he and his bride to live together. For more detail on Jewish marriage customs of the day, see the article by Dr. Renold Showers, "Jewish Marriage Customs," http://www.biblestudymanuals.net/jewish_marriage_customs.htm.

everything."[3] Advancements in science in the past one hundred years have done nothing to make the atheist view of the origins of the universe, the origins of life, or the uniqueness of humanity more reasonable; nor have atheists been able to offer any plausible rationale for morality, or any source of purpose, meaning, or hope. Christianity makes sense of our lived experience in a way that, as I have tried to show, atheism does not. I am not necessarily arguing that it is true because it makes sense, but that it makes sense because it is true.

There is yet one last bit of "foolishness" to consider. I must admit that, with the psalmist who writes, "what is man that thou art mindful of him,"[4] I cannot fully comprehend why, if God is indeed all-powerful, and He is good, He would leave man in charge at all. In short: what in the world was God thinking? I am talking here not quite exactly of the problem of evil, but rather of a different though related question. One message in the Bible that is plain from the very first chapters dealing with the creation of man is that man is meant to have dominion over the earth and all the creatures therein.[5] Like Denethor in J. R. R. Tolkien's *Return of the King*,[6] we are stewards, charged to rule and keep watch until our King returns.[7] It is obvious that we are not God, and our abilities are nowhere near His. One truth to which perhaps everyone would agree, from the most devout theist to the most ardent atheist, is that mankind has done a spotty job (at best) of caring for creation. So again, if God really wanted the job done, why make us so utterly and unfailingly *human*? Why give us human will, which could be (and has been) used to rebel against His perfect will, taking down everything that was good and pure and innocent into a disheartening miasma of brokenness, evil, and sin?

Co-Laborers

The simplest answer as to why God created us at all is "relationship." That is, He sought to create beings with whom He could be in meaningful relationship. As described in chapter 5, the whole of the Bible is in a sense a story of God and His relationship with His creation; and as mentioned

3. Chesterton, *Collected Works*, 534.

4. Ps 8:4.

5. Gen 1:28–29.

6. Tolkien, *Return of the King*, 26.

7. Gen 2:15.

in chapter 6, the Christian triune God is a God of relationship, having been in perfect fellowship long before anything was created. Among His other attributes, Christians uniquely believe that "God *is* love."[8] He created us to be in loving relationship with Him. This was done out of an abundance of love, and not because of any shortcoming or anything missing in God. He is complete. As noted earlier, "It is no argument of the emptiness or deficiency of a fountain, that it is inclined to overflow."[9] God chose to create us to share in His love and completeness. Having said this, it is worthwhile to point out (as have many others before me) that love cannot be compelled. If I am more powerful than you are, I can force you to obey me, at least for as long as I am paying attention. An almighty God can force us to obey Him. By sheer dint of His power and glory He can cause us to fear Him. But He cannot force us to love Him. In his book *Godforsaken*, Dinesh D'Souza speculates that perhaps man had to be given free will in order to love but creating creatures with a free will leaves open the possibility of evil. For what is evil but an encroachment of my selfish and fallen will over God's good and perfect will? Although we were created in the image of God,[10] with will, personality, and the ability to love, we also have the ability to reject God's love. Following the fall, we all choose to reject God; we all begin from a position of rebellion against His will.[11] This answer is only partly satisfying. Personality and will may be part of the image of God in man, but we humans like to understand why things are the way they are. Indeed, this desire to know and understand is behind the development in the Christianized Western world of the entire modern scientific enterprise.

Although there can be much debate about exactly what "in God's image" means, it seems that at least part of it is that we, like God, have a will to create. Part of God's image is also the urge to understand creation and the natural laws, and to undertake creations of our own. In his benchmark book on spiritual discipline Richard Foster asserts that we are in effect "co-laborers" with God.[12] Foster's assertion is not that God needed (or needs) help with His work of creation. Rather, God created

---

8. 1 John 4:8.

9. Jonathan Edwards, from "Dissertation Concerning the End for Which God Created the World," referenced in Piper, *Desiring God*, 44.

10. Gen 1:26.

11. Rom 8:28.

12. Foster, *Celebration of Discipline*, 35. See also 1 Cor 3:9: "For we are God's fellow workers."

man and created work for man to do. Part of that work has always been the creation of things that glorify God, be it the written word, visual art, musical compositions, or things of beauty like a garden or structure.[13] This work came before the biblical account of the fall, demonstrating that work has a purpose, and that it is, like all of creation, "good." This creative urge is a part of the image of God in man and, among all God's creatures, it is unique to man. What's more, man derives a sense of meaning and purpose from his work, and in a way comes to know his God better through a job well done.

However, the question I am still trying to get at here is why involve us at all? The answer may possibly be best portrayed by an example. Many people struggle with the concept of God because He is most often portrayed as a loving Father, and some have had such bad experiences with their own father (or in some cases no experience, as their biological father was absent) that they struggle to relate to God the "Father."[14] In his book *Wild at Heart*, John Eldredge makes a compelling argument for the importance our relationship with our earthly father to our Christian faith and walk.[15] I was among those fortunate ones who have been blessed with a good and loving earthly father. When I was a small boy, perhaps five or six, I received for my birthday a Fisher-Price lawnmower. It was a small plastic toy that had a mechanism that made sound like a lawnmower engine when the toy's wheels turned. I would push it around the house pretending to mow. Though I have long since lost it, I remember a Polaroid picture of a day when I took my toy lawnmower outside and ran around the yard behind my father as he mowed the lawn with a real push mower. I do not recall for sure, but I suspect I got in the way. To be certain, I was not helping—my toy mower had no blade and could cut no grass. Instead, I was at best a cute but useless kid, idolizing his father and mimicking his behavior as I took my first steps toward becoming more like him. I was also a possible distraction, endangering myself, and therefore my father, who had to keep an eye on me. My father could have mowed the lawn by himself with less effort and in less time. Even when I got old enough to help out with the real mower, my father could have done a much better job than my first somewhat shoddy

---

13. Foster, *Celebration of Discipline*, 199.

14. McDowell and Wallace write, "Regardless of the particular religion . . . a warm relationship with the parents, and in particular the father, is the single most important factor in faith transmission" (*So the Next Generation Will Know*, 38).

15. Eldredge, *Wild at Heart*.

attempts to cut the lawn. So why involve me at all? Why not just do it himself?—it would have been easier and much more efficient to have me out of the way. I suspect that my earthly father had at least two reasons. Practically speaking, my father knew that I was growing up and needed to learn useful things, like how to cut the lawn. No parent wants their child to remain forever childish—part of growing up means taking the time to let us learn hard lessons. As any good parent or teacher knows, while it might be a lot quicker and more efficient to do for the child, it is ultimately more meaningful for the child to accomplish something himself. Secondly, and perhaps more importantly, I suspect it simply gave my father pleasure to have me out there tagging along; after all—he loves me. My wife and I have since had a little boy of our own. He too has a toy lawnmower, and he loves to "help" his daddy mow the lawn. At five years old he loses interest long before my real work is done, and I spend a portion of my time keeping an eye on him, making sure he doesn't get too close to the mower, making sure he doesn't run out into the street, making sure he is safe. Like my father before me, I could cut the lawn a lot more efficiently if my boy weren't there "helping," but I wouldn't change it for the world. I delight in my son wanting to be like his daddy.

In the same way, I suspect that it simply gives God pleasure to see us, even in our failing, broken way, trying to emulate Him. In another story from my own youth, I recall a day in the second or third grade when, after a fire safety lesson in school, I came home and asked my father to show me how to reset a blown fuse. I remember he was both a bit surprised that I knew what a fuse was and very pleased to teach his son a skill. Our God, the ultimate loving Father, delights to see us trying to model His behavior. Our attempts are admittedly halting, broken, and incomplete, but perhaps they are pleasing to God nonetheless. Perhaps this is what Jesus meant when He told His disciples, "Unless you change and become like little children, you will never enter the kingdom of heaven."[16]

God could have created a perfect world that did not need stewards at all. He could have created a perfect world and excluded any and all possibility that the fall could have happened. He would have had perfectly happy, perfectly innocent, and perhaps perfectly robotic children. For reasons that sometimes escape me, God chose to allow us to lose our innocence, just as a child grows up into an adolescent. But adolescents do not stay that way for ever—they eventually go on to full maturity. Just

16. Matt 18:3 (NIV).

as my earthly father and I now have a closer, more enjoyable (for me anyway—I hope he would agree) relationship than we did when I was a child, it may be that God's plan was for us to grow into something even more than that which we were initially created. It might seem easier to love God if we were in a nearly perfect, sinless Eden, with all of our needs provided for and every evil banished from ever approaching us. But perhaps, just as the first few chapters of the book of Job hint, God is acknowledging that the proof of true love is not that it is given when times are good, but that it is given even when times are difficult. When the tempter considers Job in the beginning of that book, he says to God, "Does Job fear God for naught? Hast thou not put a hedge about him and his house and all that he has on every side? Thou hast blessed the work of his hands, and his possessions have increased in the land."[17] The tempter is saying, in effect, "Of course Job loves you—he has it so good, who wouldn't love you?" Perhaps God desires for us to love as He does, through thick and through thin, for better or for worse. That is true love. That is certainly what I wanted when I was looking for a wife. If the church is indeed the bride of Christ, why would Jesus settle for anything less?

Where Was God When . . . ?

If God is truly seeking relationship with His creation, why does He sometimes seem to be so hard to find? It is said that atheist Bertrand Russell was asked what he would say to God if, upon his death, Russell were to come before Him. Russell is said to have replied that he would ask God why the evidence for His existence was so little. As I have tried to summarize in the preceding chapters, the evidence is not nearly so little or so weak as some might presume, but there is indeed a puzzle with respect to this apparent hiddenness of God. Even in the Bible God seems in some ways to progressively disappear.[18] This disappearance seems apparent on a small and on a large scale, in personal longing for meaning and purpose, and in almost daily global catastrophes that cause suffering and loss. On a small scale it is evident by the number of books written to address the questions of where God is in our suffering, and whether or not God answers prayer. On the large scale, it is apparent most often after some great tragedy, when people ask publicly, "Where was God? Why did

---

17. Job 1:9–10.
18. See for example Friedman, *Disappearance of God*.

He allow this to happen?" After the terrible events of September 11, 2001, many people sorrowfully, angrily, or indignantly wondered aloud where God was to be found in all the tragedy. At the risk of seeming judgmental, such questions were most often asked by agnostics, nominal Christians, and even atheists with "an axe to grind" with the God in whom they claim not to believe. Again, at the risk of seeming judgmental, do these same questioners ever think to look for God when everything goes well? Most likely they only curse Him when things go wrong, but do not thank or acknowledge Him when they go well; but then, when was the last time you thanked your earthly parents for all that they did for you?

None of this answers the question, "Where was God when . . . ?" At least part of the answer to this question is that God really does seem to expect His people—the church—to be His ambassadors on earth. We are called to be His hands and feet. Teresa of Avila, a Spanish saint from the fourteenth century who entered a Carmelite convent when she was eighteen, wrote, "Christ has no body but yours, No hands, no feet on earth but yours."[19] It is for this reason that Jesus said that He would send the Holy Spirit; to empower His church—His body here on earth—so that they could go into Jerusalem, and Judea and Samaria, and to the ends of the earth to be His witnesses.[20] Serving as a witness to Christ includes loving our neighbor, working toward justice, and providing for those in need. In a parable Jesus told concerning the kingdom of heaven, Jesus said that upon reaching the afterlife, God would say to those on His right hand, "as you did it to one of the least of these my brethren, you did it to me," where "it" refers to feeding the hungry and giving drink to the thirsty, welcoming strangers, clothing those in need, and visiting the sick and those in prison.[21] Fulfilling the commands to serve as Christ's witnesses and love our neighbors includes sharing with them the truth of the gospel, even when it is unwelcome. Although Jesus most certainly did not forget about earthly needs, His foremost concern was to redeem His beloved, and to restore all things. His concern was the salvation of our eternal souls. He has charged His church to be His witnesses to this truth.

I say that this is only part of the answer to the question, "Where was God when . . . ?" because of the obvious failures of the church through the millennia. As noted in chapter 8, the record of the Christian church is

---

19. The poem "Christ Has No Body" is attributed to Teresa of Avila (1515–1582).

20. Acts 1:8.

21. Matt 25:31–46.

spotty at best. Although not nearly so uniformly bad as her most ardent critics would have you believe, neither is it even remotely as good as we would wish. Although according to contemporary culture the church's greatest sin seems to be being closed-minded and judgmental, in fact its greatest sins are failing to be Christ's witnesses here on earth and making disciples of all nations, as Christ told us to do,[22] and failing to "go and do likewise," as Christ told the lawyer to whom He told the parable of the Good Samaritan.[23] As pastor and author Erwin McManus has said, "The church does not exist for us. We are the church, and we exist for the world."[24] Max Lucado has written, "Faith is at its best, not in three-piece suits on Sunday mornings or at V.B.S. on summer days, but at hospital bedsides, cancer wards, and cemeteries."[25] In spite of its obvious shortcomings, the fact remains that the church is called to be the hands and feet of Christ here on earth until His return. In spite of its obvious shortcomings, the church, empowered by God's Holy Spirit, truly is the last best hope for positive change in the world. After the atrocities, violence, and terror of the twentieth century and the first twenty years of this century, can anyone truly believe that any merely human institution can possibly save us? Do you really believe that either political party will usher in a new era of wholeness and truth?

Perhaps, taking the analogy of an earthly father-child relationship farther still, just as a father must step back to allow his child to make his own choices and learn from his own mistakes, so too perhaps God is slowly stepping back to allow us to make our own choices. If God truly does seek to be in a loving relationship with His children, He cannot awe us into love—it almost seems as though He cannot (or will not) even awe us into obedience. One clear conclusion after reading the Old Testament is that a very real and present God does not necessarily excite love and devotion, or even obedience. During those times in the Old Testament when God's presence was most palpable, the people were no less likely to ignore His Law and turn toward other gods. The Israelites during their exodus from Egypt saw the Shekinah glory of God every day over the tabernacle in the wilderness,[26] and after Solomon's blessing they

22. Matt 28:19.

23. Luke 10:25–37.

24. Cited in Groeschel, *Christian Atheist*, 220.

25. Lucado, *No Wonder They Call Him the Savior*, 77.

26. See for example Exod 33.

saw it descend upon the temple in Jerusalem,[27] but they continued to rebel against Him and turn to false idols and false teachings. For reasons known only to God, He allows us to exert our will, perhaps until such time as things here are so badly broken that more of us will turn to Him and cry out, "Even so, come Lord Jesus." One thing at least is clear, it is part of our human nature that good times rarely cause us to turn in gratitude to the source of those blessings.

It is not uncommon to see the church portrayed as little more than a fund-raising machine for a giant propaganda effort. In the band U2's Rattle and Hum World Tour, Bono criticized televangelists and exclaimed to the audience that "the God I believe in ain't short of cash, mister."[28] Of course the crowd went wild, screaming their approval of this indictment of "closed-minded" and "judgmental" Christianity. Bono was right; God is not short of cash. He "owns the cattle on a thousand hills."[29] He could create cash from nothing. He could fix all the problems of the world such that we would not need to give cash to charitable organizations. But He chooses to work in us and through us. We are blessed to be a blessing— just as God told Abraham, "I will make of you a great nation, and I will bless you, and make your name great, so that you will be a blessing."[30] I do not mean to criticize Bono, a charitable man who has done much good with his wealth and fame. Of course, he makes a valid point that many of the most public and vocal televangelists, some of whom are an embarrassment to most rank-and-file Christians, seem to be little more than snake oil salesmen and shysters. But this is not real Christianity as taught to us in God's Word and by the words and life of Jesus Christ Himself. The media is no more interested in showing real, true Christianity than they are in showing anything that does not support their own cynical agenda. Mike Bryan writes, "The press does stories on Christians like Pat Robertson and Jim Bakker mainly in order to denigrate them and, by extension, their beliefs."[31] The media often selectively shows only the most vocal and controversial groups claiming to speak for Christianity and trumpets Christianity's failures and foibles. It is easy to criticize the lunatic fringe of any movement, but this is not an honest assessment

27. 2 Chr 7:1.

28. Bono, from U2's tour supporting the album *Rattle and Hum* (Island, 1988).

29. Ps 50:10.

30. Gen 12:2.

31. Bryan, *Chapter and Verse*, 9.

of that movement; nor is it a fair treatment of its influence. God does not always step in and make things happen; or rather, in many cases, it seems as if He waits until one of His own takes a step of faith, and then He blesses their efforts, often beyond their own abilities. Furthermore, although God is indeed not short of cash, His ambassadors often are. This is in part because too few of His followers are tithing, and too few of us humans are even saved to begin with (again, because we in the church are not doing our job). Yet some still do His will. As noted in chapter 8, millions of individual Christians, and Christian organizations, in big and small ways, are quietly carrying out the mission that was given by Christ to His followers. Since Jesus sent the Holy Spirit, there have been some who have caught His vision and continued the work that He began of serving and making disciples of all nations. Thanks be to God, because it is truly frightening to imagine the state our planet would be in except for those faithful few.

You and Love and I

In 2009 the musical group the Avett Brothers released a pretty but somewhat sad love song called "I and Love and You." In the refrain, the singer sings that these three words have become hard to say. Although the song is about difficulties in a human relationship that has failed to live up to expectations for a perfect and fulfilling love, as so many songs are, when I first heard the song, my thoughts went in a different direction. Taken in reverse order, with the "You" being God, what happens when we cannot or will not believe in the divine "You"? Absent a transcendent reality—absent a spiritual realm over and above the merely physical world of our immediate experience—there is no God to whom we can address our worries and our cares and our longings. There is no divine object for our spiritual longings. There is no divine "You" with whom we can be in relationship.

Furthermore, absent the triune Christian God, love is at best an afterthought, mere neurochemistry. Love—indeed, all emotion—is merely a sensation related to electrochemical impulses firing within our brains that has evolved for some yet-to-be-determined adaptive advantage. In response to some external stimuli, neurotransmitters are released and bind to their cognate receptors. The signal is transmitted across synapses triggering additional chemical changes resulting in the appearance of love, or peace, or consciousness. Love is not real; it is nothing more than a release of the neuropeptide oxytocin.[32] It is an adaptation in response to the complex social hierarchies typical of the most advanced primate species. Without the divine "You," there is no "love," and every love song, every sonnet, every moving act of love is foolishness—"A tale told by an idiot . . . signifying nothing."[33]

What's more, if the material world is all that there is, what has been referred to as the "mind-brain problem" comes to the fore. As distinguished Johns Hopkins psychiatrist Paul McHugh points out, "we do not have a clue how a material object—even one as complicated as our brain—can produce the light of consciousness in which we experience our thoughts, carry out our enterprises, and in so many different ways conduct our lives."[34] Many have concluded that consciousness is merely the result of the extremely complex neurological activity in the human brain, and thus the individual self is a myth. As Julian Baggini said, "There isn't actually a 'you' at the heart of all of these experiences."[35] Without the transcendent, we may search hard and long for a "ghost in the machine," but there is none. There is only deterministic nature, and nature cares only for species, never individuals.[36]

> Dumbed down and numbed by time and age
> Your dreams that catch the world, a cage
> The highway sets the traveler's stage
> All exits look the same.
> Three words that became hard to say:
> I and love and you.[37]

Without the divine "You," three words become impossible to say: "You" and "love" and "I." Truly the triune God of the Bible is the great I Am, the Creator and Sustainer of life and the universe, a merciful Judge, a beautiful Savior, a wonderful Counselor, and a loving Father. The triune God of Christianity is unique among all other belief systems in providing a cogent and cohesive rationale for existence, order, scientific enquiry, consciousness, morality, forgiveness, love, and relationship. He cannot be

---

32. Carter and Porges, "Biochemistry of Love," 12–16.

33. Excerpted from William Shakespeare, *MacBeth*, act 5, scene 5, lines 16–27.

34. McHugh, *Mind Has Mountains*, 201.

35. Baggini, "Is There a Real You?"

36. Paglia, *Sexual Personae*, 10.

37. Excerpt from the Avett Brothers, "I and Love and You," from the album *I and Love and You* (American Recordings, 2009).

proved by empirical methods, but neither can He be denied by anyone who honestly evaluates the evidence. Jesus Christ, the second person of the Trinity, says, "I am the way, and the truth, and the life; no one comes to the Father, but by me."[38] All that it takes to know this God is to believe something that makes more sense than any of the alternatives—to accept Him at His Word.

Creation, Fall, Redemption, Restoration

Put simply, Christianity makes sense. The evidence of history and of reason are witnesses to the truth of the Christian faith. "He is no fool who gives what he cannot keep to gain that which he cannot lose."[39] He is no fool who clings to a religious faith that, at first blush, may seem madly irrational, but is in fact more internally consistent than any of the alternatives. Although there are still hard questions in a Christian worldview, these are no more than with an atheist worldview. Although there are some spectacular and difficult beliefs that one must accept in order to be an adherent of the Christian faith, there are many more challenging and contradictory things that must be accepted to be an atheist. Although belief in an admittedly unfathomable creator God may be difficult, an honest assessment reveals that all of the alternatives are no less incredible.

The Christian narrative is experientially true. The Christian worldview, based upon the Bible, can be summarized as a story in four parts: creation, fall, redemption, and restoration. These four parts cohere and make sense of the world as it actually is. Although the creation account in Genesis 1 and 2 (or the fall in Genesis 3) cannot be proven empirically, neither can the creation myths of any religion (including atheism) be empirically proved or disproved—we simply were not there. Whether it is a monotheistic God, a pantheistic universal force, or inanimate matter and energy, something is eternal. Something has always been there, for if there was a beginning, then there was a Beginner. The alternative—the

38. John 14:6.

39. This quote is most often attributed to Jim Elliot, a missionary and martyr who gave his life trying to share the gospel with the reclusive and violent Huaorani (also called "Auca," the Quechua word for "savage") tribe (see for example Elliot, *Through Gates of Splendor*). The quote, found in Elliot's journal, is close to the words of an English preacher named Philip Henry (1631–1696), who said, "He is no fool who parts with that which he cannot keep, when he is sure to be recompensed with that which he cannot lose."

hypothesis that everything arose from nothing—is demonstrably irrational and unscientific. Nothing comes from nothing; everything does not. If humans were not created in God's image, then we are in fact no different than the animals that we eat, the vermin we extinguish, and the bacteria we wash away in their billions. We are smarter, to be sure, but our one value then is simply a function of how smart or how productive we are. If we evolved from single-celled organisms in a materialistic, mechanistic world, then individuality is a myth. If humanity arose from impersonal forces, then personality is an aberration, a deviation from the ultimate truth of the universe. But if we were created in the image of a personal-infinite God, then we have value, because He says we do. Knowing whose we are, we can know who we are.

If there was no fall, then what humanity is now is what we have always been. There is no answer for the remarkable cruelty of which humans are capable. If the God of deism, or of Islam, or the many gods of pantheism created us this way, attempts to overcome our obviously flawed human nature are in effect attempts to go against God's created order and improve upon God's design. If, again, we evolved from lower organisms and there was no fall, then there is only the pitiless and indifferent march to advance our species. Our species' remarkable (and singular) cruelty must have coevolved with our increased intelligence, resulting in our evolutionary success. If so, instead of wringing our hands at all of the evil and subjugation we witness, we should celebrate the inexorable march of humanity to become even more successful as a species. Efforts to improve ourselves are doomed to fail, as should be obvious from the fruit of the various atheistic political regimes of the nineteenth and twentieth centuries. If there was no fall, then everything that we need to be saved from is everything that has made us a successful species. But if there was an actual, historical fall, then things are not as they should be. If there was a fall, then we need to be redeemed, to be bought back and made right.

If there is no God-anointed Redeemer, then we are our own saviors. It is left to man to try to become more than we are, to overcome millennia of evolution, and become more humane. But what does that look like? Success from an evolutionary perspective does not mean more kindness or more generosity; it means survival of the fittest and death for those who are unfit to advance the species. And the quicker the weaklings die, the better for the survival of the species. It does not mean each one of us living "our best life now"; it means the strong and the able and the intelligent and the wealthy subjugating those less fortunately endowed by the random processes of the evolutionary mechanism. If Jesus was just a man, then His death on the cross was a meaningless mistake and we should yield to the inexorable march of evolution to become even crueler and more successful. But if Jesus is God incarnate, as He clearly claimed to be, then God has done what only God could do. He took on flesh and redeemed us, paying the price for all sin so that we can be clothed in Christ's righteousness and made holy by His holiness.

If there is no restoration, then our lives are truly without meaning. We are not invited by anyone to advance a new kingdom, because all of our efforts at the improvement of our species are doomed to break against the truth that the strong will survive and the weak will perish. Any other ethic is contrary to the "truth" that our species' success is due to the pitiless indifference of chance mutation, adaptation, and reproductive success. But if the gospel is true, then God in Christ through the power of His Holy Spirit invites us to be a part of His efforts to restore this broken world and make all things new.

As I have tried to describe in this book, the Christian faith is more internally consistent, and more consistent with the external evidence of reality, than any of the alternative beliefs. If the Bible is to be believed, the Christian God is a God of covenant; even when we break our part of the deal, He is faithful to His promise. This means that our salvation, once given, cannot be lost. It cannot be earned; it is given by God's grace as a free gift, but once given, it cannot be lost. Science cannot promise immortality. If science is your ultimate truth, perhaps you could put your faith in science and freeze your brain after death like Robert Ettinger, founder of the Cryonics Institute, in the hope that one day science will enable us to cure terminal diseases or download our being into indestructible cyborgs so that we have immortality. No materialist believes in life after death. If you think the idea of a creator God is foolish, you must accept that you will one day die, and that will be your end. You cannot keep this life. You can perhaps extend it, but you cannot keep it. At first blush, it may seem like you ought to "live for now." Go out and eat, drink, and be merry; fornicate, make as much money as you can by whatever means and spend it and enjoy it, because in a few short years you'll be dead. YOLO (you only live once). Many atheists and agnostics (and, sadly, far too many who claim to be Christians) live just this way. They cannot be bothered with moral rules that might impede their pleasure seeking.

Text Box 17. The previous paragraph and the one following are really just a restatement of Pascal's wager.[40] Simply, if I wager that Christianity is true and I am correct, I gain everything—including eternity in paradise. If I am wrong, I have at worst enjoyed slightly fewer earthly pleasures for the span of my life before dying and falling into nothingness. Conversely, if I wager that Christianity is false and I am correct, I may have enjoyed more earthly pleasures during my short span on earth (though there is no evidence that atheists or agnostics are actually any happier or more content than evangelical Christians) before dying and falling into nothingness. But if I reject Christianity and I am wrong, the price I will pay upon my death is dire. Pascal claimed that no one is exempt from this wager, but far too many are entirely unaware that they have placed a bet.

But what if there is a God—a God who offers a path to eternal life? What if eternal life is a gift that, once given, cannot be taken from you? The cost of this gift is simply faith in the gift and in the Giver, and following Him daily. It cannot be earned, and once given it cannot be lost, though it can be squandered by pursuing empty pleasures and meaningless goals. What if our very purpose for existing on this earth is to bring glory to God—to glorify God by enjoying him forever?[41] That can be done in two ways: glorifying God in my life, and glorifying God with my life by serving as a vessel for the Spirit of the living God and sharing His love for others.[42] That means being called to help others see the foolishness of their ways and to accept that God and Jesus are True, and that the Christian faith is the only belief system that makes sense. For some seemingly foolish, crazy reason our Father in heaven has chosen to invite us into His story, to involve us, if we wish to be involved, in His work, and to make us "co-laborers" in this present reality. As G. K.

40. Pascal, *Pensees* (233), 66.

41. Piper, *Desiring God*, 18.

42. This is, of course, captured in the two great commandments that Jesus spoke in response to a question from a skeptical lawyer. As recorded in Matt 22:34–40, Jesus said, "you shall love the Lord your God with all your heart and with all your soul and with all your mind," and "you shall love your neighbor as yourself." The first is a quote from the Shema in Deut 6:5, while the second is found in Lev 19:18.

Chesterton said, "Truth, of course, must of necessity be stranger than fiction, for we have made fiction to suit ourselves."[43]

Additional Reading

For additional reading on God's extravagant love, mercy, and grace, please consider these outstanding books, all of which have spoken to me when I was a new Christian and still do now that I am maturing in my faith. As a new Christian, *What's So Amazing about Grace?*[44] by Philip Yancey spoke to my heart and began me on a lifelong journey of learning about the beauty and wisdom of the living Christ. *The Jesus I Never Knew*,[45] also by Philip Yancey, is a compelling and biblical meditation on the life and ministry of Jesus Christ. Finally, *Desiring God*[46] by John Piper is a compelling read in which Piper argues that the purpose of life is to "glorify God by enjoying Him forever."

43. Chesterton, *Essential Gilbert K. Chesterton*, 145.

44. Yancey, *What's So Amazing about Grace?*

45. Yancey, *Jesus I Never Knew.*

46. Piper, *Desiring God.*

Epilogue

But we preach Christ crucified, a stumbling block to Jews and folly to Gentiles, but to those who are called, both Jews and Greeks, Christ the power of God and the wisdom of God. For the foolishness of God is wiser than men, and the weakness of God is stronger than men.

—1 Corinthians 1:23–25

For what can be known about God is plain to them, because God has shown it to them. Ever since the creation of the world His invisible nature, namely, His eternal power and deity, has been clearly perceived in the things that have been made. So they are without excuse.

—Romans 1:19–20

Seek the LORD while he may be found, call upon him while he is near; let the wicked forsake his way, and the unrighteous man his thoughts; let him return to the LORD, that He may have mercy on him, and to our God, for He will abundantly pardon. For My thoughts are not your thoughts, neither are your ways My ways, says the LORD. For as the heavens are higher than the earth, so are My ways higher than your ways and My thoughts than your thoughts.

—Isaiah 55:6–9

Simon Peter answered him, "Lord, to whom shall we go? You have the words of eternal life."

—John 6:68

Bibliography

Akbar, Arifa. "Mao's Great Leap Forward 'Killed 45 Million in Four Years.'" *The Independent*, September 17, 2010.

Alcorn, Randy. *Heaven: A Comprehensive Guide to Everything the Bible Says about Our Eternal Home*. Carol Stream, IL: Tyndale, 2004.

"Alexander Reads about Himself in the Book of Daniel." *Good News*, January–February 2005. https://www.ucg.org/the-good-news/alexander-reads-about-himself-in-the-book-of-daniel.

Alighieri, Dante. *The Divine Comedy—Inferno*. Translated by Henry Wadsworth Longfellow. New York: Modern Library, 2003.

Augustine of Hippo. *Confessions*. Translated by Albert C. Outler. Grand Rapids: Christian Classics, 1955.

———. *Enchiridion: On Faith, Hope and Love*. Translated by Albert Outler. Louisville: Westminster, 1955.

Bada, Jeffrey L. "New Insights into Prebiotic Chemistry from Stanley Miller's Spark Discharge Experiments." *Chemical Society Reviews* 42:5 (2013) 2186–96.

Baggini, Julian. "Is There a Real You?" TED talk, 2011.

Bailey, Mark. "Christmas Means More than You've Realized." *Decision Magazine*, December 1, 2019.

Barrow, John. *The Constants of Nature*. New York: Vintage, 2002.

Baumgardt, Carola, and Jamie Callan. *Johannes Kepler Life and Letters*. New York: Philosophical Library, 1953.

Beckford, Martin. "Richard Dawkins Interested in Setting Up 'Atheist Free School.'" *The Telegraph*, June 24, 2010.

Behe, Michael J. *Darwin's Black Box: The Biochemical Challenge to Evolution*. New York: Free Press, 1996.

Belmonte, Kevin. *Hero for Humanity: A Biography of William Wilberforce*. Colorado Springs, CO: Navpress, 2002.

Bhagavad Gita (The Song of God). Translated by Swami Prabhavananda and Christopher Isherwood. New York: Mentor, 1944.

Birnbaum, Robert. "Camille Paglia." *The Morning News*, August 3, 2005. https://themorningnews.org/article/camille-paglia.

Black, Edwin. *War Against the Weak: Eugenics and America's Campaign to Create a Master Race*. New York: Basic Books, 2003.

Bloom, Allan. *The Closing of the American Mind: How Higher Education Has Failed Democracy and Impoverished the Souls of Today's Students.* Chicago: Simon and Schuster, 1987.

Bodhi, Bhikkhu. *The Numerical Discourses of the Buddha: A Translation of the Anguttara Nikaya.* Somerville, MA: Wisdom, 2012.

Borg, Marcus. *Jesus and Buddha: The Parallel Sayings.* Berkeley, CA: Ulysses, 2002.

Boyd, Robert T. *Boyd's Handbook of Practical Apologetics.* Grand Rapids: Kregel, 1997.

Brand, Paul, and Philip Yancey. *Fearfully and Wonderfully Made.* Grand Rapids: Zondervan, 1987.

Breslin, James. *Mark Rothko: A Biography.* Chicago: University of Chicago Press, 1993.

Brix, Shawn. "A Childhood Prayer." *Today Magazine*, April 18, 2011.

Broglie, Louis de. "Recherches sur la Théorie des Quanta." Doctoral thesis, Paris University, 1924.

Bryan, Mike. *Chapter and Verse: A Skeptic Revisits Christianity.* New York: Random House, 1991.

Butterfield, Rosaria Champagne. *Openness Unhindered: Further Thoughts of an Unlikely Convert on Sexual Identity and Union with Christ.* Pittsburgh: Crown and Covenant, 2015.

Callaway, Ewen. "The Coronavirus Is Mutating—Does It Matter?" *Nature* 585 (2020) 174–77.

Camus, Albert. *The Myth of Sisyphus.* Paris: Gallimard, 1942.

———. *The Stranger.* Paris: Gallimard, 1942

Carpenter, Siri. "Government Sanctions Harvard Psychologist." *Science* 337 (2012) 1283.

Carrington, Philip. *The Early Christian Church.* Vol. 1. Cambridge: Cambridge University Press, 2011.

Carter, Brandon. "Large Number Coincidences and the Anthropic Principle in Cosmology." From the IAU symposium " Confrontation of Cosmological Theories with Observational Data." Dordrecht, Netherlands: Reidel, 1974.

Carter, C. Sue, and Stephen W. Porges. "The Biochemistry of Love: An Oxytocin Hypothesis." *EMBO Reports* 14:1 (2013) 12–16.

Chesterton, G. K. *Autobiography.* New York: Sheed and Ward, 1936.

———. *Charles Dickins: A Critical Study.* New York: Dodd, Mead & Co, 1906.

———. *Collected Works.* Vol. 15. Edited by Alzina Stone Dale. San Francisco: Ignatius, 1989.

———. "Concluding Remarks on the Importance of Orthodoxy." In *Heretics*, 287–308. London: Bodley Head, 1905.

———. *Orthodoxy.* New York: Doubleday, 2001.

———. *The Victorian Age.* New York: Henry Holt, 1913.

Clausius, Rudolf. "Über die bewegende Kraft der Wärme." *Annalen der Physik* 79 (1850) 368–97, 500–524.

Clouser, Roy A. *The Myth of Religious Neutrality.* Notre Dame, IN: University of Notre Dame Press, 1991.

Collins, Francis. *The Language of God: A Scientist Presents Evidence for Belief.* New York: Free Press, 2007.

Colson, Charles, and Nancy Pearcey. *How Now Shall We Live?* Carol Stream, IL: Tyndale House, 1999.

Courtois, Stephane. *The Black Book of Communism*. Cambridge, MA: Harvard University Press, 1999.

Craig, William Lane. *The Kalām Cosmological Argument*. London: MacMillan, 1979.

Crane, Stephen. "A Man Said to the Universe." In *War Is Kind & Other Lines*. 1905.

Darwin, Charles. *On the Origin of Species by Means of Natural Selection, or the Preservation of Favoured Races in the Struggle for Life*. London: John Murray, 1859.

Davies, Paul. *The Cosmic Blueprint: New Discoveries in Nature's Creative Ability to Order the Universe*. New York: Simon and Schuster, 1988.

———. *The Cosmic Jackpot: Why Our Universe Is Just Right for Life*. Boston: Mariner, 2007.

Dawkins, Richard. *The Blind Watchmaker*. New York: Norton, 1986.

———. *The God Delusion*. Boston: Houghton Mifflin Harcourt, 2006.

———. "Has the World Changed?" *The Guardian*, October 11, 2001.

———. "Richard Dawkins Hits Vack at Allegations He Is Islamophobic after Berkeley Event Is Cancelled." *The Independent*, July 26, 2017.

———. *River Out of Eden: A Darwinian View of Life*. New York: Basic Books, 1996.

———. *The Selfish Gene*. Oxford: Oxford University Press, 1976.

Deprit, Albert. "Monsignor Georges Lemaître." In *The Big Bang and Georges Lemaître*, edited by A. Barger. Dordrecht, Netherlands: Reidel, 1984.

Desmond, Adrian, and James Moore. *Darwin: The Life of a Tormented Evolutionist*. New York: Norton, 1991.

Dikötter, Frank. *Mao's Great Famine: The History of China's Most Devastating Catastrophe, 1958–1962*. New York: Walker, 2010.

Dostoevsky, Fyodor. *The Brothers Karamazov*. Translated by Constance Garnett. New York: Modern Library, 1996.

Downing, David C. *Looking for the King*. San Francisco: Ignatius, 2013.

Dowson, Ernest. "Vitae Summa Brevis Spem Nos Vetat Incohare Longam." In *The Complete Poems of Ernest Dowson*. New York: Medusa Head, 1928.

D'Souza, Dinesh. *Godforsaken: Bad Things Happen. Is There a God Who Cares? Yes. Here's Proof*. Carol Stream, IL: Tyndale House, 2012.

Eden, Murray. "Heresy in the Halls of Biology—Mathematicians Question Darwin." *Scientific Research* November (1967) 59–66.

———. "Inadequacies of Neo-Darwinian Evolution as Scientific Theory." In *Mathematical Challenges to the Neo-Darwinian Theory of Evolution*, edited by P. S. Moorhead and M. M. Kaplan, Philadelphia: Wistar Institute Press, 1967.

Edwards, William D., et al. "On the Physical Death of Jesus Christ." *JAMA* 255:11 (1986) 1455–63.

Efird, James. *Daniel and Revelation: A Study of Two Extraordinary Visions*. Eugene, OR: Wipf & Stock, 2001.

Ehrman, Bart D. *God's Problem*. New York: HarperOne, 2008.

———. *Misquoting Jesus: The Story Behind Who Changed the Bible and Why*. New York: HarperCollins, 2005.

Einstein, Albert. "Zur Elektrodynamik bewegter Körper." *Annalen der Physik* 17 (1905) 891–921.

Eldredge, John. *Wild at Heart: Discovering the Secret of a Man's Soul*. Nashville: Thomas Nelson, 2001.

Elliot, Elisabeth. *Through Gates of Splendor*. Carol Stream, IL: Tyndale House, 1981.

Evans, Richard J. *The Third Reich at War*. New York: Penguin, 2009.

Falcon, Andrea. "Aristotle on Causality." In *The Stanford Encyclopedia of Philosophy*, Spring 2022 edition, edited by Edward N. Zalta. https://plato.stanford.edu/archives/spr2022/entries/aristotle-causality/.

Feder, Don. "Atheism Isn't the Final Word." *USA Today*, April 16, 2007.

Finegan, Jack. *The Archaeology of the New Testament*. Princeton, NJ: Princeton University Press, 1992.

Flew, Anthony. *There Is a God: How the World's Most Notorious Atheist Changed His Mind*. New York: HarperCollins, 2007.

"For Camille Paglia, the Spiritual Quest Defines All Great Art." *The Daily Beast*, December 17, 2012. Available at https://www.fisheaters.com/forums/showthread.php?tid=60647.

Foster, Richard. *Celebration of Discipline: The Path to Spiritual Growth*. San Francisco: Harper Collins, 1978.

Friedman, A. "Über die Krümmung des Raumes." *Zeitschrift für Physik* 10:1 (1922) 377–86.

Friedman, Richard Elliott. *The Disappearance of God: A Divine Mystery*. Boston: Little, Brown, 1995.

Gabriel, S. E., et al. "Cystic Fibrosis Heterozygote Resistance to Cholera Toxin in the Cystic Fibrosis Mouse Model." *Science* 266 (1994) 107–9.

Gay, Peter. *Deism: An Anthology*. Princeton, NJ: Van Nostrand, 1968.

Geisler, Norman L., and William E. Nix. *A General Introduction to the Bible*. Chicago: Moody, 1968.

Geisler, Norman, and Frank Turek. *I Don't Have Enough Faith to Be an Atheist*. Wheaton, IL: Crossway, 2004.

Gishlick, Alan D. "Icons of Evolution? Why Much of What Jonathan Well Writes about Evolution Is Wrong." National Center for Science Education, 2003.

Goldberg, Bernard. *Bias: A CBS Insider Exposes How the Media Distort the News*. Washington, DC: Regnery, 2002.

Gonzalez, Guillermo, and Jay W. Richards. *The Privileged Planet: How Our Place in the Cosmos Is Designed for Discovery*. Washington, DC: Regenery, 2004.

Greene, Albert E. *Reclaiming the Future of Christian Education*. Colorado Springs, CO: Purposeful, 1998.

Groeschel, Craig. *The Christian Atheist: Believing in God but Living as If He Doesn't Exist*. Grand Rapids: Zondervan, 2010.

Guinness, Os. *The Call: Finding and Fulfilling God's Purpose for Your Life*. Nashville: W Publishing, 1998.

———. *Carpe Diem Redeemed: Seizing the Day, Discerning the Times*. Downers Grove, IL: InterVarsity, 2019.

Harran, Marilyn J. *The Holocaust Chronicle: A History in Words and Pictures*. Lincolnwood, IL: Publications International, 2000.

Harris, Sam. "God's Dupes." *Los Angeles Times*, March 15, 2007. https://www.latimes.com/la-oe-harris15mar15-story.html.

———. "Sam Harris Extended Interview." *Religion and Ethics Newsweekly*, PBS, January 5, 2007. https://www.pbs.org/wnet/religionandethics/2007/01/05/january-5-2007-sam-harris-extended-interview/3736/.

Hawking, Stephen. *A Brief History of Time*. New York: Bantam, 1996.

Heeren, Fred. *Show Me God*. Wheeling, IL: Searchlight, 1995.

Hein, David. "In War for Peace: General George C. Marshall's Core Convictions and Ethical Leadership." *Touchstone*, March–April 2013. https://www.touchstonemag.com/archives/article.php?id=26-22-041-f.

Heisenberg, Werner. *Physics and Philosophy*. New York: HarperCollins, 2007. Originally published 1958.

Heller, Joseph. *Good as Gold*. New York: Simon and Schuster, 1999.

Hesser, Leon. *The Man Who Fed the World: Nobel Peace Prize Laureate Norman Borlaug and His Battle to End World Hunger*. Dallas: Park East, 2010.

Hill Kent R. "The Sweet Grace of Reason: The Apologetics of G. K. Chesterton." In *The Riddle of Joy: G. K. Chesterton and C. S. Lewis*, edited by Micheal H. Macdonald and Andrew A. Tadie, 226–45. Grand Rapids: Eerdmans,1989.

Hillenbrand, Laura. *Unbroken: A World War II Story of Survival, Resilience, and Redemption*. New York: Random House, 2010.

Hitt, Russell. *Jungle Pilot: The Life and Witness of Nate Saint*. Grand Rapids: Discovery House. 1997.

Hogan, Michael J. *The Marshall Plan: America, Britain, and the Reconstruction of Western Europe, 1947–1952*. Cambridge, UK: Cambridge University Press, 1987.

Holt, Bradley P. *Thirsty for God: A Brief History of Christian Spirituality*. Minneapolis: Augsburg, 1993.

Hoyle, Fred. "The Universe: Past and Present Reflections." *Engineering and Science*, November 1981, 8–11.

Hubble, Edwin. "A Relationship between Distance and Radial Velocity among Extra-Galactic Nebulae." *PNAS* 15:3 (1929) 167.

Human Whole Genome. GRCh38.p13 (Genome Reference Consortium Human Build 38), INSDC Assembly. Ensembl Project, European Bioinformatics Institute (EMBL-EBI), December 2013. https://uswest.ensembl.org/Homo_sapiens/Info/Annotation.

Hume, R. E., ed. and trans. *The Thirteen Principal Upanishads*. Oxford: Oxford University Press, 1954.

Hybels, Bill. *Courageous Leadership*. Grand Rapids: Zondervan, 2002.

Jastrow, Robert. *God and the Astronomers*. New York: Warner, 1978.

Jeremiah, David, *The Prophecy Answer Book*. Nashville: Thomas Nelson, 2010.

John Paul II, Pope. "We Remember: A Reflection on the Shoah." Pontifical Commission for Religious Relations with the Jews, 1998. https://www.bc.edu/content/dam/files/research_sites/cjl/texts/cjrelations/resources/documents/catholic/We_Remember.htm.

Johnson, A. P., et al. "The Miller Volcanic Spark Discharge Experiment." *Science* 32:5900 (2008) 404.

Johnson, Phillip E. *Darwin on Trial*. Downers Grove, IL: InterVarsity, 1993.

Josephus, Flavius. *The New Complete Works of Josephus*. Translated by William Whiston and Paul L. Maier. Grand Rapids: Kregel Academic, 1999.

Kates, Graham. "Lori Loughlin and Felicity Huffman among Dozens Charged in College Bribery Scheme." *CBS News*, retrieved March 27, 2022.

Katoh, K., et al. "MAFFT: A Novel Method for Rapid Multiple Sequence Alignment Based on Fast Fourier Transform." *Nucleic Acids Research* 30 (2002) 3059–66.

Kazantzakis, Nikos. *The Last Temptation of Christ*. New York: Simon and Schuster, 1960.

Kean, Sam. *The Violinist's Thumb and Other Lost Tales of Love, War, and Genius as Written by Our Genetic Code.* New York: Back Bay, 2012.

Kekulé, Auguste. *Benzolfest: Rede, Berichte der Deutschen Chemischen Gesellschaft* 23:1 (1890) 1302–11.

Keller, Timothy. *The Reason for God: Belief in an Age of Skepticism.* New York: Riverhead, 2008.

Kelly, Cathal. "The Gospel According to Paglia." *The Toronto Star*, June 13, 2009. https://www.thestar.com/news/insight/2009/06/13/the_gospel_according_to_paglia.html.

Kershaw, Ian, and Moshe Lewin. *Stalinism and Nazism: Dictatorships in Comparison.* Cambridge, UK: Cambridge University Press, 1997.

Kline, Morris. *Mathematics for the Nonmathematician.* New York: Dover, 1967.

Kolodiejchuk, Brian, ed. *Mother Teresa: Come Be My Light: The Private Writings of the Saint of Calcutta.* New York, NY: Doubleday, 2009.

Kreeft, Peter. "Argument from Design." http://www.peterkreeft.com/topics/design.htm.

———. *Heaven, the Heart's Deepest Longing.* San Francisco: Ignatius, 1989.

———. "The Problem of Evil." http://www.peterkreeft.com/topics/evil.htm.

Kumar, Sudhir, et al. "An Evolutionary Portrait of the Progenitor SARS-CoV-2 and Its Dominant Offshoots in COVID-19 Pandemic." *Molecular Biology and Evolution.* 38:8 (2021) 3046–59.

Lanzer, Rick. "Did Ezra Come to Jerusalem in 457 BC?" https://biblearchaeology.org/abr-projects-main/the-daniel-9-24-27-project-2/4549-did-ezra-come-to-jerusalem-in-457-bc.

Lavoisier, *Traité Élémentaire de Chimie.* Paris: Cuchet, 1789.

Layman, Jack. "Early History of Educational Philosophy." In *Foundations of Christian School Education*, edited by James Braley et al., 20–32. Colorado Springs, CO: Purposeful Design, 2003.

Lee, Richard G. *In God We Trust.* Nashville: Thomas Nelson , 2009.

Lemaître, Georges. "Un Univers Homogène de Masse Constante et de Rayon Croissant Rendant Compte de la Vitesse Radiale des Nébuleuses Extra-Galactiques." *Annales de la Société Scientifique de Bruxelles* A47 (1927) 49–59.

Lennox, John C. *God's Undertaker: Has Science Buried God?* Oxford: Lion Hudson, 2009.

———. "The Loud Absence—Where Is God in Suffering?" The Veritas Forum, Harvard Medical School, December 19, 2014.

Lewis, C. S. *The Great Divorce.* New York: Harper Collins, 2001. Originally published 1946.

———. "Is Theology Poetry?" In *The Weight of Glory and Other Addresses*, 63–78. New York: HarperCollins, 2001.

———. *The Last Battle.* London: Bodley Head, 1956.

———. *Mere Christianity.* New York: Harper Collins, 1952.

———. *The Screwtape Letters.* London: Geoffrey Bles, 1942.

———. *Surprised by Joy: The Shape of My Early Life.* London: Geoffrey Bles, 1955.

———. "The Weight of Glory." In *The Weight of Glory and Other Addresses*, 1–15. New York: HarperCollins, 2001.

Lloyd-Jones, Sally. *The Jesus Storybook Bible.* Grand Rapids: Zonderkidz, 2007.

Logan, Ian. *Reading Anselm's Proslogion: The History of Anselm's Arguments and Its Significance Today.* Burlington, VT: Ashgate, 2009.

Lovelock, J. E. "Gaia as Seen Through the Atmosphere." *Atmospheric Environment* 6:8 (1967) 579–80.

Lucado, Max. *No Wonder They Call Him the Savior.* Colorado Springs, CO: Multnomah, 1986.

Lutz, Donald. *The Origins of American Constitutionalism.* Baton Rouge, LA: Louisiana State University Press, 1988.

Lutzer, Erwin. *Seven Reasons Why You Can Trust the Bible.* Chicago: Moody, 2008.

MacDonald, George. "The New Name." In *Unspoken Sermons,* 55–62. New York: Cosimo Classics, 2007.

Mandela, Nelson. *Long Walk to Freedom: The Autobiography of Nelson Mandela.* Randburg, South Africa: Macdonaldo Purnell, 1995.

Mangalwadi, Vishal. *The Book That Made Your World: How the Bible Created the Soul of Western Civilization.* Nashville: Thomas Nelson, 2011.

Maniloff, Jack. "The Minimal Cell Genome: 'On Being the Right Size.'" *PNAS* 93:19 (1996) 10004–6.

Markie, Peter, and M. Folescu. "Rationalism vs. Empiricism." In *The Stanford Encyclopedia of Philosophy,* Fall 2021 Edition, edited by Edward N. Zalta. https://plato.stanford.edu/archives/fall2021/entries/rationalism-empiricism/.

Marx, Karl. *Deutsch–Französische Jahrbücher.* Paris: February, 1844.

Mayer, Johann Christoph Andreas. *Anatomische Kupfertafeln nebst dazu gehörigen Erklärungen.* Berlin: Georg Jacob Decker, 1788.

McBirnie, William Steuart. *The Search for the Twelve Apostles.* Carol Stream, IL: Tyndale Momentum, 1973.

McDowell, Josh. *Evidence That Demands a Verdict: Historical Evidences for the Christian Faith.* Vol. 1. Nashville: Thomas Nelson, 1972.

McDowell, Sean, and J. Warner Wallace. *So the Next Generation Will Know.* Colorado Springs, CO: David C. Cook, 2019.

McHugh, Paul R. *The Mind Has Mountains: Reflections on Society and Psychiatry.* Baltimore, MD: Johns Hopkins University Press, 2006.

McLoughlin, Barry, and Kevin McDermott. *Stalin's Terror: High Politics and Mass Repression in the Soviet Union.* Basingstoke, UK: Palgrave Macmillan, 2002.

McRay, John. *Archaeology and the New Testament.* Grand Rapids: Baker, 1991.

Medved, Michael. *The 10 Big Lies about America.* New York: Crown, 2009.

Mendel, Gregor. "Versuche über Pflanzenhybriden." *Verhandlungen des naturforschenden Vereines in Brünn,* Abhandlungen (1866) 3–47.

Metaxas, Eric. *Bonhoeffer, Pastor, Martyr, Prophet, Spy.* Nashville: Thomas Nelson, 2010.

———. *Is Atheism Dead?* Washington, DC: Salem, 2021.

Miller, Stanley L. "A Production of Amino Acids under Possible Primitive Earth Conditions." *Science* 117(3046) (1953) 528–29.

Miller, Stanley L., and Harold C. Urey. "Organic Compound Synthesis on the Primitive Earth." *Science* 130:3370 (1959) 245–51.

Montgomery, John Warwick. *History and Christianity.* Minneapolis: Bethany, 1965.

Moody, Robert. *The Saltonstall Papers, 1607–1815.* Vol. 1: *1607–1789.* Massachusetts Historical Society Collections 80. Boston: Massachusetts Historical Society, 1972.

Murray O'Hair, Madalyn. *What on Earth Is an Atheist?* Cranford, NJ: American Atheist, 2004.

Myerson, Joel. *Transcendentalism: A Reader.* New York: Oxford University Press, 2000.

Newbigin, Lesslie . *Foolishness to the Greeks: The Gospel and Western Culture.* Grand Rapids: Eerdmans, 1986.

The New England Primer. Boston: Edward Draper, 1777. Available from WallBuilders, Aledo, Texas. www.wallbuilders.com.

Nietzsche, Friedrich. *The Gay Science.* Translated by Walter Kaufmann. New York: Vintage, 1974. Originally published 1882.

Nostradamus. *Les Propheties.* Compiled by Arcanaeum, 2003. Originally published 1555.

O'Connor, Clare. "Human Chromosome Translocations and Cancer." *Nature Education* 1:1 (2008) 56.

Onfray, Michel. *Atheist Manifesto: The Case against Christianity, Judaism, and Islam.* New York: Arcade, 2007.

Ortlund, Dane. *Gentle and Lowly: The Heart of Christ for Sinners and Sufferers.* Wheaton, IL: Crossway, 2020.

Outler, Albert C. "The Wesleyan Quadrilateral in Wesley." *Wesleyan Theological Journal* 20:1 (1985) 7–18.

Paauw, Glen. *Saving the Bible from Ourselves: Learning to Read and Live the Bible Well.* Downers Grove, IL: InterVarsity, 2016.

Packer, J. I. *Knowing God.* Downers Grove, IL: InterVarsity 1973.

Paglia, Camille. *Sexual Personae: Art and Decadence from Nefertiti to Emily Dickinson.* New Haven, CT: Yale University Press, 1990.

Pascal, Blaise. *Pensees.* Translated by A. J. Krailsheimer. New York: E. P. Dutton, 1958.

Pearcey, Nancy. *Total Truth: Liberating Christianity from Its Cultural Captivity.* Wheaton, IL: Crossway, 2005.

Penrose, Roger. *The Emperor's New Mind.* Oxford: Oxford University Press, 1989.

Penzias, Arno. "Creation Is Supported by All the Data So Far." In *Cosmos, Bios, Theos: Scientists Reflect on Science, God, and the Origins of the Universe, Life, and Homo Sapiens,* edited by Margenau and Varghese, 81–87. La Salle, IL: Open Court, 1992.

Perry, John, and Marvin Olasky. *Monkey Business: True Story of the Scopes Trial.* Nashville: Broadman and Holman, 2005.

Pier, Gerald B., et al. "Salmonella Typhi Uses CFTR to Enter Intestinal Epithelial Cells." *Nature* 393 (1998) 79–82.

Piper, John. *Desiring God: Meditations of a Christian Hedonist.* Colorado Springs, CO: Multnomah, 1986.

———. *Don't Waste Your Life.* Wheaton, IL: Crossway, 2003.

Pomper, Philip. "Lomonosov and the Discovery of the Law of the Conservation of Matter in Chemical Transformations." *Ambix* 10:3 (1962) 119–27.

Popper, Karl, and John Eccles. *The Self and Its Brain.* Berlin: Springer, 1977.

Qureshi, Nabeel. *No God but One: Allah or Jesus? A Former Muslim Investigates the Evidence for Islam and Christianity.* Grand Rapids: Zondervan, 2012.

Radbill, Samuel X. "A History of Child Abuse and Infanticide." In *Violence in the Family,* edited by Suzanne K. Steinmetz and Murray A. Straus, 173–79. New York: Dodd, Mead, 1974.

Ramsay, William M. *The Bearing of Recent Discovery on the Trustworthiness of the New Testament.* London: Hodder and Stoughton, 1915.

———. *St. Paul the Traveler and the Roman Citizen.* 3rd ed. London: Hodder and Stoughton, 1897.

Rees, Martin. *Just Six Numbers: The Deep Forces That Shape the Universe.* New York: Basic, 2000.

Robinson, Marilynne. *The Death of Adam: Essays on Modern Thought.* New York: Picador, 2005.

Rosefielde, Stephen. "Stalinism in Post-Communist Perspective: New Evidence on Killings, Forced Labour and Economic Growth in the 1930s." *Europe-Asia Studies* 48:6 (1996) 959–87.

Rousseau, Jean-Jacques. *Du Contrat Cocial: Ou Principes du Droit Politique.* Amsterdam: 1762.

Sartre, Jean Paul. *Being and Nothingness.* Translated by Hazel Barnes. Secaucus, NJ: Citadel, 1957.

Schäfer, Peter. *Jesus in the Talmud.* Princeton, NJ: Princeton University Press, 2007.

Schaeffer, Francis. "Escape from Reason." In *The Francis A. Schaeffer Trilogy.* Wheaton, IL: Crossway, 1990.

———. "The God Who Is There." In *The Francis A. Schaeffer Trilogy.* Wheaton, IL: Crossway, 1990.

———. "He is There and He is Not Silent." In *The Francis A. Schaeffer Trilogy,* Wheaton, IL: Crossway, 1990.

———. *How Should We Then Live? 50th L'Abri Anniversary Edition.* Wheaton, IL: Crossway, 2005.

Schmidt, Alvin J. *How Christianity Changed the World.* Grand Rapids: Zondervan, 2001.

Schrödinger, Erwin. *What Is Life?* Cambridge, UK: Cambridge University Press, 1992.

"A Scientist's Case against God." *The Independent,* April 20, 1992.

Shalev, Baruch Aba. *100 Years of Nobel Prizes.* New York: Atlantic, 2003.

Short, Philip. *Pol Pot: Anatomy of a Nightmare.* New York: Henry Holt, 2005.

Smolin, Lee. *The Life of the Cosmos.* Oxford: Oxford University Press, 1997.

Sommerville, C. John. *The Decline of the Secular University: Why the Academy Needs Religion.* Oxford: Oxford University Press, 2006.

Sowell, Thomas. *Black Rednecks and White Liberals.* Jackson, TN: Encounter, 2006.

Spears, Paul. "Introduction to Philosophy." In *Foundations of Christian School Education,* edited by James Braley, et al., 5–15. Colorado Springs, CO: Purposeful Design, 2003.

Spencer, Herbert. *Principles of Biology.* London: Williams and Norgate, 1864.

Spiro, Ken. "The Bible as History." http://www.simpletoremember.com/articles/a/bible-as-history/.

Sproul R.C. "The Adversary." In Angels and Demons, Sanford, FL: Ligonier Ministries, https://www.ligonier.org/learn/series/angels-and-demons/the-adversary.

———. *The Holiness of God.* Wheaton, IL: Tyndale House, 1985.

Stark, Rodney. *The Victory of Reason: How Christianity Led to Freedom, Capitalism, and Western Success.* New York: Random House , 2007

Stewart, Ian. *In Pursuit of the Unknown: 17 Equations That Changed the World.* New York: Basic Books, 2012.

Stökl, Jonathan, and Caroline Waerzegger. *Exile and Return: The Babylonian Context.* Berlin: Walter de Gruyter , 2015.

Stoner, Peter W. *Science Speaks: Scientific Proof of the Accuracy of Prophecy and the Bible."* Chicago: Moody, 1969.

Stott, John. *Why I Am a Christian.* Downers Grove, IL: InterVarsity, 2003.

Strobel, Lee. *The Case for a Creator: A Journalist Investigates Scientific Evidence That Points toward God.* Grand Rapids: Zondervan, 2004.

————. *The Case for Christ: A Journalist's Personal Investigation of the Evidence for Jesus*. Grand Rapids: Zondervan, 1998.

————. *The Case for Christmas: A Journalist Investigates the Identity of the Child in the Manger*. Grand Rapids: Zondervan, 2005.

Sunshine, Glenn S. *Why You Think the Way You Do: The Story of Western Worldviews from Rome to Home*. Grand Rapids: Zondervan, 2009.

Swinburne, Richard. *Is There a God?* Oxford: Oxford University Press, 2010.

Taylor, Fred, trans. *The Goebbels Diaries 1939–41*. London: Hamish Hamilton, 1982.

Thompson, Peter. "Karl Marx, Part 1: Religion, the Wrong Answer to the Right Question." *The Guardian*, April 4, 2011.

Tolkien, J. R. R. *The Return of the King*. London: Allen and Unwin, 1955.

Tutu, Desmond. *The Book of Forgiving: The Fourfold Path for Healing Ourselves and Our World*. New York: HarperOne, 2015.

————. *No Future Without Forgiveness*. Colorado Springs, CO: Image, 2000.

Union of Catholic Christian Rationalists. "Early Date of Mark's Gospel: What the Dead Sea Scrolls Say?" April 13, 2018. https://www.uccronline.it/eng/2018/04/13/early-date-of-marks-gospel-what-dead-sea-scrolls-say/.

Varki, Ajit, and Tasha K. Altheide. "Comparing the Human and Chimpanzee Genomes: Searching for Needles in a Yaystack." *Genome Research* 15 (2005) 1746–58.

Veith, Gene E., Jr. *Postmodern Times: A Christian Guide to Contemporary Thought and Culture*. Wheaton, IL: Crossway, 1994.

Vermes, Geza. *The Complete Dead Sea Scrolls in English*. 2nd ed. New York: Penguin, 1975.

Wallace, Daniel B. *Revisiting the Corruption of the New Testament: Manuscript, Patristic, and Apocryphal Evidence*. Text and Canon of the New Testament. Grand Rapids: Kregel Academic, 2011.

Wallace, Daniel B., and Bart D. Ehrman. "Can We Trust the Text? A Debate between Daniel B. Wallace and Bart D. Ehrman." Center for the Study of the New Testament, October 1, 2011.

Wallace, J. Warner. *Cold Case Christianity: A Homicide Detective Investigates the Claims of the Gospels*. Colorado Springs, CO: David C. Cook, 2013.

Walvoord, John F. *Daniel: The Key to Prophetic Revelation*. Chicago: Moody, 1971.

Warren, Rick. *The Purpose Driven Life: What on Earth Am I Here for?* Grand Rapids: Zondervan, 2005.

Weinberg, Steven. "A Designer Universe?" *Physics and Astronomy Online*. https://www.physlink.com/education/essay_weinberg.cfm.

Williams, Peter, and David Wallace. *Unit 731: The Japanese Army's Secret of Secrets*. London: Grafton, 1989.

Wilson, Andrew. *World Scripture: A Comparative Anthology of Sacred Texts*. New York: Paragon House, 1991.

Wilson, Ian. *Jesus: The Evidence*. San Francisco: Harper, 1988.

Wright, N. T. *Evil and the Justice of God*. Downers Grove, IL: InterVarsity, 2006.

Yancey, Philip. *The Bible Jesus Read*. Grand Rapids: Zondervan, 1999.

————. *Disappointment with God: Three Questions No One Asks Aloud*. Grand Rapids: Zondervan, 1988.

————. *The Jesus I Never Knew*. Grand Rapids: Zondervan, 2002.

————. *Prayer: Does It Make Any Difference?* Grand Rapids: Zondervan, 2016.

———. *Reaching for the Invisible God: What Can We Expect to Find?* Grand Rapids: Zondervan, 2002.

———. *What's So Amazing about Grace?* Grand Rapids: Zondervan, 2002.

Zacharias, Ravi. *The End of Reason: A Response to the New Atheists.* Grand Rapids: Zondervan, 2008.

———. *Jesus among Other Gods: The Absolutist Claims of the Christian Message.* Nashville, TN: Thomas Nelson, 2000.

———. *A Shattered Visage: The Real Face of Atheism.* Grand Rapids: Baker, 1990.

Subject Index

Scripture Index

Luke (*cont.*)

18:18–27	253
19:10	183
20:27	255
21:27	179
22:37	188
22:42	185
22:44	185
23:2–9	125
23:4, 14–15	125
23:14–15	190
23:32	125
23:39–43	156
23:46	139
23:50	125
24:44	188
24:46	188

John

1:1–3	178
1:14	178
1:18	167
1:29	124
1:45–46	257
3:16	183, 191
3:16–18	150
5:2–8	176
5:27	249, 260
6:1–14	182
6:35	124
6:60, 66	183
6:68	281
7:53—8:11	136
8:12	179
8:19	73
8:23–24	260
8:44	189
8:58	178
10:10	183, 260
10:30	73, 178, 258
10:33, 36	152
11:25	180, 260
12:8	183
14:1–2	264
14:6	180, 259, 261, 275
14:15	261
14:15–17	73

14:16–18	167
14:26	167
15:5	180, 260
15:13	222
18:36	163
19:17	123
19:30	260
19:32–33	126

Acts

1:5	189
1:8	270
1:15	256
2:4	73
2:38	73
2:41	75
16:10	116
16:17	xii
17:28	33, 62

Romans

1:19–20	281
1:20	62, 130
3:23	110
3:24	130
3:28	163
4:15	114
5:5	73
5:8	205
6:1–15	132
6:20–23	128
6:23	110, 191
8:11	73
8:11–16	190
8:12	190
8:13	191
8:28	103, 266
10:9	260
10:13	110

1 Corinthians

1:23	259
1:23–25	281
1:25	xvii
3:9	266
3:16	73, 74

Made in United States
Troutdale, OR
09/05/2024